Windows Troubleshooting Series

Mike Halsey, MVP
Series Editor

Apress®

Windows Group Policy Troubleshooting

A Best Practice Guide for Managing Users and PCs Through Group Policy

Kapil Arya, MVP
Edited by Andrew Bettany, MVP

Apress®

Windows Group Policy Troubleshooting: A Best Practice Guide for Managing Users and PCs Through Group Policy

Kapil Arya
Bhopal, India

ISBN-13 (pbk): 978-1-4842-1885-3   ISBN-13 (electronic): 978-1-4842-1886-0
DOI 10.1007/978-1-4842-1886-0

Library of Congress Control Number: 2016957646

Managing Director: Welmoed Spahr
Lead (in-house) Editor: Gwenan Spearing
Development Editor: Laura Berendson, Douglas Pundick
Technical Reviewer: Matt Hitchcock
Editorial Board: Steve Anglin, Pramila Balan, Laura Berendson, Aaron Black,
     Louise Corrigan, Jonathan Gennick, Todd Green, Robert Hutchinson,
     Celestin Suresh John, Nikhil Karkal, James Markham, Susan McDermott,
     Matthew Moodie, Natalie Pao, Gwenan Spearing
Coordinating Editor: Jill Balzano and Melissa Maldonado
Copy Editor: Mary Behr
Compositor: SPi Global
Indexer: SPi Global
Artist: SPi Global

Distributed to the book trade worldwide by Springer Science+Business Media New York, 233 Spring Street, 6th Floor, New York, NY 10013. Phone 1-800-SPRINGER, fax (201) 348-4505, e-mail orders-ny@springer-sbm.com, or visit www.springer.com. Apress Media, LLC is a California LLC and the sole member (owner) is Springer Science + Business Media Finance Inc (SSBM Finance Inc). SSBM Finance Inc is a Delaware corporation.

For information on translations, please e-mail rights@apress.com, or visit www.apress.com.

Apress and friends of ED books may be purchased in bulk for academic, corporate, or promotional use. eBook versions and licenses are also available for most titles. For more information, reference our Special Bulk Sales–eBook Licensing web page at www.apress.com/bulk-sales.

Any source code or other supplementary materials referenced by the author in this text is available to readers at www.apress.com. For detailed information about how to locate your book's source code, go to www.apress.com/source-code/.

Printed on acid-free paper

This book is dedicated to my beloved mother, who died due to cancer four years ago. Mom, thanks for all the blessings you bestowed upon me. I love you and will always miss you.

—Kapil Arya

Thank you, Mike Halsey, for the opportunity to work on your Windows Troubleshooting Series. You owe me.

—Andrew Bettany

Contents at a Glance

About the Author xv

About the Editor xvii

About the Technical Reviewer xix

Windows Troubleshooting Series xxi

Acknowledgments xxiii

Introduction xxv

■Chapter 1: Getting Started with Group Policy 1

■Chapter 2: Group Policy Management Console 31

■Chapter 3: Managing the Windows Environment with
Group Policy 71

■Chapter 4: Managing Microsoft Office with Group Policy 105

■Chapter 5: Basics of Group Policy Troubleshooting 129

■Chapter 6: Advanced Group Policy Management 151

■Chapter 7: Group Policy Tips and Tricks 179

■Index 209

Contents

About the Author xv

About the Editor.. xvii

About the Technical Reviewer xix

Windows Troubleshooting Series xxi

Acknowledgments xxiii

Introduction xxv

■Chapter 1: Getting Started with Group Policy 1

Introduction 1

Using the Local Group Policy Editor 2

How to Configure a GPO 4

How Group Policy Works in Detail 8

Connecting Windows to a Server 9

Relationship Between Group Policy and the Registry 15

Advanced Uses of Group Policy.. 19

    Enhancing Security of Clients and Servers.. 19

    Deploying Policies to Manage User Actions.. 20

    Managing Microsoft Office in Your Corporate Environment..................................... 21

    Network Connections Management 22

Additional Concepts 23

    Block GPO Inheritance 23

    Enforcing GPOs.. 24

Copying GPOs 25

Importing GPOs 26

WMI Filter for GPOs 26

Security Filtering of GPOs 28

GPO vs. DSC (Desired State Configuration) 29

Setting Permissions for GPOs 30

Key Points 30

Summary 30

■Chapter 2: Group Policy Management Console 31

Introducing GPMC 31

Installing the GPMC 32

Configuring GPMC 42

How to Customize the GPMC Window 42

How to Use GPMC 43

Create and Edit GPOs in GPMC 43

Linking GPOs in GPMC 46

Deleting GPOs Using the GPMC 48

Backup and Restore GPOs in GPMC 49

Using GPMC Reports for Troubleshooting 53

GPMC Results 62

GPMC Scripts 66

Group Policy Preferences 66

What's New in Group Policy for Windows Server 2012 R2 67

Key Points 68

Summary 69

■Chapter 3: Managing the Windows Environment with
Group Policy 71

Using GPOs for Windows Customization 71

    Customizing the Start Menu or Start Screen Layout 72

    Enabling or Disabling the Password Reveal Button from Appearing 75

    Preventing Users from Customizing Windows Using Registry Manipulation 77

    Other Important Policy Settings for Windows Customization 80

Managing Windows Features with GPOs................................. 84

Enhancing System Security by Using Security Policies (GPO Subset)... 87

    Changing the Impact of User Account Control (UAC) Prompts.............................. 90

Key Points 104

Summary.. 104

■Chapter 4: Managing Microsoft Office with Group Policy........... 105

Introduction to Managing Microsoft Office with Group Policy............. 105

    Installing Microsoft Office Group Policy Administrative Templates...................... 107

Important Office-Dedicated Policy Settings and Effects 112

Troubleshooting Office Issues Using Group Policy 117

    Issue: This File Can't Be Previewed Because There Is No Previewer Installed..... 117

    Issue: The Add-In You Have Selected Is Disabled by Your System Administrator . 120

    Issue: This Feature Has Been Disabled by Your Administrator............................. 122

    Issue: Performance and Display Problems with Office Clients............................. 125

Key Points 127

Summary.. 128

■Chapter 5: Basics of Group Policy Troubleshooting.................... 129

Getting Started with Troubleshooting.. 129

    Basic Troubleshooting Approaches.. 130

Common Group Policy Issues and Resolutions 140

Group Policy Not Being Applied 140

No User Policies in Group Policy Loopback Processing 143

Misallocation of User Accounts in Organization Units (OUs) 144

All Accounts Not Receiving the Same GPO Settings 144

Issues Arising Due to Folder Redirection 145

Common Issues Faced by Local Users Regarding GPO 146

Key Points 148

Summary 149

■Chapter 6: Advanced Group Policy Management 151

Introducing the Advanced Group Policy Management Tool 151

Installing and Configuring AGPM 153

Taking Control of GPOs Using AGPM 154

Editing GPO Using AGPM 155

Deleting and Restoring GPOs 156

Restoring GPOs to Previous Versions 157

Troubleshooting AGPM Problems 157

Additional Information About AGPM 162

Advanced Group Policy Troubleshooting 162

Understanding Group Policy Processing 163

Tools to Help Identify Group Policy Issues 166

Troubleshooting Group Policy Issues 169

Key Points 176

Summary 177

■Chapter 7: Group Policy Tips and Tricks 179

Popular GPO Tweaks for Windows 180

Customizing the Way You Receive Windows Updates in Windows 10 180

Forcing Windows to Display the Delete Confirmation Prompt 184

Renaming the Administrator Account 186

Restricting a Particular Tab in the Internet Properties Window 187

Disabling Help Tips in Windows 8.1 189

Disabling Access to the Control Panel and Settings App 190

Requiring a Password When Resuming From
Hibernate/Sleep Mode 192

Setting Custom Logon Screen Background Wallpaper 193

Displaying a Custom Message to Users During Attempted Logon 194

Opening File Explorer with the Ribbon Minimized 196

Enabling Sideloading of Apps 198

Preventing Deletion of Download History for Internet Explorer and
Microsoft Edge 200

Useful Tweaks for Office Apps 201

Allowing or Blocking Access to the Office Store 201

Configuring Telemetry Data Collection in Office 202

Forcing Outlook to be the Default Program for E-Mail,
Contacts, and Calendar 203

Disabling All Application Add-ins For Office 205

Assigning Your Choice of Key to Open Menus in Excel 205

Key Points 206

Summary 207

Index 209

About the Author

Kapil Arya is currently a Microsoft MVP (Most Valuable Professional) in the Windows and Devices for IT category. He is Microsoft MVP since 2014 and is presently a Windows Insider MVP as well. He became a Microsoft Community Contributor due to his active and consistent contributions to the Microsoft Answers and TechNet IT Pro forums over the last four years. Kapil loves to help Windows users to troubleshoot the various issues they face on their systems. He is very passionate about technology blogging and running his Windows-dedicated blog called **Kapil Sparks**™ (http://www.kapilarya.com) since 2010. He also created a Group Policy site to learn and explore policy settings online; you can access it at http://gp.kapilarya.com.

About the Editor

Andrew Bettany is a Microsoft MVP recognized for his Windows expertise. As a Microsoft Certified Trainer, Andrew delivers learning and consultancy to businesses in a number of technical areas including Windows deployment and troubleshooting. He is a frequent speaker at conferences worldwide.

He co-founded and manages the IT Masterclasses series of short technical courses (www.itmasterclasses.com) and is passionate about learning and helping others. In 2011 and 2013, he delivered a training boot camp in earthquake-hit Haiti to help those in the community rebuild their technology skills.

Very active on social media, Andrew can be found on LinkedIn, Facebook, and Twitter. He lives in a village just outside of the beautiful city of York in Yorkshire in the UK.

About the Technical Reviewer

Matthew Hitchcock is a Cloud and Datacenter Management MVP and works as a Consultant at Microsoft Singapore. He specializes in datacenter operations and management, and security and identity. Matthew has spent most of his career in the identity and directory services space, dealing with complex identity and migration scenarios including roles-based access, directory services automation, federation, mergers and divestment, and provisioning processes.

Matthew leads the Singapore PowerShell User Group and contributes to the Windows IT Pro User Group. He has written for multiple blogs including TechNet's "Hey, Scripting Guy" and The DevOps Collective. He has spoken at international conferences and events in Asia and Europe.

Windows Troubleshooting Series

When something goes wrong with technology, it can seem impossible to diagnose and repair the problem, and harder still to prevent a recurrence. In this series of books, we'll take you inside the workings of your devices and software, and we'll teach you how to find and fix the problems using a simple step-by-step approach that helps you understand the cause, the solution, and the tools required.

—Mike Halsey, MVP
Series Editor

As a Microsoft MVP awardee since 2011, the author of more than ten books on Microsoft Windows, and a teacher for many years, Mike Halsey understands the need to convey complex subjects in clear and non-intimidating ways.

He believes that the Windows Troubleshooting Series is a great example of how quality help, support, and tutorials can be delivered to individuals of all technical ability. He hopes you enjoy reading this and the many other books in this series, both now and for years to come.

Acknowledgments

I would like to express my deepest gratitude to Mike Halsey, series editor of the Apress Windows Troubleshooting Series, for his full support, expert guidance, and valuable corrections throughout the completion of this book. Without his incredible patience and timely wisdom, I would not have been able to complete this book.

Very special thanks to Andrew Bettany for pointing out where I'm wrong. His precious corrections, quality editing, and expert content implementations have made this book something you'll enjoy learning from. His guidance was truly inspiring to me and I consider myself lucky to work under his supervision. He deserves great credit for the creation of this book. I submit my heartiest gratitude to Matthew Hitchcock, for providing his expert guidance and suggestions, which took this book to the standard level.

I would also like to thank Gwenan Spearing, my editor at Apress, for her valuable suggestions and immense support on this project. Special credits to Jill Balzano and Melissa Maldonado, coordinating editors, and Laura Berendson and Douglas Pundick, development editors, for giving this book the shape it is in today.

Credits to SPi Global team finalizing this project and publication of this book.

Finally, thanks to my family, my blog readers, and my forum contributors for always supporting me. Their love, motivation, and encouragement inspire me to keep going on in my work.

Introduction

Group Policy is a very special tool that greatly simplifies the life of administrators by making it easy to manage their work environment. Even for local devices, Group Policy is the simplest way to manage and configure your device with the various features found in Windows.

Group Policy can be a weapon that works to customize, tweak, and troubleshoot your installation of Windows. Unlike the registry, you do not need to delve into complex editing. With the help of UI and Group Policy Preferences, you can manage equivalent registry settings conveniently. Another advantage of Group Policy is that it is normally possible to revert back to the default state if you configure something incorrectly.

This book is our best practice guide to using Group Policy. Our aim in creating this book is to encourage readers to learn about the possibilities of Group Policy, how to apply settings, and how to troubleshoot issues that may arise. We have included plenty of additional content, such as the section on advanced tools for GPO management (Group Policy for Office), which we hope will extend your understanding deeper into Group Policy. We finish the book with a tips and tricks section, which may encourage you to experiment with Windows and configure it just the way you like.

CHAPTER 1

■ ■ ■

Getting Started with Group Policy

This chapter introduces Group Policy and explains how it can be used and configured via its editor, the Group Policy snap-in. With the help of Group Policy, you can save a huge amount of time deploying software on different machines, restricting access to a particular program or feature, enhancing the security and networking of your corporate environment, and making management easier and smoother.

This chapter will cover the following:

- What Group Policy is and how to use it

- How to use the Local Group Policy Editor to configure a policy

- How Group Policy works in detail

- The relationship between the registry and Group Policy

- Advanced applications of Group Policy

- Additional concepts regarding Group Policy

Introduction

The Microsoft Windows operating systems allows you to influence either or both of the two types of typical interaction: computer and user. This means that you can configure settings that apply to only the computer, or only the user, or both. This allows administrators to deploy settings for different scenarios. For example, a device that is used by multiple users, such as a computer in a hot desk role, can have settings that relate to each user who logs on to the device based on their role within the organization. Additionally, the device may have computer-specific settings that affect any user of the device; that is, the settings affect the computer.

The feature that allows you to deploy these configurations is called **Group Policy**. Group Policy can be set a local level, which affects the local device, or from within Active Directory, which applies to devices connected to a domain environment. Local Group Policy settings are configured using the Local Group Policy Editor, shown in Figure 1-1.

© Kapil Arya 2016
K. Arya, *Windows Group Policy Troubleshooting*, DOI 10.1007/978-1-4842-1886-0_1

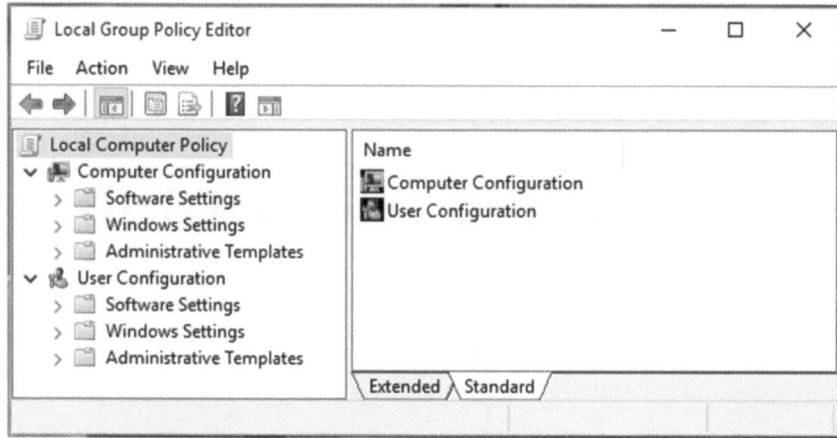

Figure 1-1. *Local Group Policy Editor*

It is worth noting that when Group Policy settings are applied to a device they are applied to the registry. An advanced user could use the Registry Editor to directly edit configurations for computers and users within the registry, but this is not recommended because making mistakes within the registry can affect the system adversely. Group Policy is the preferred and recommended method for effectively editing the registry. Once you have become proficient with both Group Policy and the registry, you will appreciate that they can be considered as mirror images of each other. If you make alterations to one, the other will also reflect the change.

Using the Local Group Policy Editor

Group Policy settings are configured and saved within a **Group Policy Object** (GPO). The Microsoft Management Console (MMC) or snap-in provided to edit these local GPOs is called the **Local Group Policy Editor** (LGPO) on local machines, while on domain based-systems you use the **Group Policy Management Console** (GPMC) to edit GPOs that are distributed within the domain.

To manage local GPOs, you must launch the Local Group Policy Editor. You can access the Local Group Policy Editor in several ways. The actual GPO editor is a Microsoft Management Console (MMC) snap-in called **gpedit**, which is stored within the **C:\Windows\System32** folder and is a Microsoft Common Console Document (**.msc** file format), as shown in Figure 1-2.

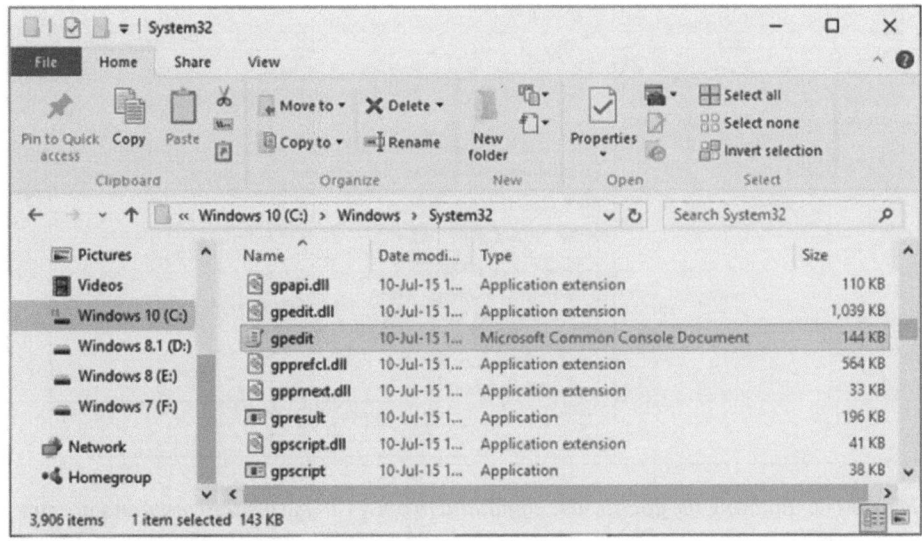

Figure 1-2. *The **gpedit.msc** file is located under the system root drive*

In Windows 10, you can open Group Policy Editor by searching for **gpedit** via Cortana. The traditional way to open the same editor is by running the **gpedit.msc** command in the Run utility (by pressing the **Windows Key + R),** as shown in Figure 1-3.

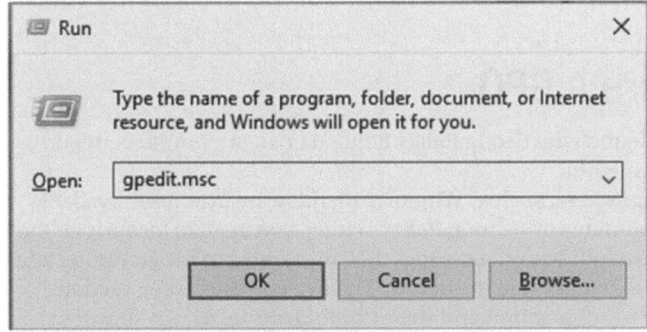

Figure 1-3. *The **gpedit.msc** command in the Run utility*

In order to open GPO via the command prompt, all you need to do is run the same command (**gpedit.msc**), as shown in Figure 1-4.

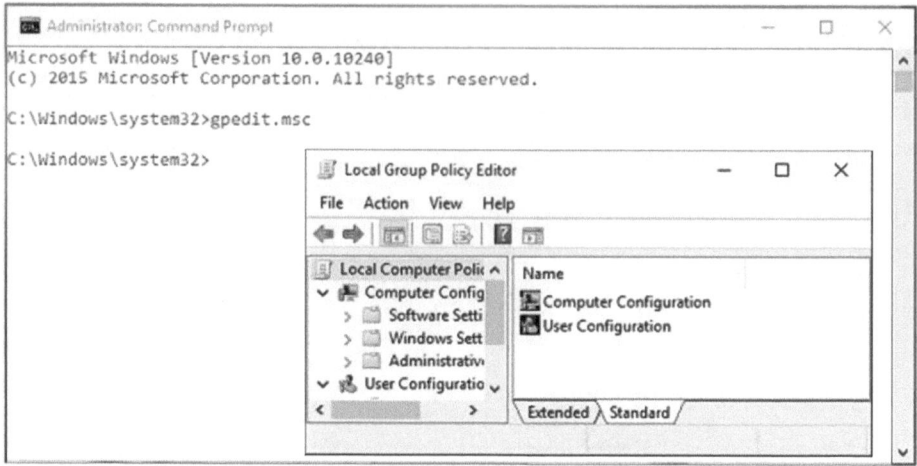

*Figure 1-4. Running the **gpedit.msc** command to open GPO using the command prompt*

■ **Note**   The Local Group Policy Editor is available on Windows desktop editions, but on Windows Server editions you can manage Group Policy through the Group Policy Management Console. To open it, run the **gpmc.msc** command via the Run menu item or a command prompt.

How to Configure a GPO

You should now be able to launch the Group Policy Editor. Let's learn how to configure a Group Policy Object in the snap-in.

On a modern operating system, such as Windows 10, there are over 3,500 available GPOs. In order to modify the status of a Group Policy setting, you need to locate it on the editor. The editor policies are split between settings that are applied to the computer and settings that affect the user that logs on to the device. The two corresponding sections of the policy are **Computer Configuration** and **User Configuration,** as was shown in Figure 1-1. If a setting is configured within the Computer Configuration tree, it will affect system-wide operations and is applied to all users that use the system. In other words, you can think of it as deploying a global setting for your system. Alternatively, if the policy setting is located within the User Configuration tree, then it will only affect operations for the logged-in user. You can configure settings in both areas. Many settings can be found in both areas; this allows you to control how the settings are applied.

The majority of GPO settings are used to modify the behavior of Windows. **Administrative templates** are used to provide logical groupings of settings such as Windows components, Internet Explorer, printers, networking, and the like. Administrative templates are basically registry-based policy settings, and each GPO setting can be configured with the help of them. These files have an **.admx** extension and utilize XML markup. There are two types of admx files used in GPOs. First, the language-neutral file, **.admx**, determines the policy settings, the location, and the category. The **.adml** file is the language resource file. It provides language-specific information to the language-neutral **.admx** file.

By default, there are three status options that a Group Policy Setting can exhibit: **Enabled**, **Not Configured**, and **Disabled**. The default status for all Group Policy settings is *Not Configured*. This is the state when you view a GPO for the first time, such as just after installing Windows.

To understand how and why you should configure a policy setting, let's use an example. Suppose you want to block third-party cookies in the Microsoft Edge browser. You want to achieve this by configuring a Group Policy setting. Luckily, there is a Group Policy setting available for this, and the setting is available for both the computer and user area separately. Follow these steps to configure this policy:

1. Launch GPO by typing **gpedit.msc** into the Search box and pressing Enter.

   If you want to configure the policy for computer, navigate to Computer Configuration ➤ Administrative Templates ➤ Windows Components ➤ Microsoft Edge.

   If you want to configure the policy for the user, navigate to User Configuration ➤ Administrative Templates ➤ Windows Components ➤ Edge UI.

2. Within the **Microsoft Edge** folder on either configuration, you will notice several settings listed on the right pane. On a newly installed device, all of the settings will exhibit the Not Configured status by default, as shown in Figure 1-5.

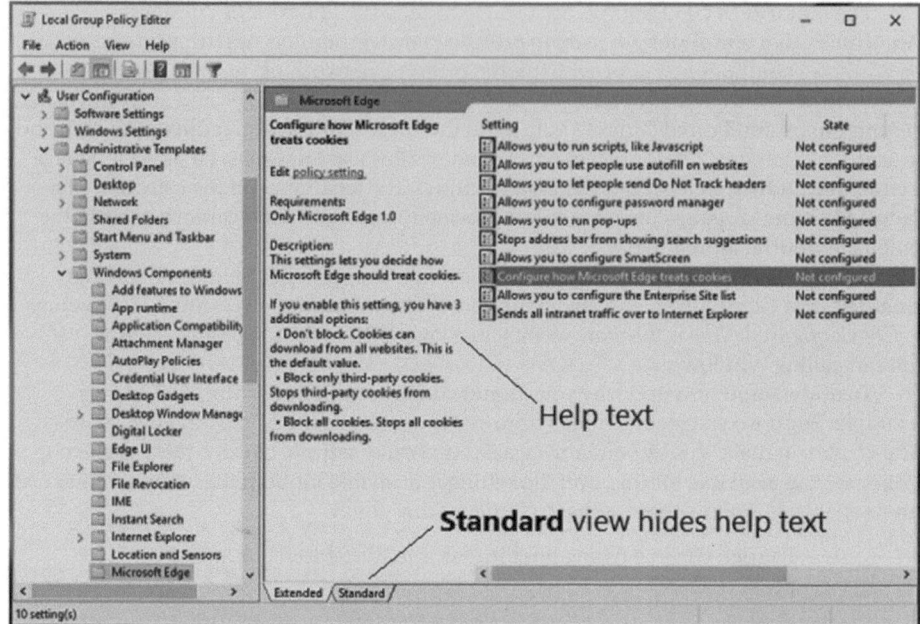

Figure 1-5. *Locating the Configure how Microsoft Edge treats cookies policy in Local Group Policy Editor*

3. Locate the *Configure how Microsoft Edge treats cookies policy* and double-click the setting to modify its status.

4. The window shown in Figure 1-6 allows you to configure the status for the *Configure how Microsoft Edge treats cookies* policy. The text mentioned under the **Help** section is useful when determining the effect of each configuration option. To illustrate how to set the GPO, select the *Enabled* option to turn on the policy and then under the *Configure Cookies setting* section, select *Block only 3rd-party cookies* option.

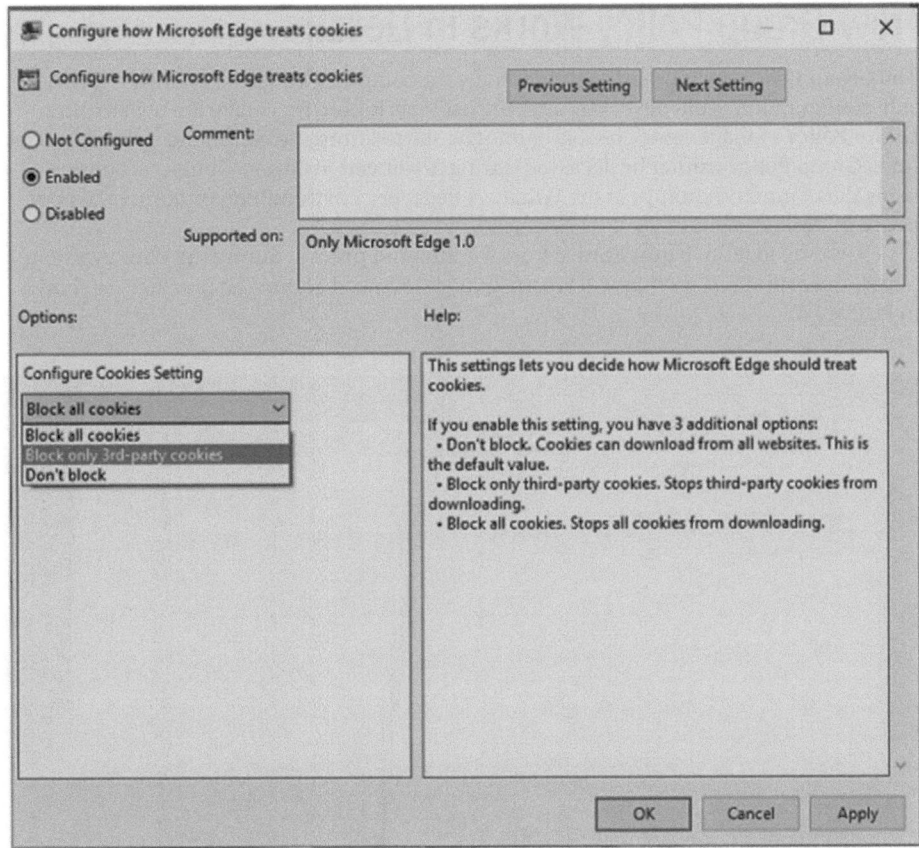

Figure 1-6. *GPO configuration setting options. To save the GPO, click the **OK** button*

In this way you have successfully configured a policy for your Windows system, under which third-party cookies are blocked for the Microsoft Edge browser.

■ **Tip**   You can download the Group Policy Settings reference available for your operating system from the Microsoft Download Center at `www.microsoft.com/en-in/download/details.aspx?id=25250`. The Windows 10 reference contains details about more than 3,500 Group Policies you can configure.

How Group Policy Works in Detail

The Group Policy engine starts acting when your computer boots up. However, the user side configuration is effective only after the user has logged in. Unlike the registry, the Group Policy Management Console cannot be started from the command prompt at boot time. Group Policy cannot be accessed during Advanced Recovery Options scenarios, using the command prompt in the Windows Recovery Environment, or during the boot phase of Windows.

If you try to launch **gpedit.msc** from a command prompt during the Windows boot phase, the command prompt will return an unrecognized command message, as shown in Figure 1-7.

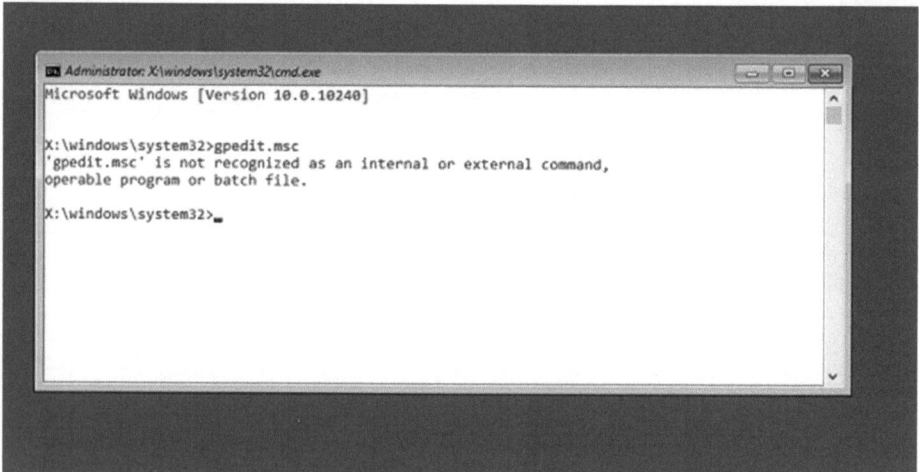

*Figure 1-7. Running **gpedit.msc** produces an error during the boot process*

Within a domain environment, Active Directory Directory Services (AD DS) controls how Group Policy settings are applied.

The engine that processes Group Policy settings is also referred as the core of Group Policy. The subsets of this engine are client-side extensions (CSEs) and server-side snap-in extensions (SSEs). The Group Policy engine on the client evaluates Active Directory to understand and prioritize the policies it should apply.

■ **Note**   For user-dedicated Windows operating systems, Group Policy is only provided on Professional and Enterprise editions. This means if you've got a Windows 10 Home or Basic version, you won't be able to access Group Policy.

Let's look "under the hood" to see how the Group Policy engine works. After reading this section, you will have a better understanding about how GPOs work.

Connecting Windows to a Server

Before delving deeper into how GPOs are applied to your system, let's review the steps required to connect a Windows 10 machine to a domain.

1. On a Windows 10 machine, go to Settings app ➤ System ➤ About. In the right pane of the window (see Figure 1-8), click the **Join a domain** button.

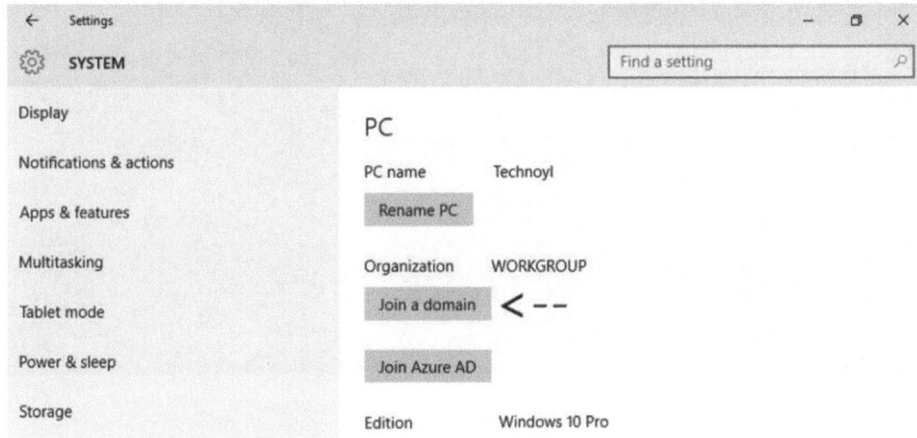

Figure 1-8. *Joining a domain*

2. In the *Join a domain* prompt, type the domain name and click **Next**.(see Figure 1-9).

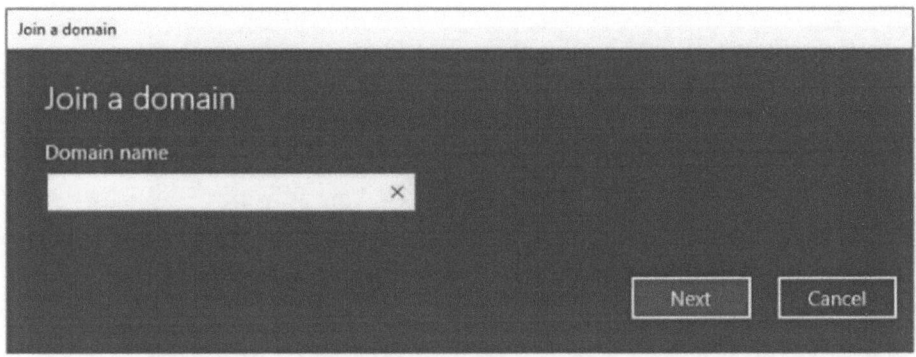

Figure 1-9. *Entering a domain name*

3. Next, you'll be asked to enter you domain credentials in order to verify your identity. Enter your details and hit **OK** (see Figure 1-10).

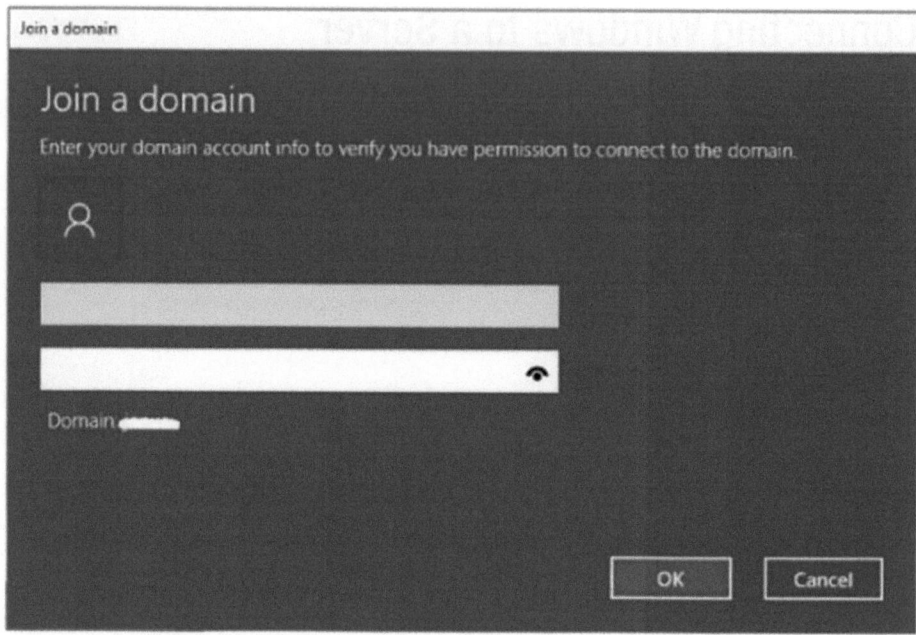

Figure 1-10. Adding your domain credentials

4. You can then add an account for the person who is using the machine. The Account type can be chosen on the screen, depending upon the situation (see Figure 1-11). Click **Next**.

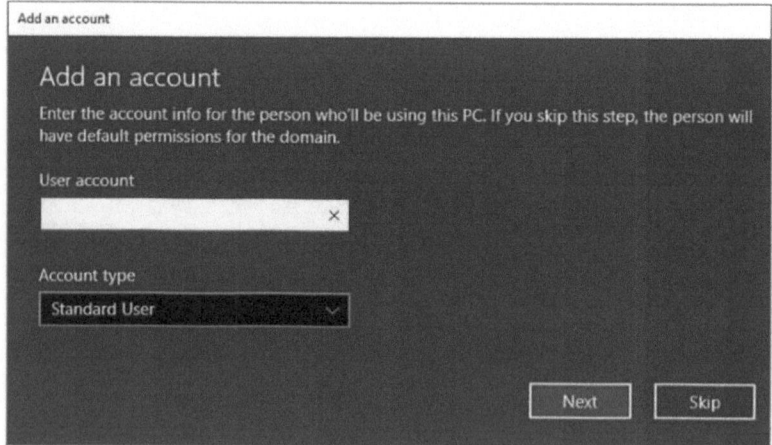

Figure 1-11. Adding the account you want to use

5. Then you will be asked to restart your machine, as shown in Figure 1-12, so that your connection to domain can be completed.

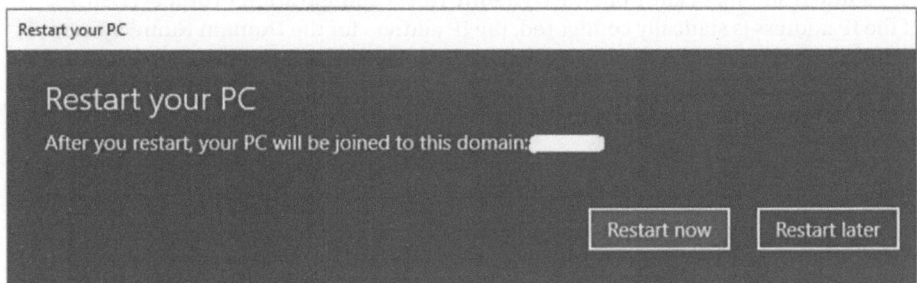

Figure 1-12. *Restart prompt*

6. After rebooting the system, the login screen will ask you to input your domain credentials (see Figure 1-13). After entering valid details, you can finally log in as a domain user.

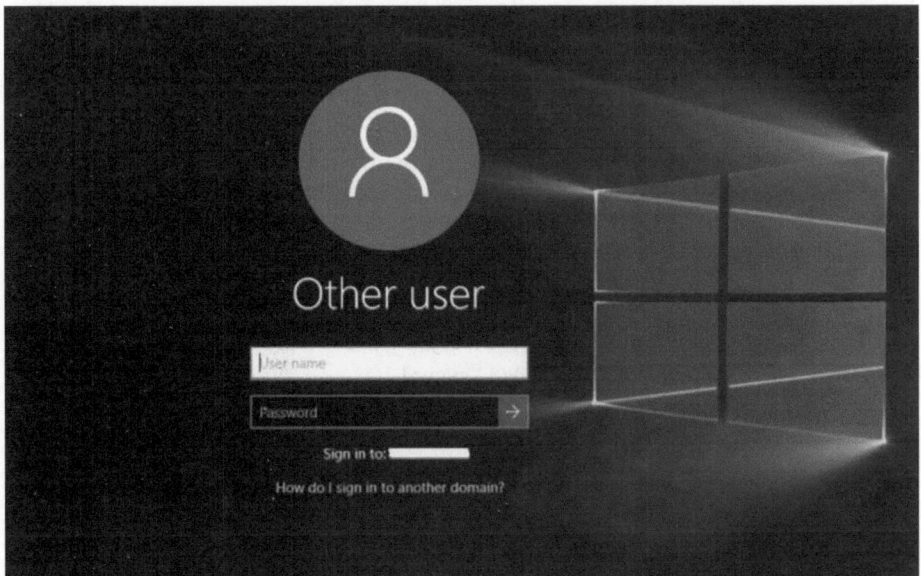

Figure 1-13. *Windows 10 logon screen for domain accounts*

Now that you have joined your workstation to AD DS, let's explore how GPOs work within a domain environment.

During the computer boot-up process:

When your domain-joined workstation boots up, it will obtain an **Internet Protocol** (IP) address automatically from the **Dynamic Host Configuration Protocol** (DHCP). If the IP address is statically configured, the IP address for the **Domain Name System** (DNS) must be the DNS server that relates to your Domain Controller (DC) server itself, for example dc.*apress.com*.

At this point, your workstation will be configured with the correct IP address information, which will include:

- IP address and **subnet mask**

- DNS Server IP address for the AD

Once the desktop has the IP address for the DNS server, it will look up the necessary records in DNS and will try to establish a connection to the **NETLOGON** service running on a DC. The DCs are listed in the DNS database under the **Service Resource Locator** (SRV) records. When the domain controller is upgraded from a server to a domain controller for that domain, the entries are entered dynamically.

■ **Note**   You can locate the NETLOGON service under the *Services* snap-in, which can be found by running the **services.msc** command. If this service is not running, you will not be able to connect to a DC.

Communication between the desktop and DC:

After obtaining list of DCs and identifying a DC, the desktop will then communicate with it to authenticate. This communication occurs via a secure channel between the desktop and the DC. The communication occurs through the shared folders available on the DC. These folders are generally found at the following locations:

Share	Location
SYSVOL	%SYSTEMROOT%\SYSVOL\sysvol
NETLOGON	%SYSTEMROOT%\SYSVOL\sysvol\<domain name>\SCRIPTS

The GPOs are stored under the *SYSVOL* share and the logon scripts are stored under the *NETLOGON* share. Once the computer and user have been authenticated and a connection to these shares has been established, the appropriate GPO settings are made available for download.

Identifying Group Policy Objects for devices:

This section focuses on the policies that will affect the computer. Only GPOs found in the *Computer Configuration* portion of the Group Policy tree will affect the computer object. The DC which the computer is connected to will determine which GPOs should apply to the device based on the computer account status and location within Active Directory. An administrator is able to create three distinct logical boundary areas within Active Directory, and the computer account object can exist at one of the following levels:

- **Domain:** A logical group of network objects such as computers, users, and devices sharing the same Active Directory database.

- **Site:** A logical grouping of a set of well-connected subnets.

- **Organizational Unit (OU):** This is the smallest logical unit within Active Directory that can contain users, groups, computers, and other organizational units.

The DC will also determine which site the computer belongs to, so the GPOs linked to this site are also applied to the device.

All of the GPOs that are linked to the domain, site, and organizational unit where the computer account resides will be delivered to the device. For more advanced control of objects within Active Directory, there are several other factors that can come into play, including security filtering, nested OUs, network topology considerations, and more. These topics will be explored later in this book.

■ **Info**   When talking about Active Directory, you should be familiar with the concepts of domain, tree, and forest. All of these components are the levels in AD that hold objects. The domain is the smallest entity and a collection of domains makes up a tree. A forest is collection of many trees sharing the same directory information, directory schema, global catalog, etc. This can be easily understood with the help of Figure 1-14.

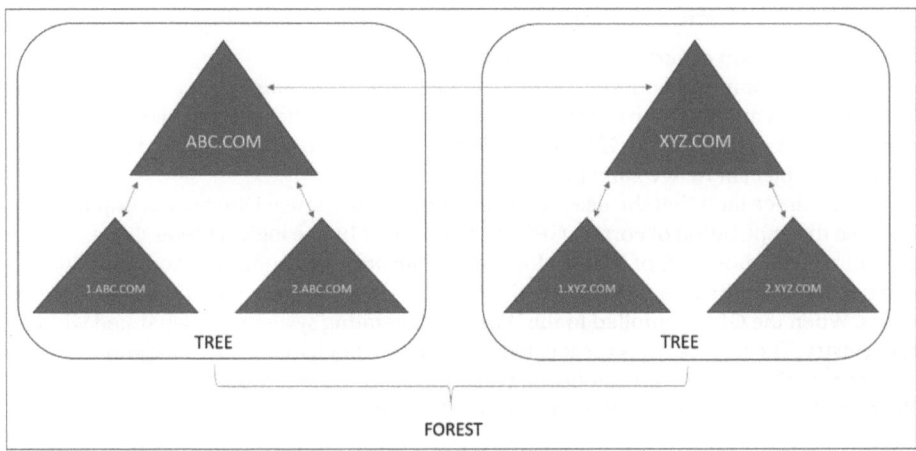

Figure 1-14. *Relationship between domain, tree, and forest*

The GPOs that are delivered to the machine are tracked; once applied, you can see that they have been stored on the computer within the registry. This list of GPOs applied to a device can be seen in Figure 1-15 and found in the registry at following location:

HKEY_LOCAL_MACHINE\Software\Microsoft\Windows\CurrentVersion\Group Policy\ History.

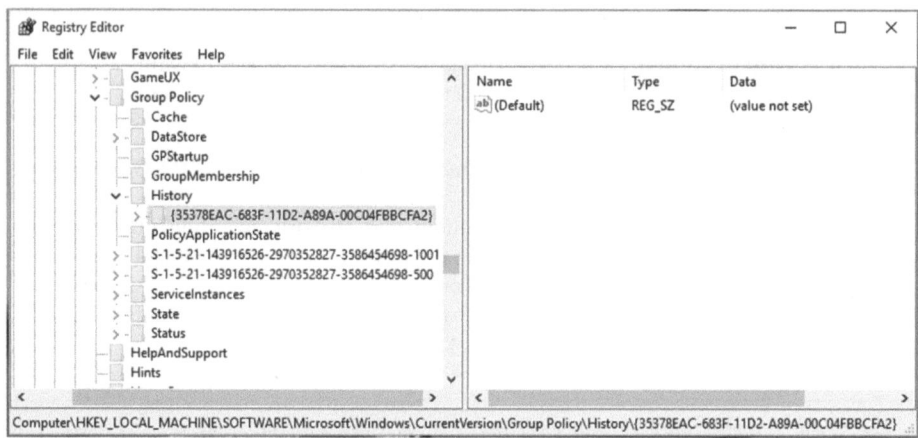

Figure 1-15. *List of applied computer-specific GPOs stored in the registry*

■ **Note**   Windows always uses a globally unique identifier (GUID) for GPOs, rather than a friendly name, because GUIDs are unique across applications and there is less chance of them clashing.

Determination of Group Policy Objects for users:

After the computer boots and Windows loads, the *Computer Configuration* GPOs will be applied first and then the user logon screen will appear. The GPOs stored in the *User Configuration* portion of the GPO are applied based on the user account and the location of the user object in Active Directory.

You will see later that the user object location within Active Directory is important because the application of correct GPOs is determined by the logical hierarchical structure of AD. Both sets of settings for the user account and computer configuration can be stored within a single Group Policy Object, or you can separate them into discrete GPOs. When the GPO is applied to the Windows operating system, it is separated within the registry. The user settings are located at the user branch in registry configuration, as shown in Figure 1-16 and at following location: *HKEY_CURRENT_USER\Software\ Microsoft\Windows\CurrentVersion\Group Policy\History.*

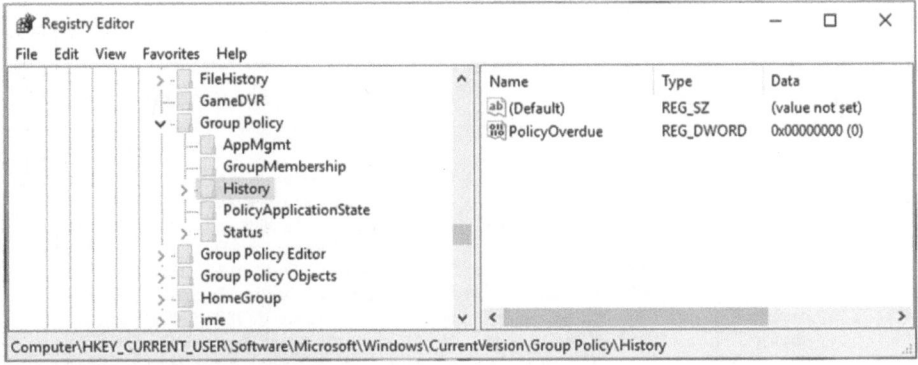

Figure 1-16. *List of user-related GPOs stored in the registry*

Relationship Between Group Policy and the Registry

You have already seen that the registry and GPOs are related to each other. The registry is a hierarchical database that stores all the computer settings that relate to Windows. Almost every component found in Windows is stored as a variable or setting (as a key and value) in the registry. Group Policy exposes over 3,500 settings that the IT Pro can configure as GPOs and these settings can then be applied to the registry database during Windows boot up and after the user has logged on.

In this section, we will demonstrate how the registry and GPO settings are related to each other. For this example, we will use the free Process Monitor tool from Sysinternals. Process Monitor allows us to see the changes being made to Windows. To investigate the low-level configuration that is being applied by Group Policy to the registry, carry out the following steps:

■ **Note** You can download Process Monitor from Sysinternals at `https://technet.` `microsoft.com/en-us/sysinternals/bb896645.aspx`.

---

1. Run the **Procmon.exe** executable to launch Process Monitor, as shown in Figure 1-17.

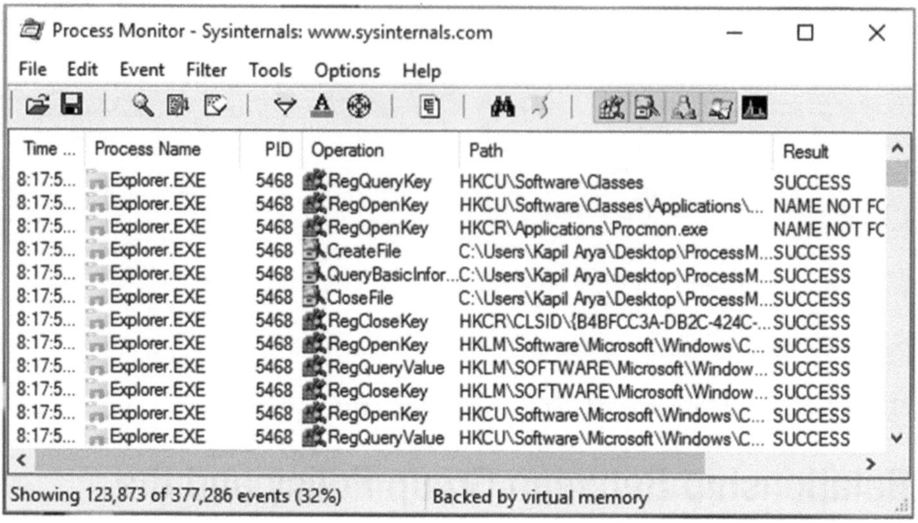

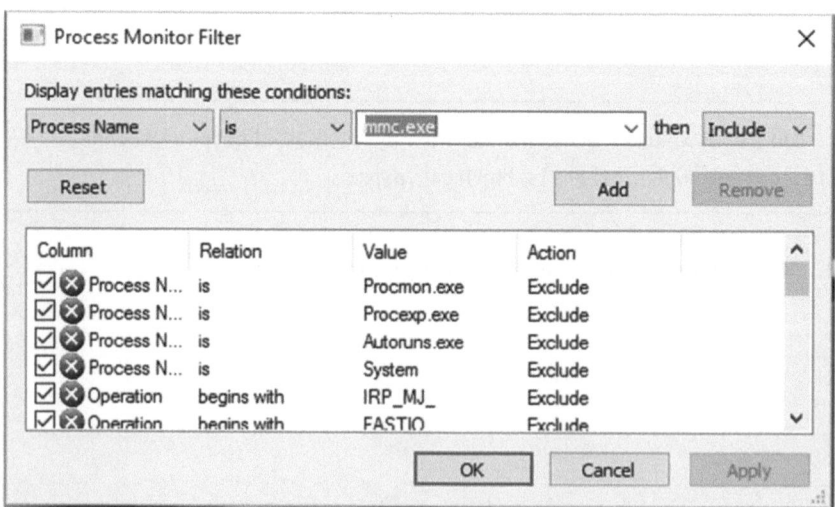

Figure 1-17. *Process Monitor*

2. Press **Ctrl + L** and the Process Monitor Filter dialog box appears. Create a new filter with a process name of **mmc. exe**. You can use the drop-down list if you prefer to select the process. Set the *Include* option to display entries matching these conditions.

3. Click **Add** to confirm the filter, as shown in Figure 1-18.

Figure 1-18. *Process Monitor Filter prompt for adding the process name of **mmc.exe** and then adding the Include rule*

4.   Let's focus on the registry changes, so create another filter rule. The second rule uses the *Operation is RegSetValue* criteria shown in Figure 1-19. Click **OK.**

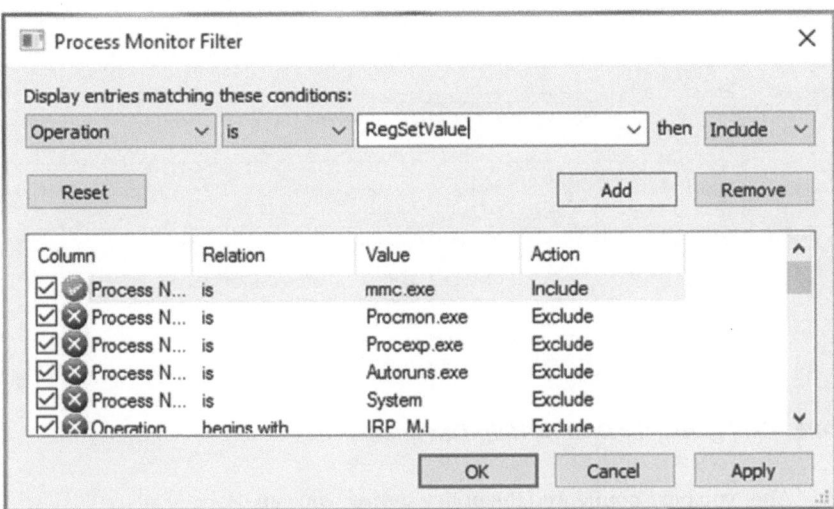

Figure 1-19. *Process Monitor Filter prompt to filter registry changes*

5.   Process Monitor should have a clear results pane. If it is not empty, press the **Ctrl + X** key combination in the Process Monitor window to clear the log.

6.   Open *Run* by pressing the **Windows Key + R**, type **gpedit. msc**, and press **Enter** to launch the Group Policy snap-in.

7.   Now configure a GPO setting. Navigate to the *Disable help tips* GPO setting in the Computer Configuration ➤ Administrative Templates ➤ Windows Components ➤ Edge UI folder, and configure the local GPO policy as shown in Figure 1-20, and click **OK.**

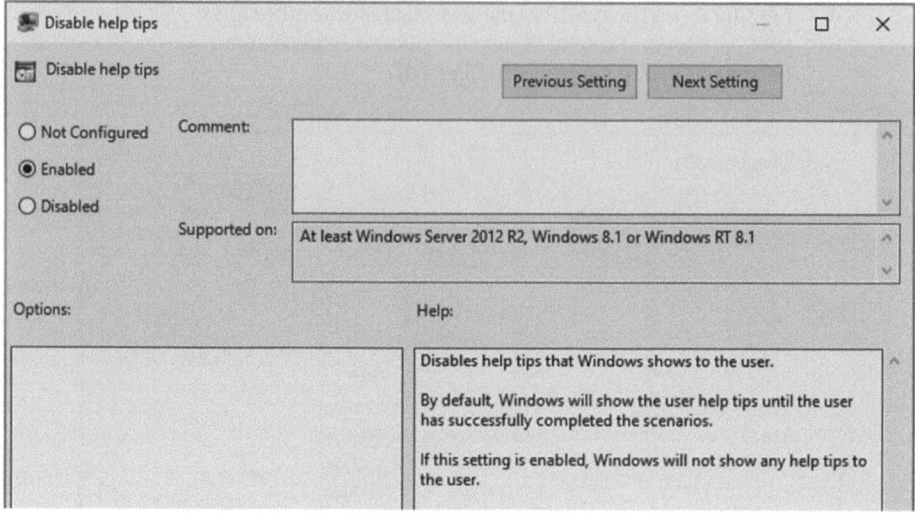

Figure 1-20. *Configuring the **Disable Help Tips** group policy*

8. After you have configured the policy setting, you can minimize or close the Group Policy window. In Process Monitor you'll now find the entry for the policy change you made. You can easily identify the entry by the time displayed, which should be the same time as when you made changes.

9. Right-click the entry and select **Jump To** in the context menu, as shown in Figure 1-21.

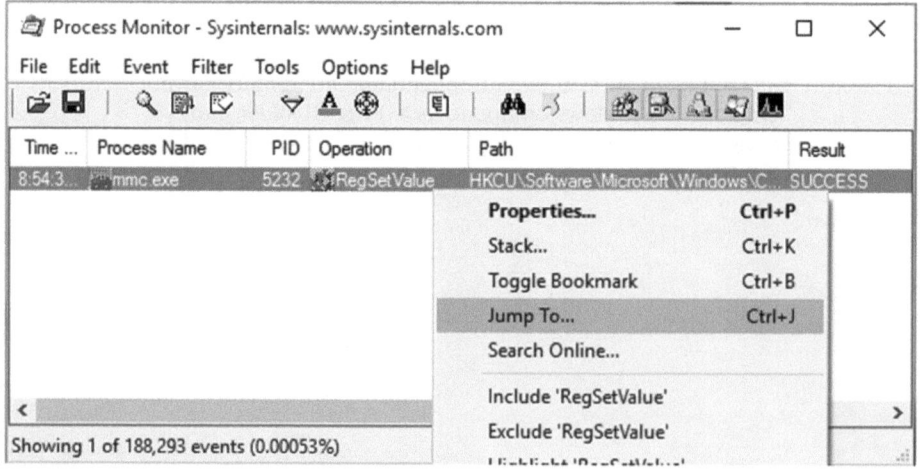

Figure 1-21. *Process context menu to jump directly to associated registry key*

10. The Registry Editor window will open and display the registry key location that is reflected as a result of the policy setting you just changed, as shown in Figure 1-22.

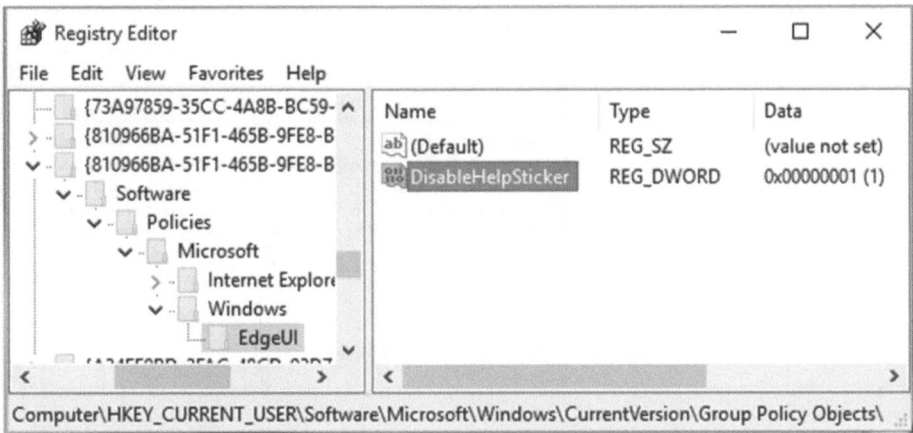

Figure 1-22. *Registry Editor window showing the key modified by Group Policy*

So the summary is, Group Policy and the registry are directly related to each other, which is useful when troubleshooting system problems.

Advanced Uses of Group Policy

There are many uses for Group Policy. It can be used to harden clients and servers, manage user activities in a domain environment, manage features on local computer, and so on. For quick reference, the following sections lists some well-known applications of GPOs.

Enhancing Security of Clients and Servers

GPOs support security templates, and by using them you can harden servers and client installations in a domain environment and also on a standalone local machine. This set of security templates is commonly known by the name **Local Security Policy** and can be accessed by running the **secpol.msc** command on the system.

In a client Windows operating system, security templates are stored in the **C:\Windows\Security\Templates** file location. These files are basically text files and they can be configured using the snap-in shown in Figure 1-23.

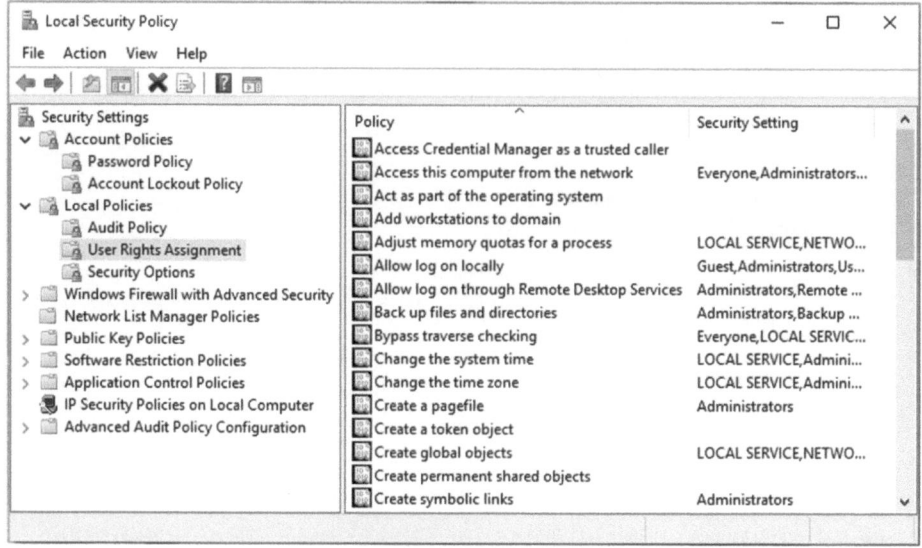

Figure 1-23. *Local Security Policy snap-in on Windows 10*

We will discuss Local Security Policy in detail in Chapter 3.

Deploying Policies to Manage User Actions

Sometimes you need to restrict user activities whether you are in a domain environment or using a standalone local computer with multiple users. GPOs can be applied easily and reliably to manage hundreds of settings that affect users.

For example, if you want to restrict users from customizing the Start Menu or Screen in Windows 10, you can define a policy setting for that. Open the snap-in and configure **Start Layout**, which is located under User Configuration ➤ Administrative Templates ➤ Start Menu and Taskbar ➤ Start Layout, as shown in Figure 1-24.

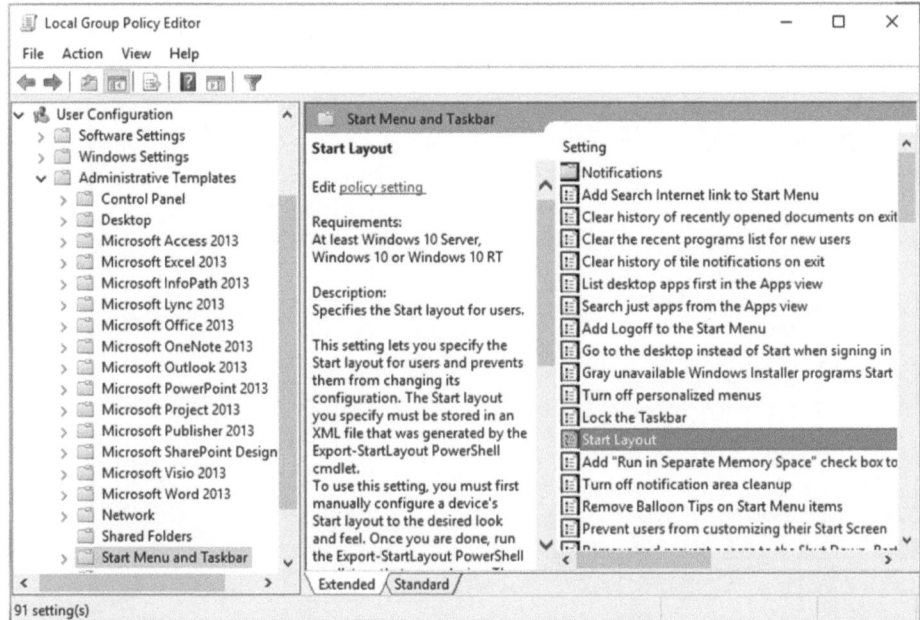

Figure 1-24. *Deploying Group Policy to restrict Start Menu/Screen customization by users*

Similarly, you can also configure this policy on a local computer with multiple users. In this way, Group Policy is easy to use and deploy due to its simplified behavior, as compared to modifying settings directly using the registry.

Managing Microsoft Office in Your Corporate Environment

The Microsoft Office productivity suite includes hundreds of configurable settings that administrators can use to customize the various applications. Managing these settings in a corporate environment individually can be quite challenging. Microsoft provides GPO templates for the Office application for administrators to use to centrally configure policies that are applied to user machines. Microsoft Office 2013 includes more than 2,100 settings for administrators to use, some which are shown in Figure 1-25. We will discuss Group Policy management for Microsoft Office applications in detail in Chapter 4.

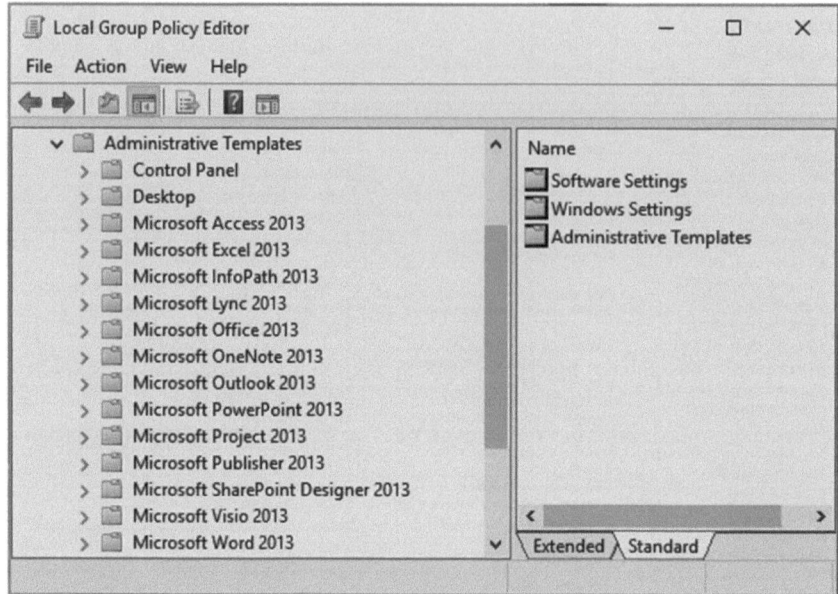

Figure 1-25. *Group Policy window with Microsoft Office GPO administrative templates installed*

Network Connections Management

Group Policy can play a vital role in maintaining secure network connections on a Windows device. Using policies that are applied to networked devices within a domain environment, administrators can deploy settings that can control network-related operations for the device and user.

The network management policies are found in the following GPO location: Computer or User Configuration ➤ Administrative Templates ➤ Network.

To alter these policies on a local computer, you need to be a member of the administrative users group. If you are in a domain, you must belong to domain administrators group to perform these operations. Figure 1-26 shows the policy settings to manage network connections inside a GPO.

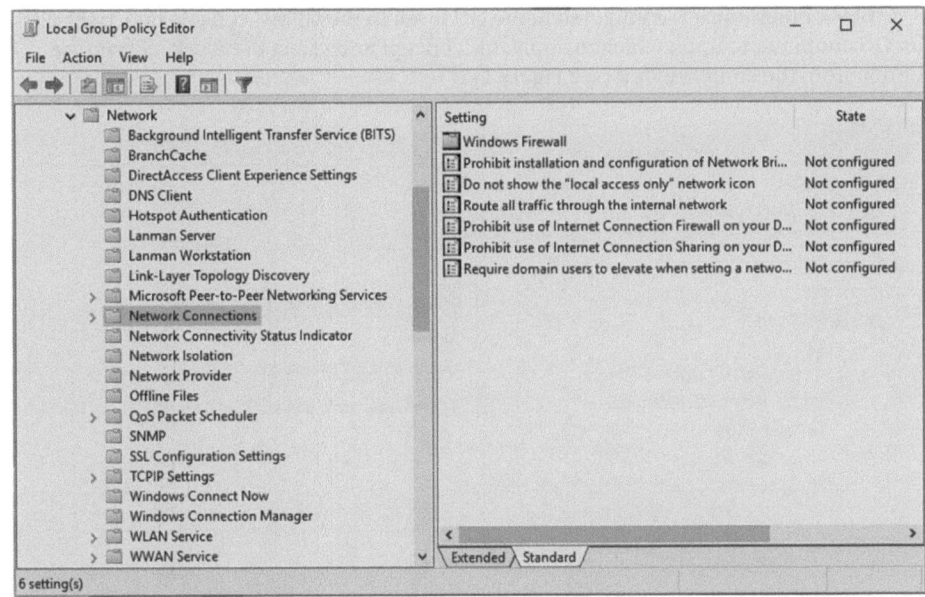

Figure 1-26. *Group Policy window with network connections administrative templates*

■ **Note** To verify if you belong to the administrators group on local computer, open the *Local Users and Group Users* snap-in by running the **lusrmgr.msc** command. Then expand **Users** and double-click on **your Name**. On the account property dialog box, switch to the **Member of** tab. If you belong to administrative group, you should see **Administrators** indicated.

Additional Concepts

There are various terms used in regards to Group Policy. To manage GPO, administrators require information about these terms. This section covers some additional GPO concepts in brief.

Block GPO Inheritance

Actually, Group Policies are cumulative in nature, so all of the GPOs will apply to site, domain, and OU as well as locally for both user and machine configurations. When you need to stop this situation, block inheritance comes into play. Block inheritance means that no policy setting from higher lever containers are applied to a particular level. Hence, it is obvious that when GPO inheritance is blocked, higher-level GPOs are blocked, provided there is no policy enforcement.

Block inheritance is configured at the OU level. In the GPMC console tree, right-click an OU container to upon which to apply this concept and select the *Block inheritance* option from the context menu (see Figure 1-27).

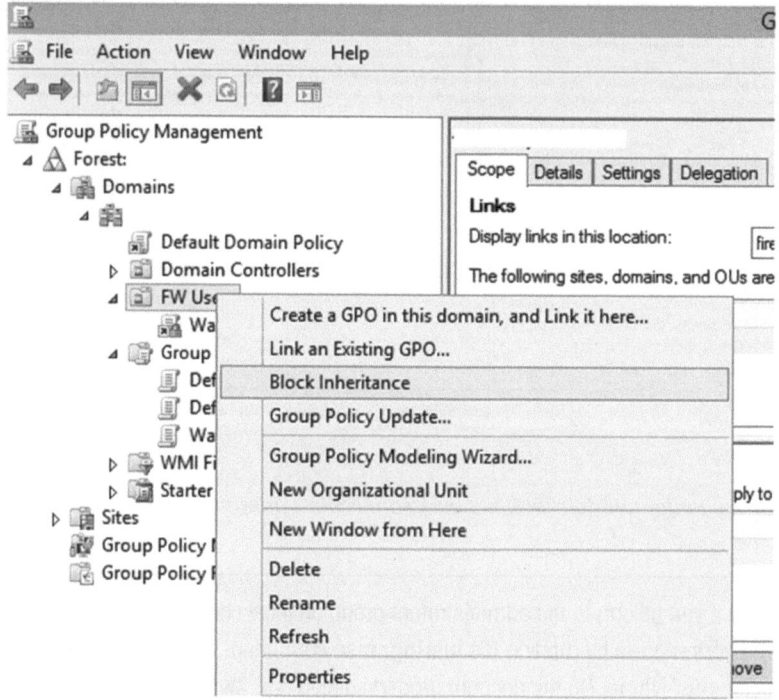

Figure 1-27. *Block inheritance in a GPO*

Enforcing GPOs

After reading about block GPO inheritance, you might be thinking that when inheritance is blocked, does it mean that no higher-level policies can be applied? The answer to this question is *No*. The exceptional case for blocking inheritance is enforcing a GPO. When a GPO link (read about linking GPOs in next chapter) is *enforced*, it gets applied depending upon the level at which the GPO is configured. This is actually because the GPO is enforced at the GPO level.

To enforce a particular GPO setting, right-click on it in the console tree and select *Enforced* (see Figure 1-28).

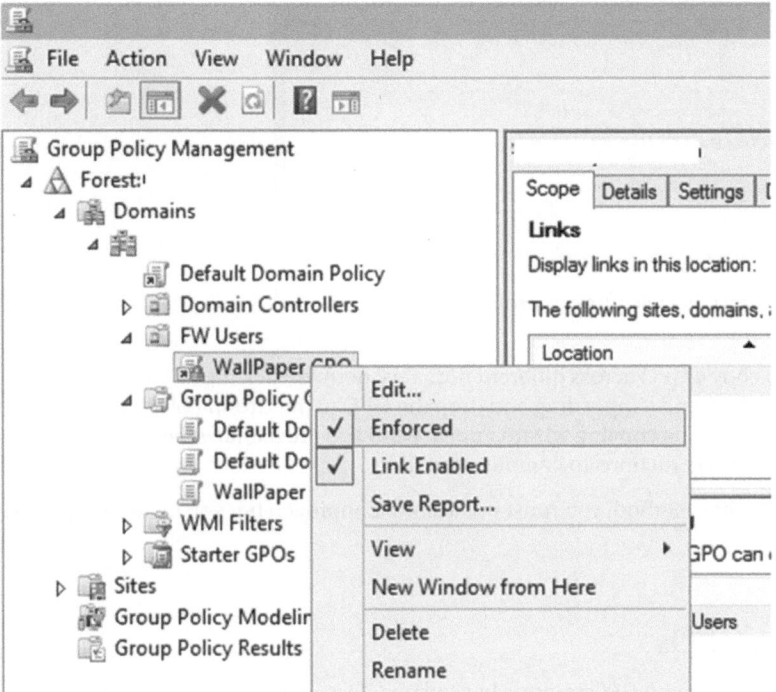

***Figure 1-28.** Enforcing GPO links*

Let's understand GPO inheritance blocking and enforcing with the help of an example. Say that X and Y GPOs are applied at the domain and OU levels, respectively. If neither inheritance blocking is configured nor enforced, then the X and Y GPOs get applied on the OU. But when you enable inheritance blocking on the OU level, only Y will be applied and X is blocked. The twist comes when you enforce X GPO. After enforcing X, no matter whether you have block inheritance applied on OU or not, X will be applied in parallel to Y, as it is enforced now.

Copying GPOs

Sometimes it happens that you need to use same GPO setting in different domains and forests. In that case, you can avoid wasting time creating a new GPO and just copy a GPO from another domain/forest. Copying is also used for creating new versions of an existing GPO that you can test without affecting the existing one. Copying GPOs works in two ways: either the right-click method or the drag-and-drop method. The drag-and-drop method is as follows:

- When you are copying GPOs in same domain, simply drag and drop the GPO across Group Policy Objects. You may be asked to assign permissions for copied or resulted GPO (see Figure 1-29).

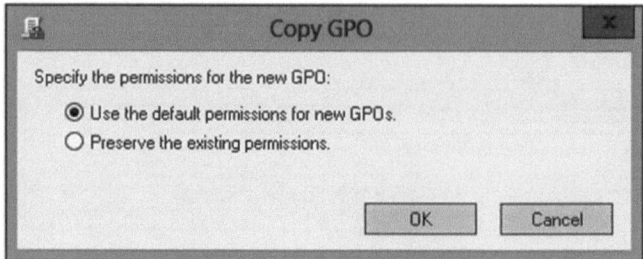

Figure 1-29. Copy GPO permissions prompt

- To copy a GPO across different domains, double-click the target domain, and simply drag and drop the GPO to the Group Policy Objects. The copying wizard appears and you must follow the on-screen instructions to complete the task.

In the right-click method, you must use a similar approach but you need to copy and paste manually.

Importing GPOs

The Import operation with GPO imports backed up GPOs. Importing is generally done after creating a new GPO. This is typically done to move Group Policy settings between different environments, such as test and production. This operation can be performed using following steps:

1. In the GPMC console tree, highlight the GPO to which you want to import settings. Then go to Action ➤ Import Settings.

2. You will now see *Import Settings* wizard window. Click **Next**. Now you can back up the existing settings of the GPO to which you are importing settings. You will need to specify a backup folder on the next screen of the wizard. Then click **Next**.

3. In the next screen, you can select one of the earlier backed up GPOs and import its settings to the existing GPO. Complete the wizard by clicking **Next**. Once the wizard tasks are completed, you are done with importing.

WMI Filter for GPOs

The WMI Filter helps you decide which operating system should apply the policy. In case of a GPO, administrators often need to work with miscellaneous operating systems. Using WMI Filter queries, they can limit the OSes to which a GPO applies. Using this approach, it is possible to apply GPOs only on OSes and you can dump server operating systems in one OU. Here is how you apply WMI filter:

1. In the GPMC console tree, locate the WMI Filters node and double-click it.

2. Then in *New WMI Filter* window shown in Figure 1-30, enter the required information and click **Add**.

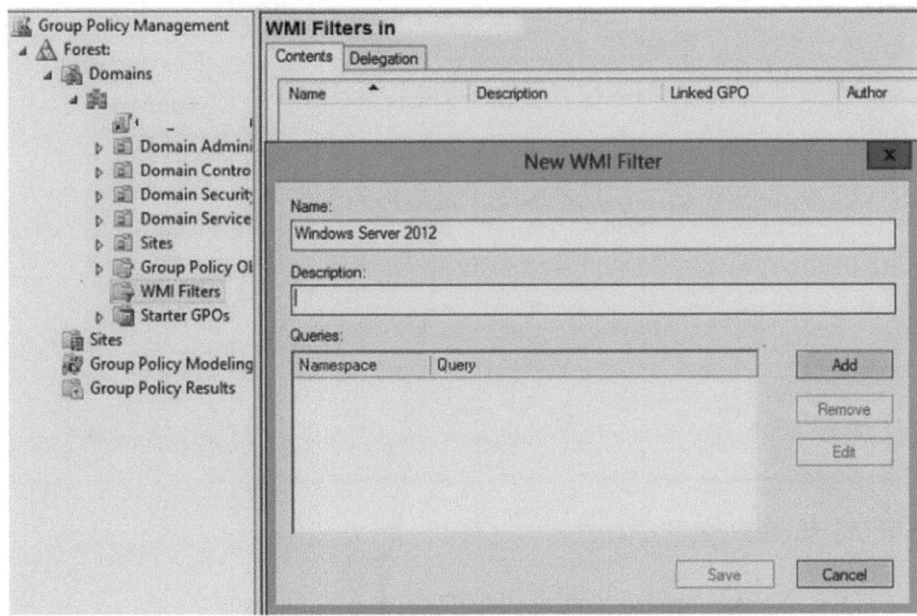

Figure 1-30. *New WMI filter window*

3. Next, add the WMI query for the filter. There are many constraints you can use in creating a WMI query, such as the OS version number. Figure 1-31 shows a typical OS version number-based WMI query. Complete the WMI filter creation wizard by clicking **OK**.

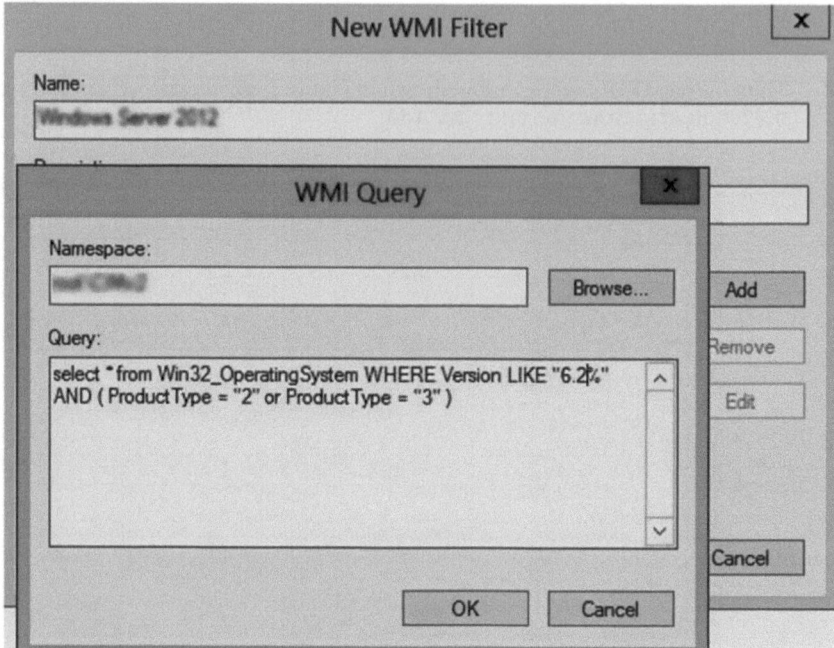

Figure 1-31. WMI Query window

4.   Now you need to configure the GPOs to use the filter you created. Click a GPO in the console tree. Then, in the corresponding right pane of GPMC window, locate the Scope tab. At the bottom, you can locate the WMI filtering option. Using the drop-down, select the filter you created.

In this way, a WMI filter is created and applied to GPOs.

■ **Info**   For an excellent article about WMI filters, in which you can read about different WMI queries in detail, go to http://blogs.technet.com/b/askds/archive/2008/09/11/ fun-with-wmi-filters-in-group-policy.aspx.

Security Filtering of GPOs

Using security filtering, administrators can apply GPOs to a particular set of users or computers. This is done by assigning appropriate permissions for correct OUs, so that only those users you are targeting receive the settings.

To apply security filtering, follow these steps:

1. In the GPMC console tree, click any GPO for which you want to configure security filtering.

2. Next, in the **Scope** tab, under **Security Filtering** (refer Figure 1-32), click **Add**, and apply the security filtering for specific users.

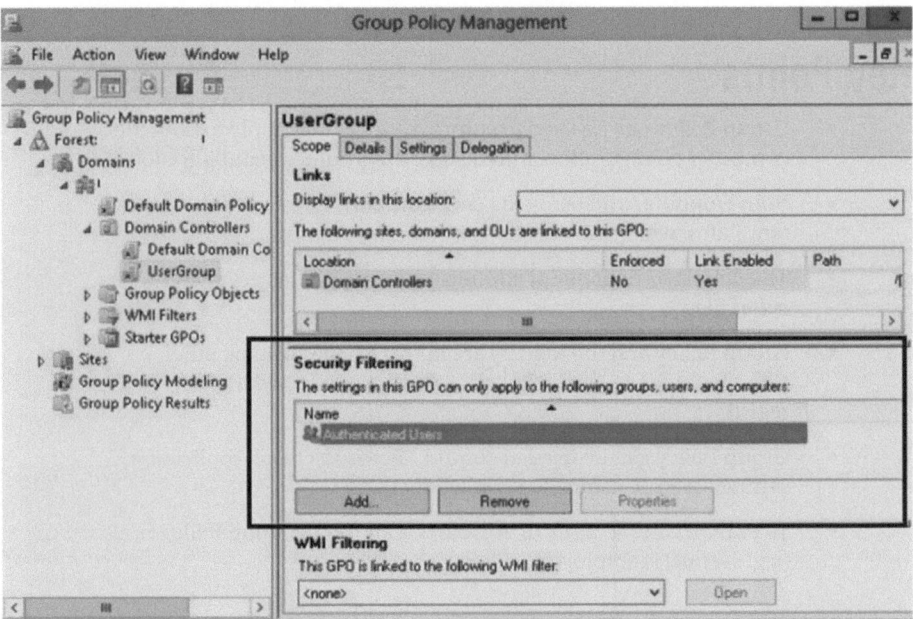

Figure 1-32. *Security filtering for GPOs*

GPO vs. DSC (Desired State Configuration)

Overall, you have seen that Group Policy has a greater ability to target computers based on their location in AD, such as an OU or AD site, WMI criteria, etc. Nowadays, there is an alternative to Group Policy called **Desired State Configuration** (DSC), which works with the base of Windows PowerShell. The major advantage of DSC is that it provides the same functionality as Group Policy and it can be used on Linux operating systems as well. However, DSC is a young tool, it's not as powerful as Group Policy because DSC is for servers, and it does not give you the ability to target machines in the exact way Group Policy does. Also, Microsoft keeps adding new policy settings with every new Windows OS build they offer, which is another advantage of keep using Group Policy as a prime tool for management.

Setting Permissions for GPOs

Whatever operation you perform with GPOs, you need appropriate permissions to do so. You have to adopt different processes to assign permissions on different kinds of objects. The following article in the TechNet library provides clear information about setting permissions on registry keys, system services, files, and folders. It also mentions the necessary conditions required for setting these permissions. Read it at `https://technet.microsoft.com/en-us/library/cc756952%28v=ws.10%29.aspx`.

Key Points

- Group Policy can be used to control settings that apply to both the computer configuration and the user environment configuration.

- Both computer and user-side configurations have administrative templates, which are registry-based policy settings.

- The language-dependent administrative templates are called *adml* files.

- Group Policy and the registry are mirror images of each other. Changes made to Group Policy settings are reflected in the registry.

- Group Policy can be used to control Microsoft Office Application settings at scale using the supplied templates.

- To enhance the security of Windows, a subset of Group Policy (e.g. *secpol*) is employed.

Summary

Group Policy is not only a graphical way of tweaking registry settings but it is effective in scenarios of more complex and versatile operations. Moreover, it can do tasks like run scripts, map drives, etc., which are not possible using the registry. In this chapter, you learned the terminology and how to configure and use GPOs effectively, you explored its relation to the registry, and you saw some examples of advanced usage. In the next chapter, you will explore how Group Policy can be useful for end users and take a deeper dive for administrators who are seeking to benefit from GPO management.

CHAPTER 2

■ ■ ■

Group Policy Management Console

When thinking of Group Policy, don't forget that there are dedicated tools for managing GPOs. One of the most useful and widely used tools is the default Microsoft Group Policy Management Console (GPMC), or Group Policy Management, which is available as a feature in Windows Server.

This chapter focuses solely on the GPMC, with the aim of describing the features and management possibilities of using GPMC. After the introduction, we will share with you the step-by-step guide to installing the GPMC in a Windows Server environment and to using the client. Once installed, we will discuss some popular scenarios for manipulating GPOs. By focusing on the day-to-day usage of the GPMC and highlighting various troubleshooting examples, we hope to build your familiarization with the management console. At the end of this chapter, we will cover the new changes that are available in Windows Server when configuring GPOs.

Let's get started with the GPMC.

Introducing GPMC

In the first chapter, you saw that Group Policy is a big feature with over 3,500 possible GPO settings for Windows and more than 2,000 GPO settings for Microsoft Office applications. With so many settings, it is highly likely that even the most proficient administrator will encounter problems from time to time. Issues are likely to happen when multiple policies are deployed on the same machine. To assist you during the configuration and deployment of GPOs, Microsoft provides the GPMC, which allows you to work with GPOs very effectively.

The GPMC is quite similar to the Local Group Policy Editor (LGPO), which you used in Chapter 1 and which is included in the business-oriented versions of Windows. In appearance, the GPMC is similar in nearly all aspects as the LGPO, as you can see in Figure 2-1. However, the GPMC is designed to work in a domain environment and the LGPO is aimed at configuring local GPO settings on standalone machines.

© Kapil Arya 2016
K. Arya, *Windows Group Policy Troubleshooting*, DOI 10.1007/978-1-4842-1886-0_2

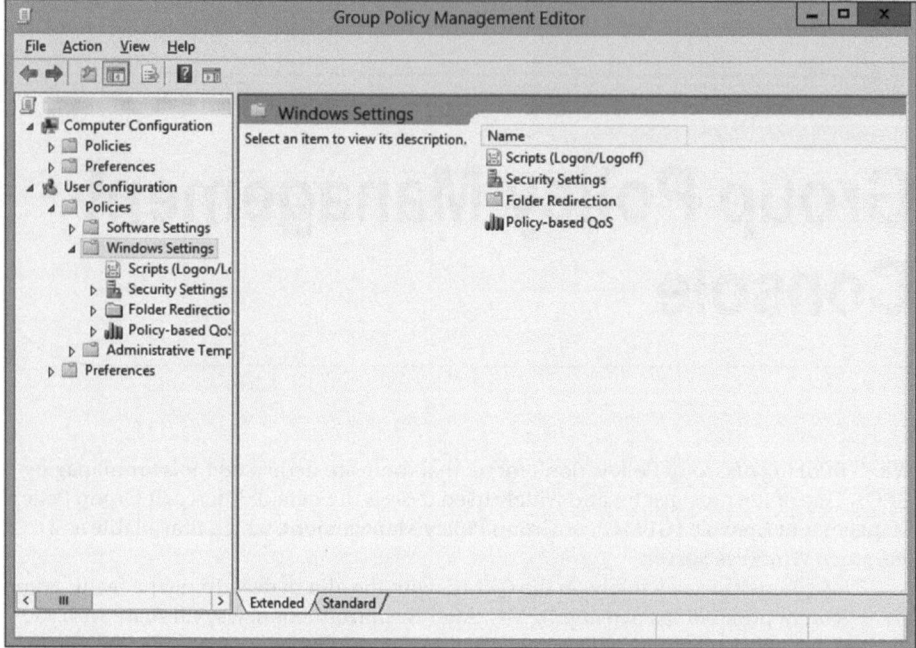

Figure 2-1. *Group Policy Management Console (GPMC) Tool*

Installing the GPMC

Group Policies should be administered from a client or an administration server. GPMC is a feature normally deployed onto a Windows Server. Once it's installed, you install the Remote Server Administration Tools (RSAT) onto a client device, which will allow you to administer domain-based GPOs from the client. On a Windows Server, you can enable the GPMC feature as follows:

1. Open Server Manager. In the Server Manager Dashboard (shown in Figure 2-2), click **Add roles and features** under the *Configure this local server* heading.

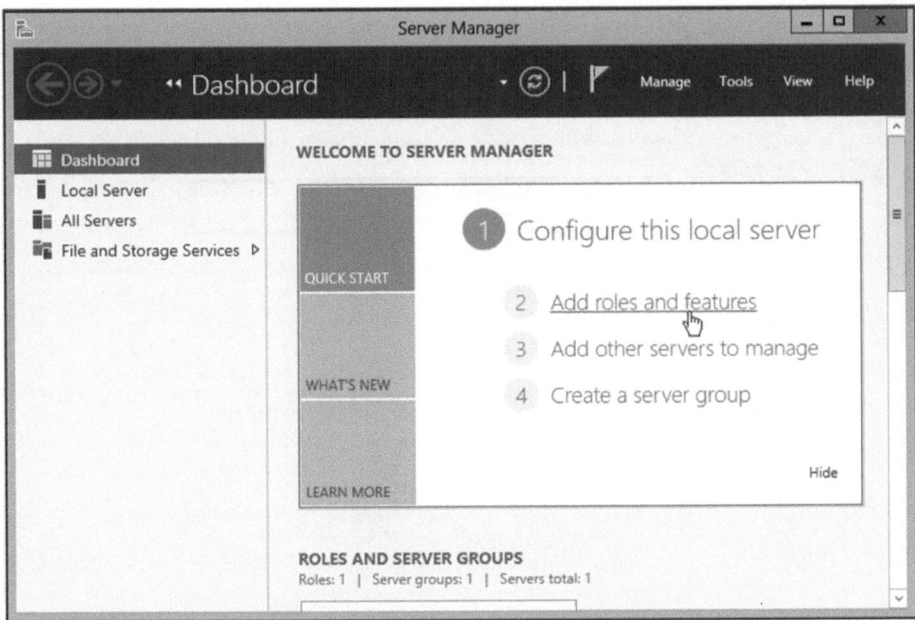

Figure 2-2. *Server Manager dashboard*

2. Now, choose the **Role-based or feature-based installation** option and click **Next**, as shown in Figure 2-3.

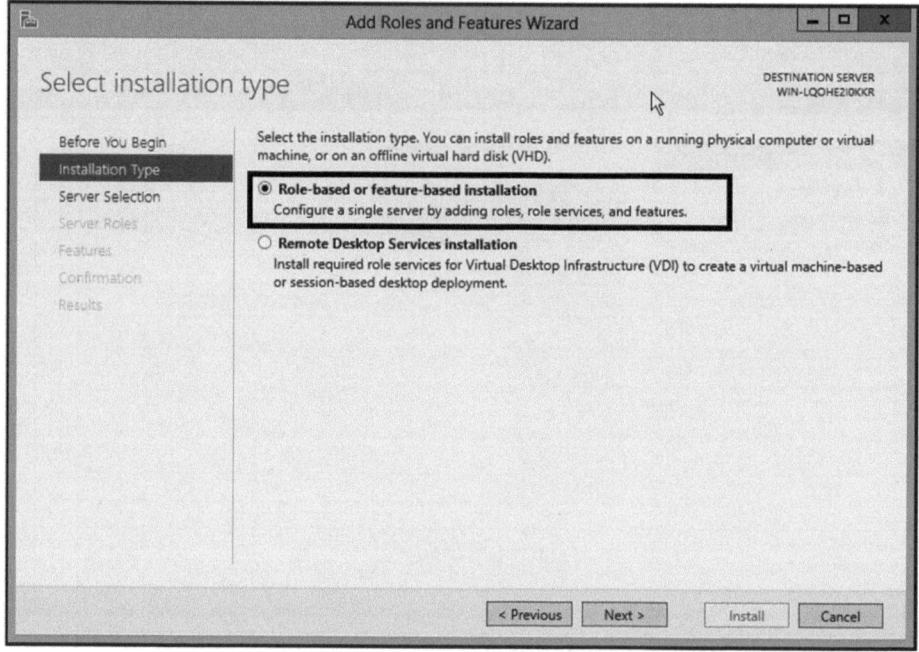

Figure 2-3. *Selecting the installation type*

3. Next, select your destination server and click **Next** (refer to Figure 2-4).

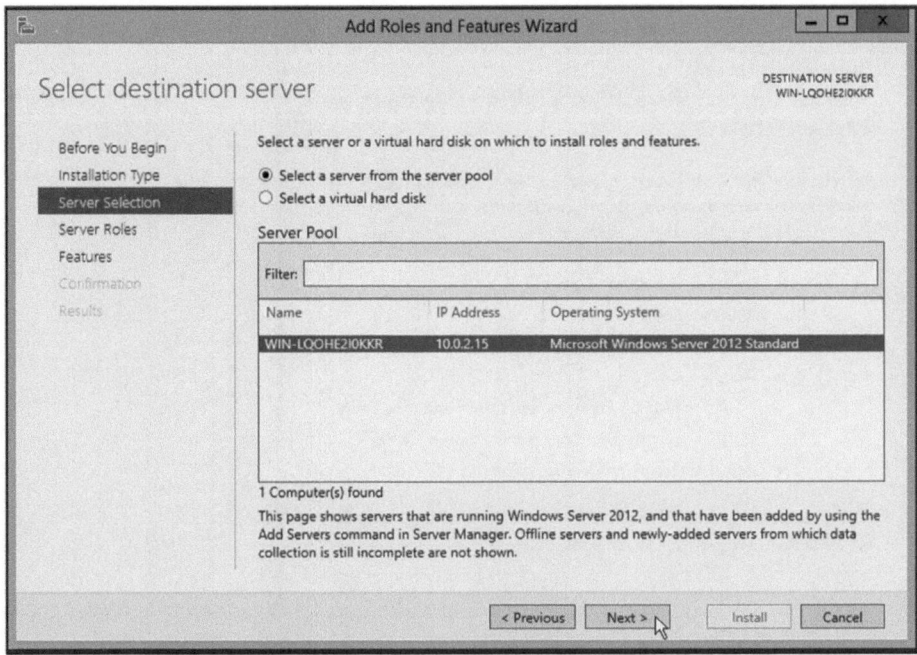

Figure 2-4. *Selecting the destination server*

4.   Now you'll see the *Add Roles and Features Wizard*, as shown
      in Figure 2-5. Click the **Add Features** button.

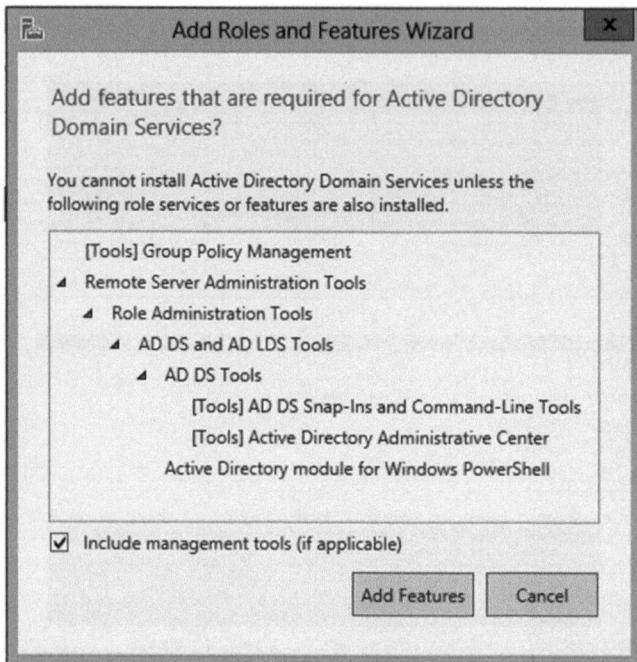

Figure 2-5. *Adding roles and features*

5. If you do not already have a domain environment configured, you will need to set this up. You first need to make sure that you're authorized to deploy AD on the machine at which you're working. In the *Server roles* section, select the **Active Directory Domain Services** option and click **Next** (see Figure 2-6).

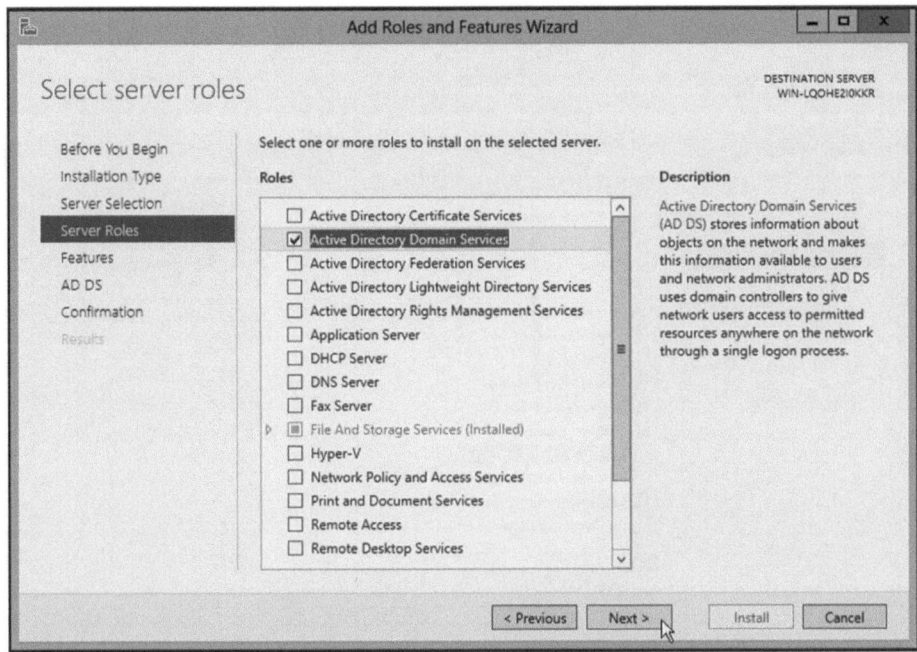

Figure 2-6. *Selecting server roles*

6. In the Features screen shown in Figure 2-7, select **Group Policy Management** and press the **Next** button. Then click **Next** on the *AD DS* screen.

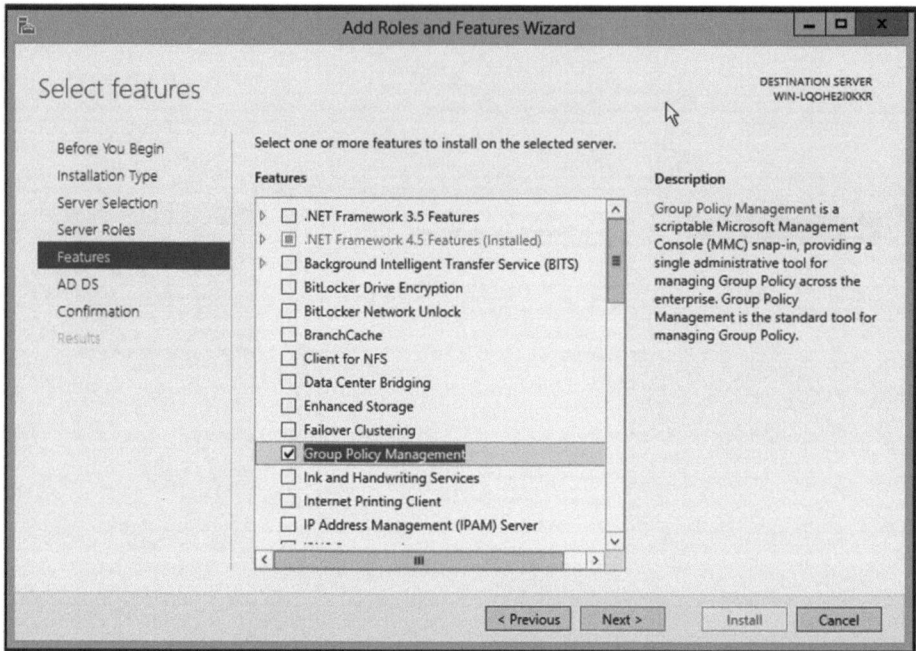

Figure 2-7. *Selecting features*

7. In the screen shown in Figure 2-8, confirm whether you want to restart the machine (recommended) or not after adding the features listed there. Click **Install**.

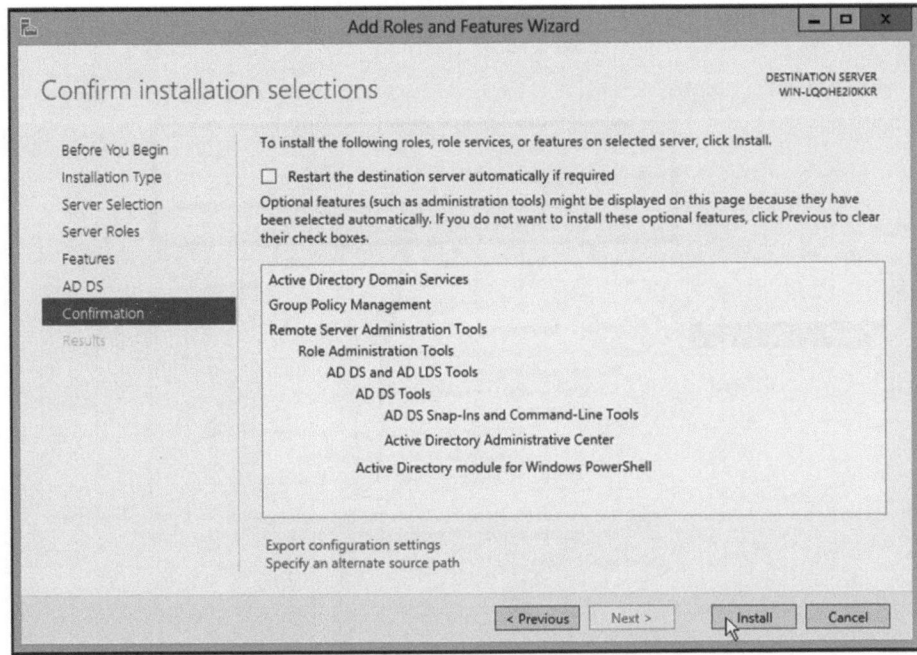

Figure 2-8. *Confirmation screen to add selected features*

8. Window Server will now complete the installation of AD DS and GPMC. You will see the installation has succeeded message, shown in Figure 2-9, once everything is finished. You can then open the GPMC using the **gpmc.msc** command.

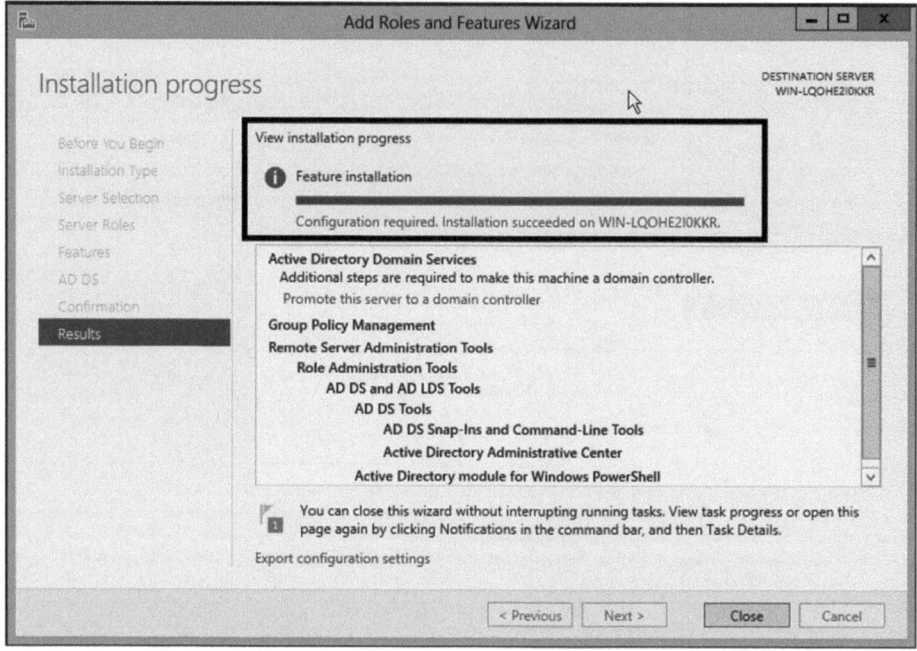

Figure 2-9. *Installation progess*

Once GPMC is installed on your Windows Server, you are ready to centrally manage your GPOs. In addition to the Server Manager GUI, you can also install GPMC using the command-line **ServerManagercmd.exe** command. To install and start the configuration, follow these steps:

1. Open the administrative/elevated command prompt.

2. Type following command and press **Enter**:

   ServerManagercmd -install gpmc

3. Now open GPMC using the **gpmc.msc** command.

Best practice advises you not to administer the server directly. You should therefore install the GPMC tool, which can be installed as part of the Remote Server Administrative Tools (RSAT), directly onto your domain-joined Windows client machine that you will use to administer your server. (The client must be running Windows 2000 or later.)

To install GPMC on a Windows machine that is part of a domain, follow these instructions:

1. Download RSAT from *Microsoft Download Center* using one of the version-specific links provided.

■ **Info**   You can download RSAT for different Windows editions using the following links:

Windows Vista with Service Pack 1 (SP1):

www.microsoft.com/en-us/download/details.aspx?id=21090

Windows 7 with Service Pack 1 (SP1):

www.microsoft.com/en-us/download/details.aspx?id=7887

Windows 8/8.1:

www.microsoft.com/en-us/download/details.aspx?id=28972

Windows 10:

www.microsoft.com/en-us/download/details.aspx?id=45520

2.   The downloaded file is in the *Microsoft Update Standalone Package* (*.msu*) format. You must double-click the file so that it can be installed utilizing the Windows Update offline installer.

3.   After successfully installing RSAT, navigate to the *Turn Windows Features on or off* section on the Control Panel, and locate the Remote Server Administration Tools entry, as shown in Figure 2-10. Make sure the **Group Policy Management Tools** option is enabled/checked here. Click **OK**.

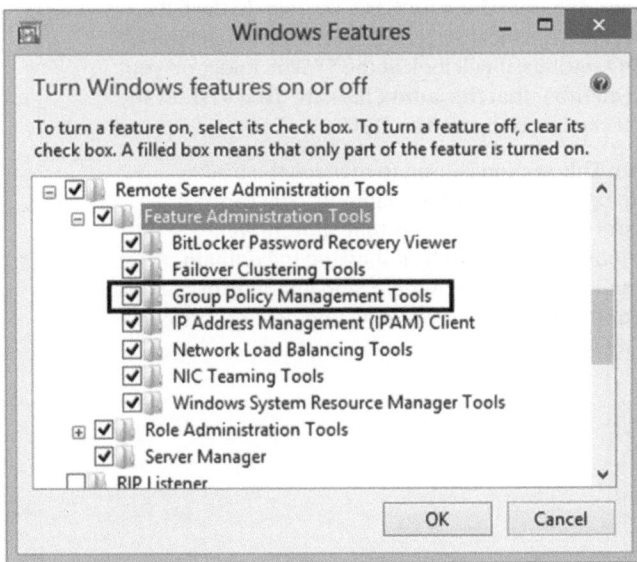

Figure 2-10.   *Windows feature page to enable GPMC from the RSAT*

41

When you now type **gpmc.msc** in Search, the Run utility, or the command prompt, you will launch the GPMC as required.

Configuring GPMC

In this section, you will discover how to configure GPMC and learn how to use the management console.

How to Customize the GPMC Window

First, let's review the user interface for GPMC. It is important that you understand the many areas of the GPMC. We'll also take a quick review of the console.

1. Open GPMC window (as shown in Figure 2-1) and click View ➤ Options.

2. In the Options window, there are three tabs which have following purposes:

• **Columns tab**: This will help you to customize the list view that you see in the GPMC window. The default order (top to bottom) is Group Policy Inheritance ➤ Group Policy Objects, Linked Group Policy Objects ➤ WMI Filters. You can allow or prevent either of these sections from being visible, and you can reorder them the way you prefer.

   • **Reporting tab**: Use this tab to configure where GPMC should look to find the administrative templates (**.admx** files) needed while searching for GPO. By default, the GP engine will check the local system only. If a local machine is missing GPO settings, it will look at the SYSVOL folder on your domain. Remember that the **.admx** files are used to show the settings that can be configured by GPO.

   • **General tab**: This section is used to manage the trust relationship between the GPMC elements. You can also configure some other options that allow more customizations to GPMC, such as showing the domain controller names within the domain, and enabling or disabling confirmation boxes while distinguishing between GPO and GPO links.

To add forests, domains, and sites you want to manage in the GPMC, follow these steps:

1. Open the GPMC, right-click Group Policy Management, and select Add Forest. Alternatively, you may click Action ➤ Add Forest.

2. A prompt will ask you to enter the forest name. Type the name (e.g. domain.com) and click **OK**. The forest will now appear beneath Group Policy Management.

3. Next, to add a domain available in this forest, right-click it and select Domains ➤ Show domains. The domains appearing in the *Show domains* dialog can be checked individually so that they are added to forest.

4. To add the site to forest, you can follow similar approach as you did for domains. Right-click the forest and select Sites ➤ Show sites. In the Show sites dialog, check the sites listed to get them added into the forest.

How to Use GPMC

This section will help you to understand how you should use the GPMC tool for day-to-day operations.

Create and Edit GPOs in GPMC

To create a new GPO, follow these steps:

1. In the Group Policy console tree shown in Figure 2-11, expand the site, domain, or OU to which you want to create a new GPO. For an instance, if you expand your domain, you can right-click the Group Policy Objects and select **New**.

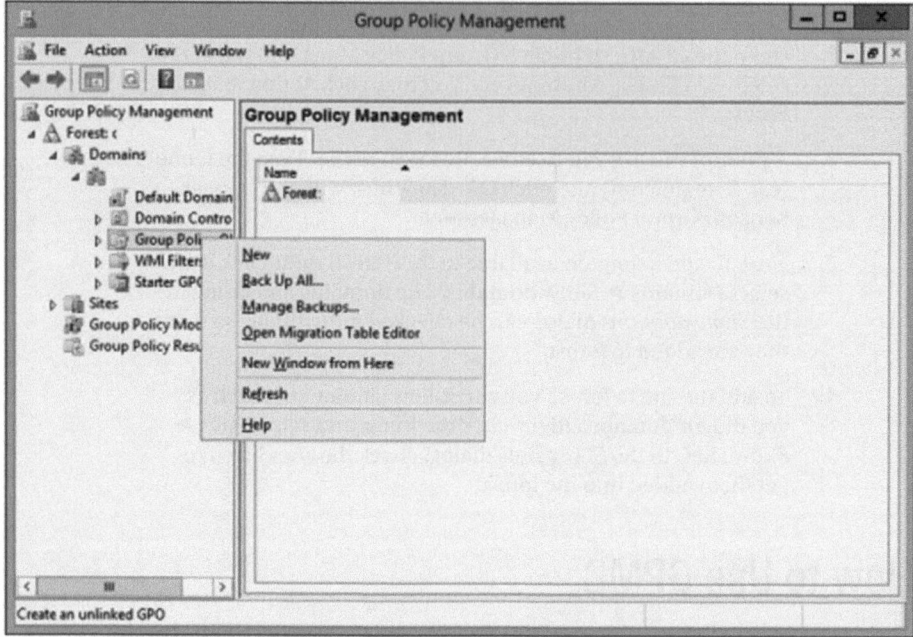

Figure 2-11. *Creating a new GPO in GPMC*

2. In the New GPO dialog box (see Figure 2-12), type the name of
    GPO and click OK. The new GPO will be linked to the object
    for which you created it.

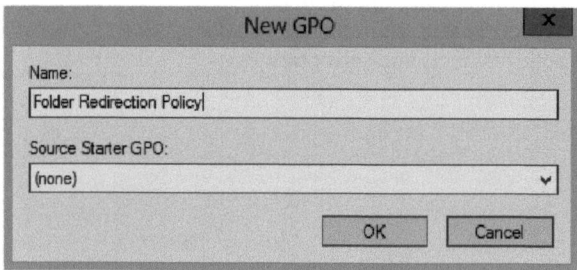

Figure 2-12. *New GPO dialog*

■ **Info** Figure 2-12 also shows a place to specify Source Starter GPOs while creating a GPO. Starter GPOs provide a template-like ability for creating new GPOs. They are usually stored in the StarterGPOs folder, found in the shared SYSVOL folder under DCs. If you create a new GPO using Starter GPOs, the newly created GPO will derive administrative policy settings from it.

In order to edit a GPO, you can use the following approach:

3. In the console tree (shown in Figure 2-13), right-click a GPO and select Edit.

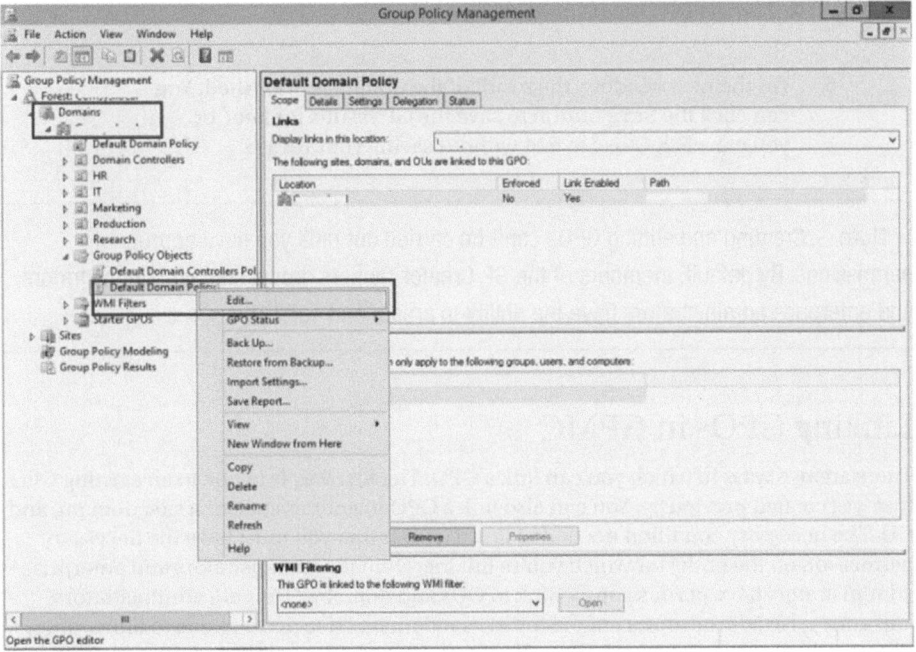

Figure 2-13. *Editing a GPO*

4. In the Group Policy Management Editor window, change the status of the corresponding policy to *Not Configured* (Default), *Enabled,* or *Disabled.* This is the same way you would configure a policy setting in LGPO, as discussed in Chapter 1.

5. To update the Group Policy, right-click the container and select the *Group Policy Update* option. In the window appearing next (see Figure 2-14), click Yes to make Windows force the update of the user and computer policy settings.

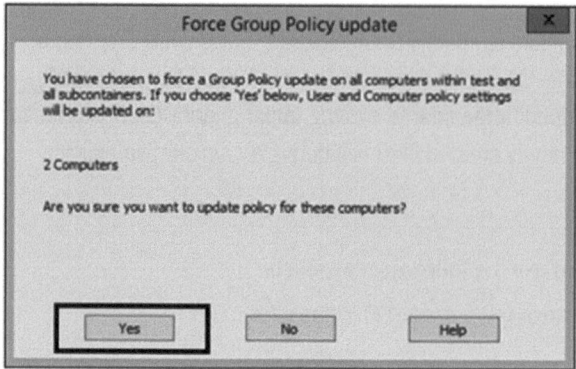

Figure 2-14. *Forcing GP Update prompt*

6. On the next window, the result of the update is published. You can click the **Save** button to save the GP results for later, or you can click **Close** to exit without saving your results.

■ **Note**   Creating and editing GPOs can't be carried out until you have appropriate permissions. By default, members of the GP Creator Owners group, domain administrators, and enterprise administrators have the ability to create and edit GPOs.

Linking GPOs in GPMC

There are two ways in which you can link a GPO. The first way is to link to an existing GPO that was created previously. You can also link a GPO to entities such as a site, domain, and OU. The necessary condition needed to link a GPO is that you must have the necessary permission on the entity for which you're linking. Domain administrators and enterprise administrators have permissions to link to OUs and domains. Domain administrators and enterprise administrators of the forest root domain have permissions to link to sites. The users and groups who have the authority to create GPOs in selected domains find themselves listed on the *Delegation* tab, under the *Group Policy Objects* node.

To link to an existing GPO, follow these steps:

1. In the console tree, right-click the domain or OU within the domain and select **Link to an existing GPO**, as shown in Figure 2-15.

2. In the *Select GPO* window, choose a GPO and click **OK** to link it.

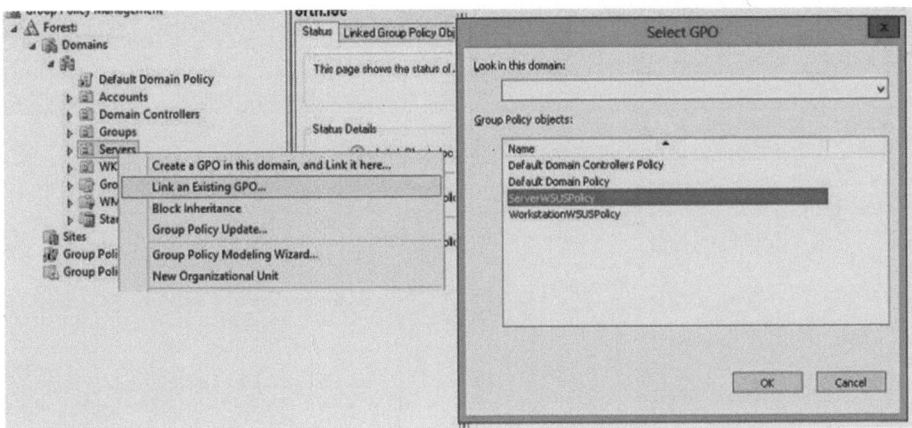

Figure 2-15. *Linking to existing GPOs*

The second way to link to GPOs is to create a link to a brand new GPO. You must have permissions to create the GPO plus manage GPO links on the object to which you are linking it. Note that this option does not exist for sites. Follow these steps to create a new GPO and link:

1. In the console tree, right-click a domain or an OU within a domain and select **Link to an existing GPO**, as shown in Figure 2-16.

2. In the *New GPO* dialog, type the name of GPO and click **OK**.

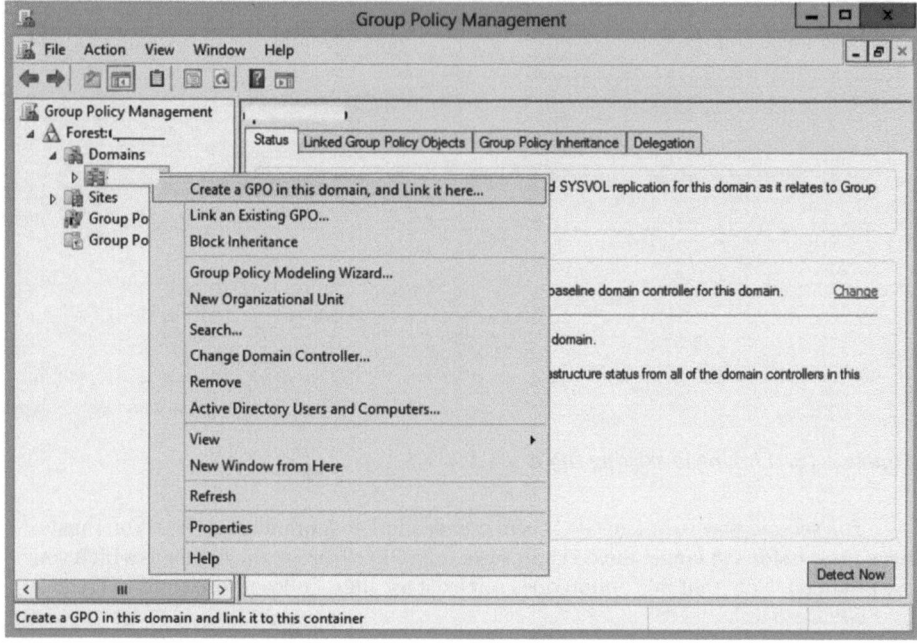

Figure 2-16. *Linking GPOs by creating new GPO*

Deleting GPOs Using the GPMC

Deleting a GPO is a simple operation similar to creating a GPO. However, when you delete GPOs, the link is deleted but not the actual GPO. The GPO is retained so that you can reuse it later. To delete a GPO (delete the link), follow these steps:

1. In the GPMC window, right-click the policy you want to erase and select **Delete** in the context menu.

2. As soon as you click Delete you will see the prompt shown in Figure 2-17, clearly stating that deleting will remove only the link and not the GPO itself.

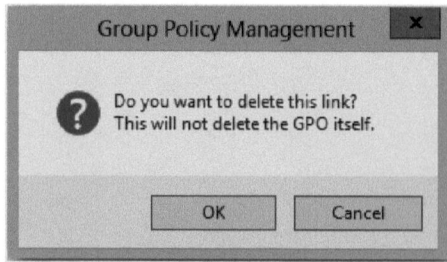

Figure 2-17. *Confirmation prompt for deleting the GPO link*

3. Click **OK** to confirm deletion.

To delete or destroy GPOs permanently, follow these steps:

1. In the GPMC window, locate the forest/domain from which you want to destroy the GPO. Press the Group Policy Objects node under this forest/domain and locate the GPO.

2. Now right-click the GPO and select **Delete**.

3. In the confirmation prompt, click **OK** and you are done.

In this way, GPO has been completely removed.

Backup and Restore GPOs in GPMC

Consider a scenario where you are managing GPOs along with different administrators. Another administrator made some changes to few GPOs and you need to restore those GPOs to their previous state. Will you restore the whole AD just to restore a few GPOs? The answer is simply *No*. If you backed up the GPOs earlier, you have an option to easily restore them back to the previous stage. This shows that backing up GPOs helps you to go back to an earlier state handily, just like System Restore in Windows.

To back up GPOs, follow these steps:

1. In the GPMC window, right-click a GPO and select **Backup**. If you want to back up all GPOs under *Group Policy Objects*, right-click it and select **Back Up All** (as shown in Figure 2-18).

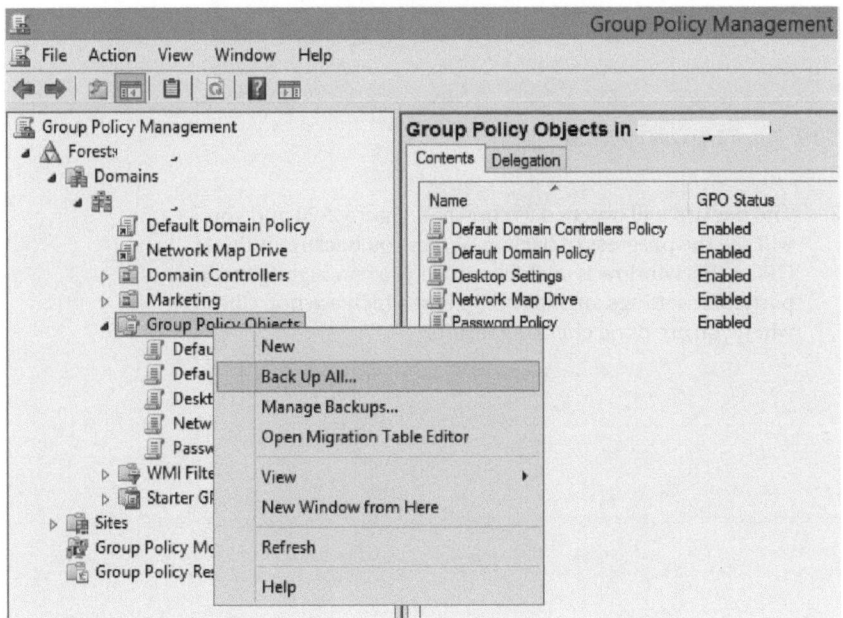

Figure 2-18. *GPO Backup option*

2. Provide a location and description in the respective fields, as shown in Figure 2-19, and click **Backup**. Any settings that are external to the GPO, such as WMI filters, IPsec policies (discussed in Chapter 3) and independent objects in AD, are not included in the backup.

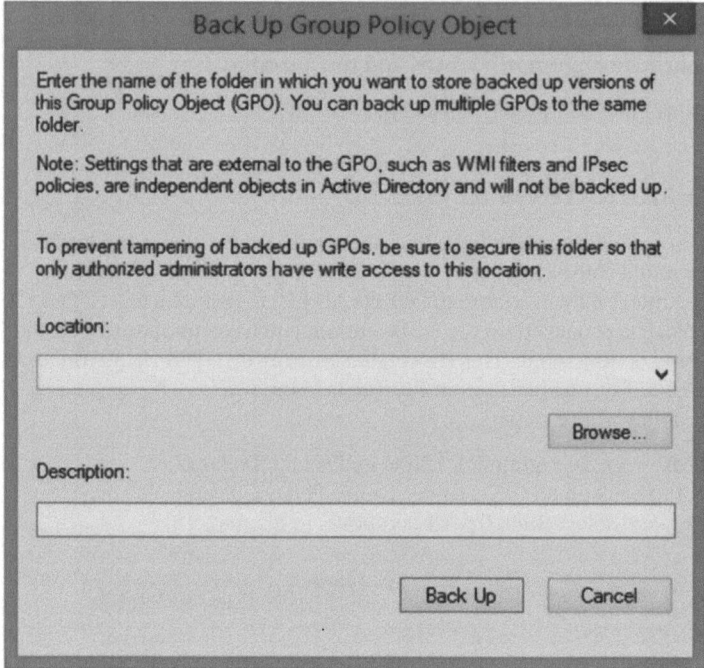

Figure 2-19. Back Up GPO wizard

3. The backup will proceed as shown in Figure 2-20 and you will see the progress of backup. When you backup multiple GPOs, this window is useful because you can highlight which particular settings are backed up and which are not. Click **OK** when you are done checking results.

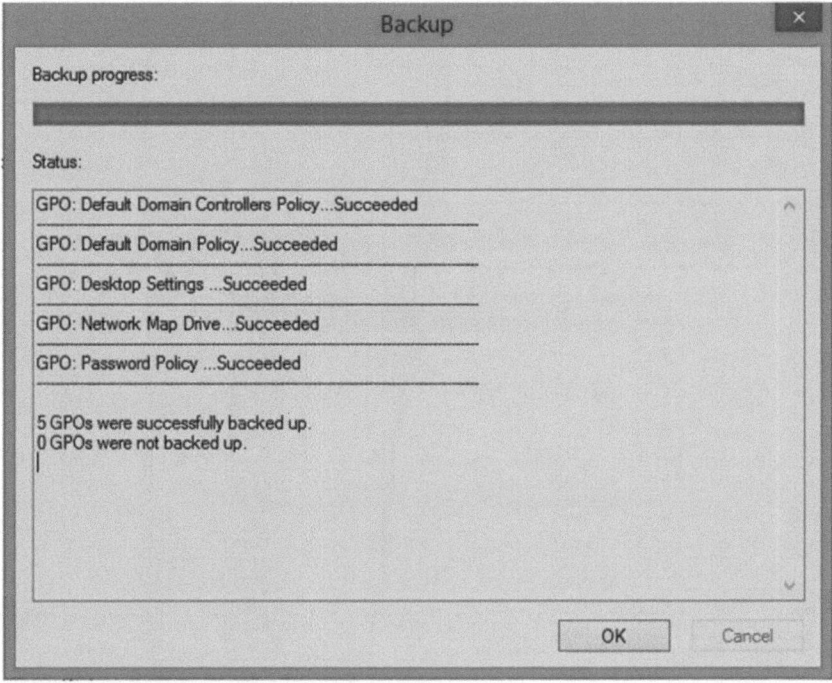

Figure 2-20. *Backup progress window*

To restore GPOs, you can use following steps:

1. In the Group Policy console tree, right-click the **Group Policy Objects** node and select **Manage Backups**.

2. In the *Manage Backups* window, shown in Figure 2-21, select the GPO setting you want to restore and click **Restore**. For this to work, you should have delete, edit, and modify security permissions for the GPO. Additionally, you must have read permissions on the backup folder to restore the GPO.

3. Click **OK** in the confirmation prompt to restore the selected backup.

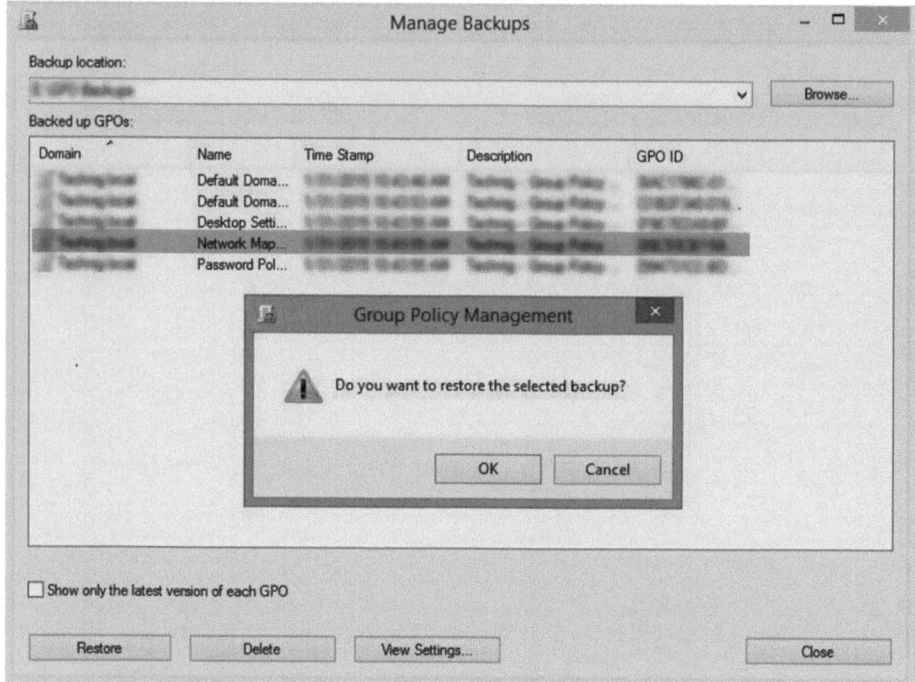

Figure 2-21. *Restoring a GPO from the backup library*

4.   In the Restore Progress window, similar to the Backup Progress window shown in Figure 2-20, you can track the status of the restore operation and view a Succeeded or Failed message.

Note   It's often challenging when you copy/import GPOs from one forest/domain to another because the destination forest/domain might not have same settings that were defined in the source domain. In such cases, you need to use migration tables. Read more about them at https://technet.microsoft.com/en-us/library/cc754682.aspx.

Using GPMC Reports for Troubleshooting

When you are troubleshooting Group Policy issues, GPMC is a very capable tool. It offers the following helpful features:

- *Group Policy Modeling* generates reports that are used to predict the policies that will be applied for a specific client. It allows you to understand what will happen before you make changes such as moving users or computers into different OUs to assess the impact before doing so. Similarly, when users log into specific computers, you can see what will happen and what will apply. It allows simulation, rather than prediction.

- *Group Policy Results* produces reports that gather information directly from the client to show the policies in effect, and include key policy events that have been logged at that client.

- *Group Policy Reports* provide very helpful details that can be used in troubleshooting problems, so you can track which GPO is applied or denied. Even if a GPO is not applied, you are provided with information about why a GPO was denied, so you can investigate the issue further. You can also see which settings are being or would be applied, and the winning GPO that supplied the value for a particular Group Policy setting. Let's delve deeper into each of these tools.

GPMC Modeling

Within a business context, it is not recommended to test major changes in a production environment; rather you would be wise to build a lab and test the changes thoroughly before rolling them out to your client devices. Using this approach also often achieves better results. It's the same case with deploying GPOs. The GPMC Modeling feature allows you to model a scenario and then report on the effects. The information provided is split into two sections: the *Summary* and *Settings* tabs are similar to what you would see for a *Group Policy Results report*. Instead of the **Policy Events** tab, a list of the conditions that were applied when creating the model appears on the **Query** tab.

A GPMC Modeling report can be generated in this manner:

1.	Right-click **Group Policy Modeling** in the left pane of the GPMC window (see Figure 2-22) and select the **Group Policy Modeling Wizard.**

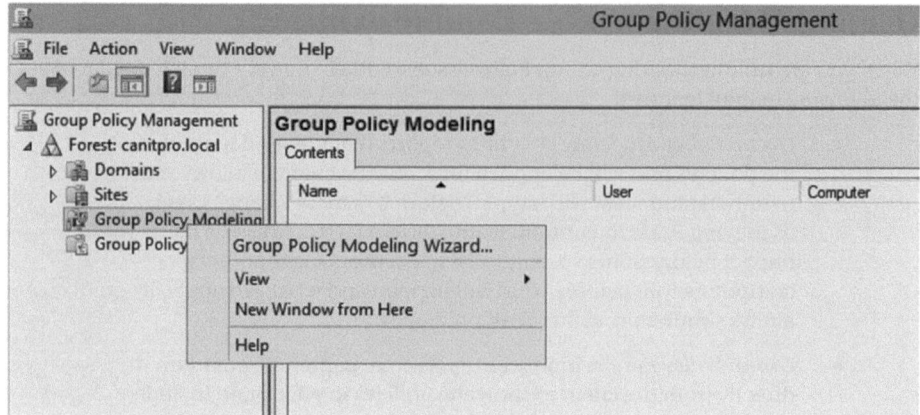

Figure 2-22. *Group Policy Modeling context menu in GPMC window*

2. The last step will launch the Group Policy Modeling Wizard and you will see the welcome prompt shown in Figure 2-23. Click **Next**.

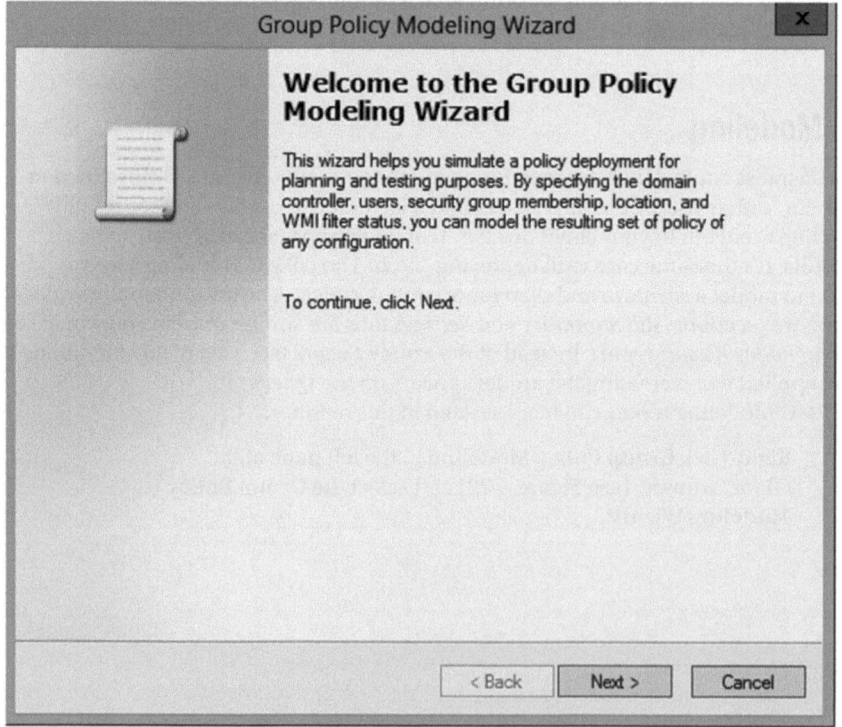

Figure 2-23. *Group Policy Modeling Wizard welcome prompt*

3. In the DC selection screen shown in Figure 2-24, choose which DC you want to use for simulation. Click **Next**.

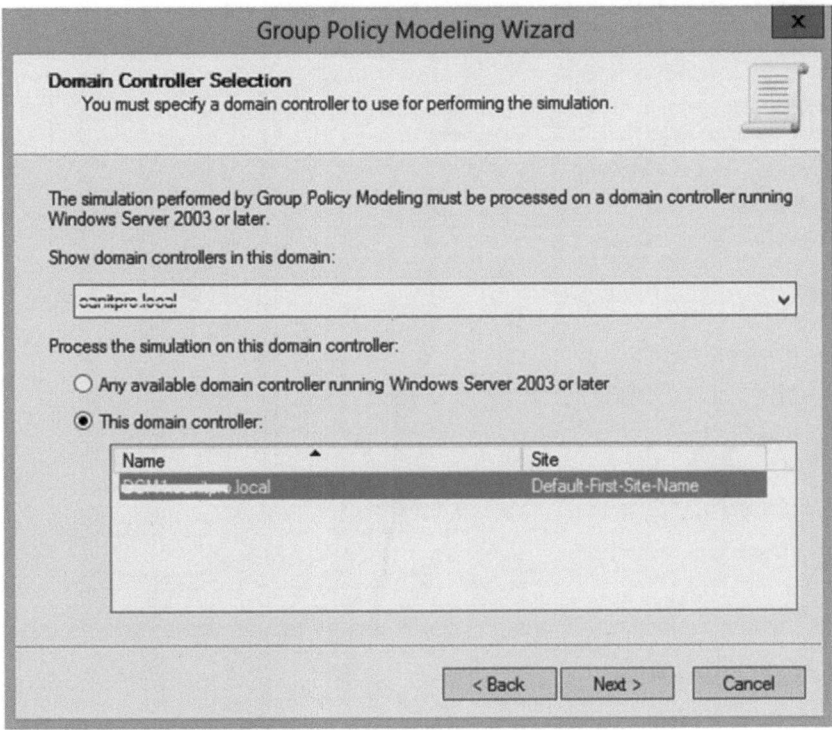

Figure 2-24. DC selection

4. Referring to Figure 2-25, you now need to make an OU selection for the user and computer sides. Click **Next** after making your choice.

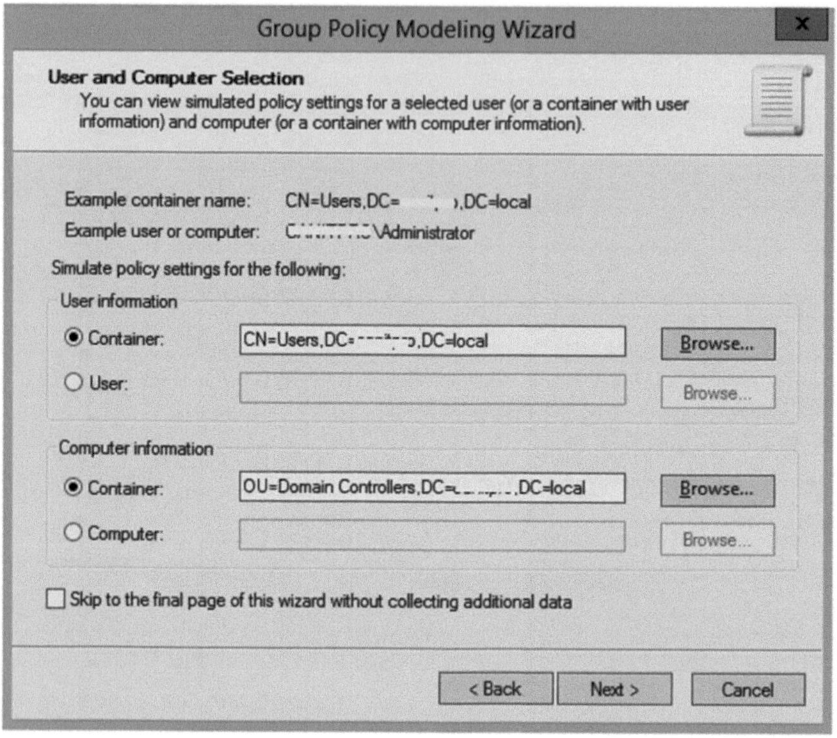

Figure 2-25. *The OU selection*

5. Moving on, the next screen (shown in Figure 2-26) gives you the ability to choose *Advanced Simulation Options* such as *Slow network connection* and *Loopback Processing* (discussed in Chapter 5). You can also specify the site you want to use. Click **Next**.

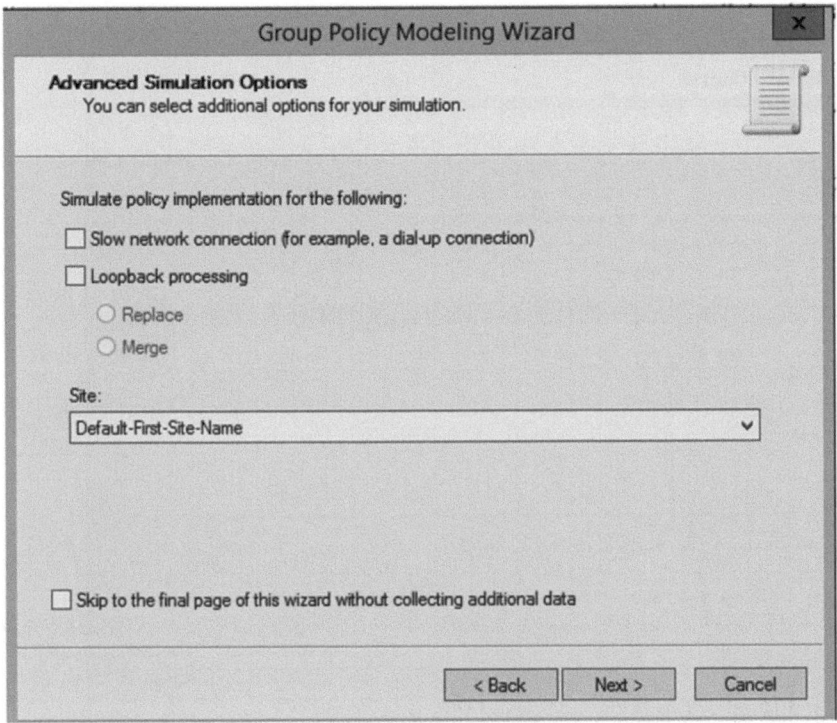

Figure 2-26. *The Advanced Simulation Options screen*

6. In the next window (shown in Figure 2-27), choose the security groups for users. Click **Next** and then select the security groups for the computer in a similar manner in the next window. Click **Next**.

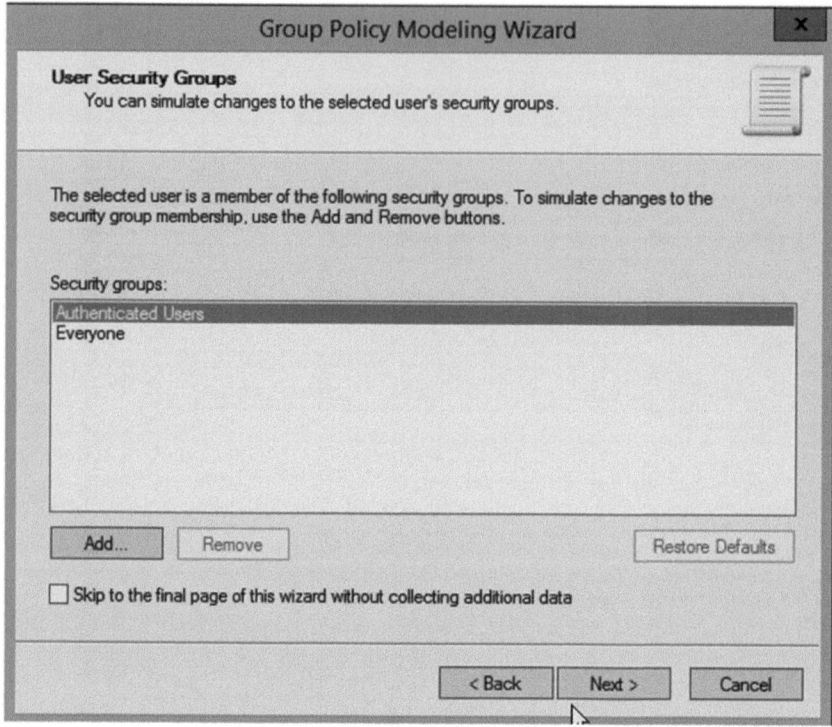

Figure 2-27. The security group selection for users

7. Then choose the WMI Filter for users, as shown in Figure 2-28. Click **Next**. Similarly, select the WMI Filter for the computer and click **Next**.

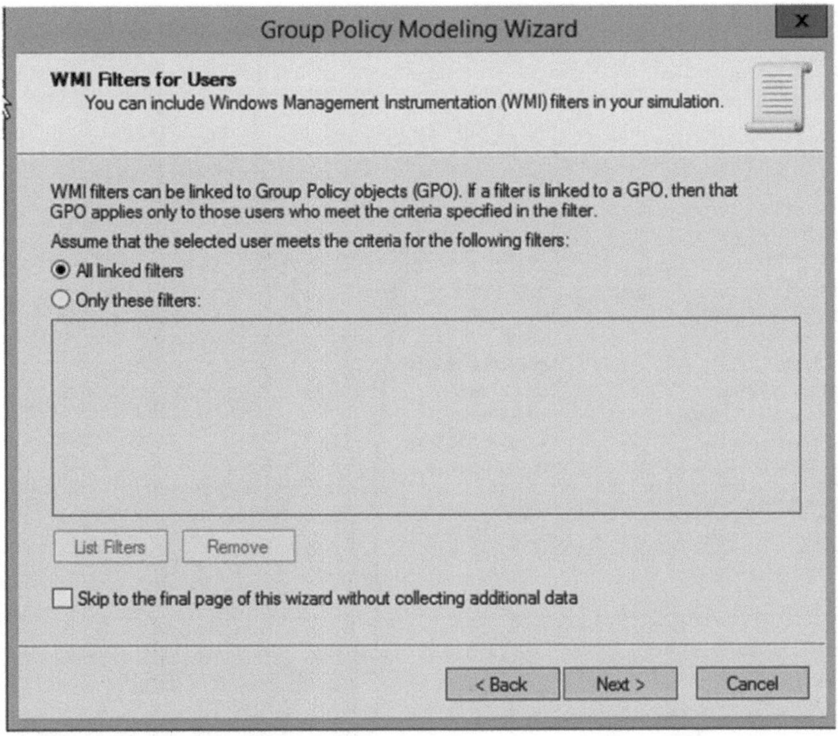

Figure 2-28. *The WMI Filter selection*

8. You'll see the summary of your selections in next window
    (Figure 2-29). Click **Next**.

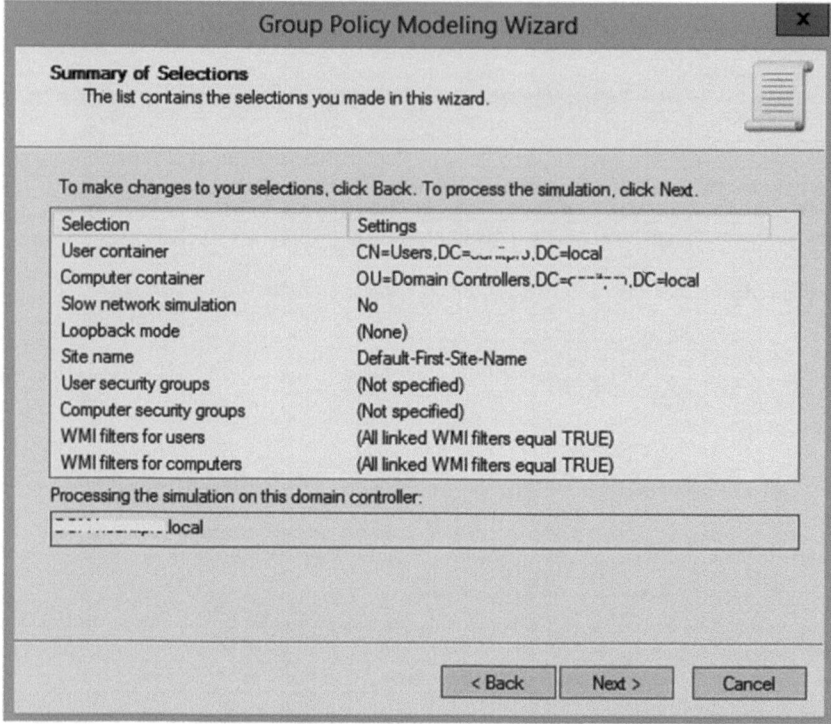

Figure 2-29. *Summary of selections*

9. Click **Finish** in window shown in Figure 2-30 to complete Group Policy Modeling Wizard.

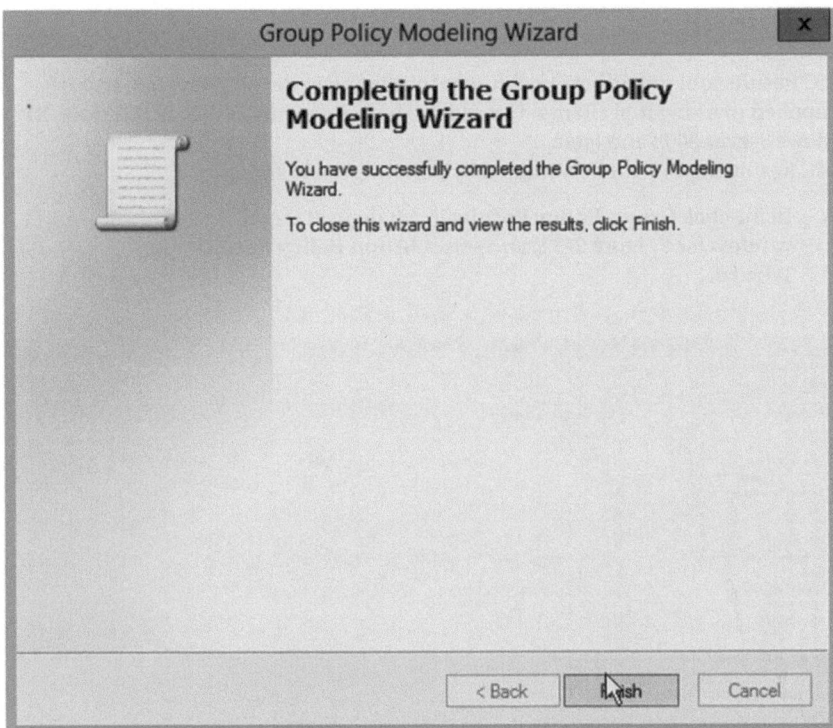

Figure 2-30. *The finishing window*

10. In the GPMC window (refer Figure 2-31), expand **Group Policy Modeling Wizard** and click the new object created by it. The right pane will display the report that appears in the *Details* pane, providing information about the anticipated Group Policy application on that client.

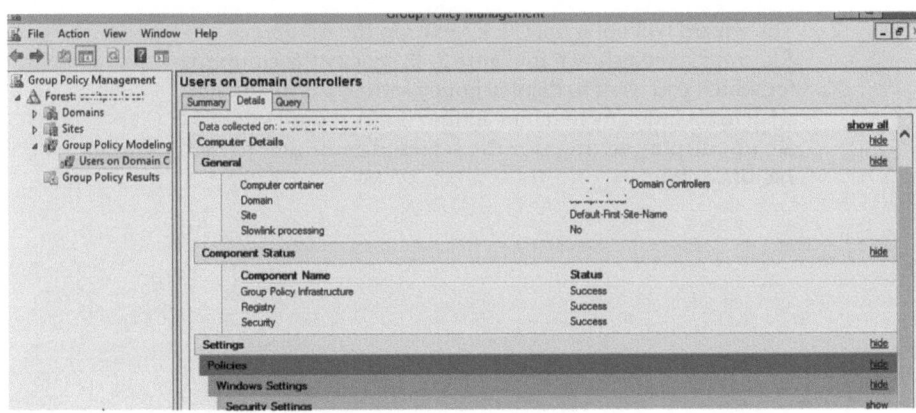

Figure 2-31. *Group Policy Modeling Report*

GPMC Results

The GPMC Results tool provides you with reports relating to the way in which Group Policy is applied to individual clients. This feature has been available since Windows XP and Windows Server 2003 and later.

GPMC Results report can be obtained by following these steps:

1. Right-click **Group Policy Results** in left pane of GPMC window (see Figure 2-32) and select **Group Policy Results Wizard.**

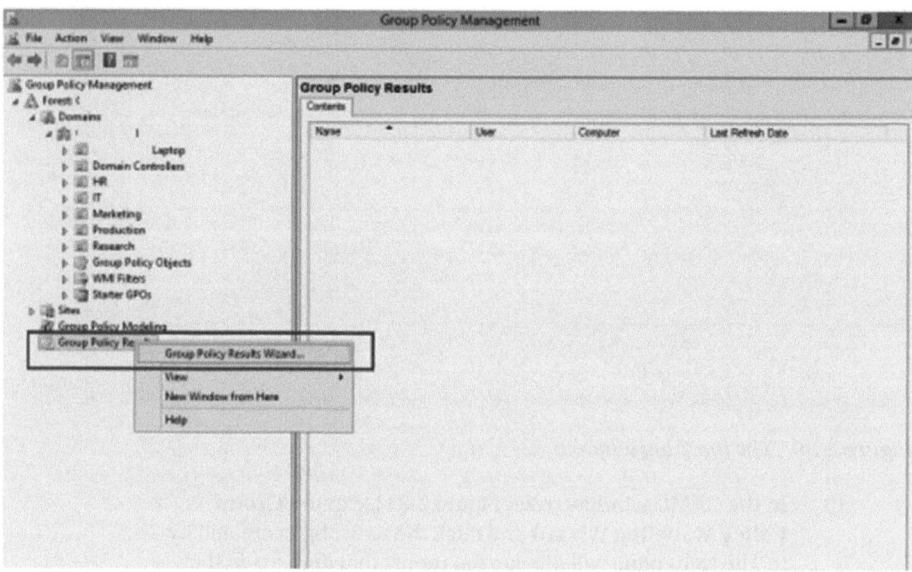

Figure 2-32. *Group Policy Results context menu in the GPMC window*

2. The wizard will open up. Click **Next**. On the *Computer Selection* screen shown in Figure 2-33 specify the computer for which you want to display policy settings. If you do not wish to include any machine in the results report, select the **Do not display settings for the selected computer in the results** option.

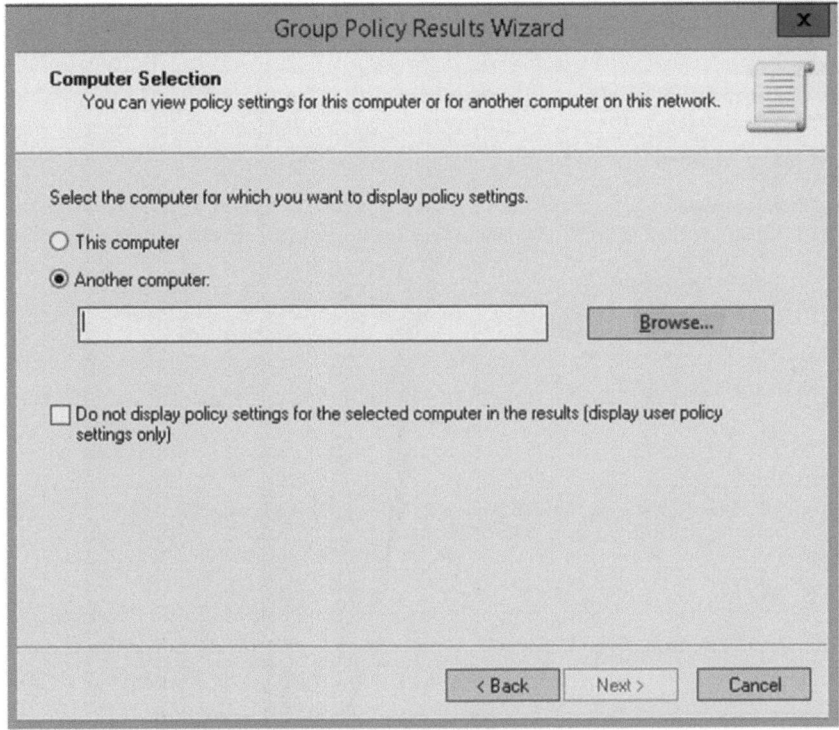

Figure 2-33. *The Group Policy Results Report Wizard*

3. Referring to Figure 2-34, select the user for which you want
    to generate the report. Check the **Do not display user policy
    settings in the results** option if you want to exclude users in your
    report so that you get a report only for computers. Click **Next**.

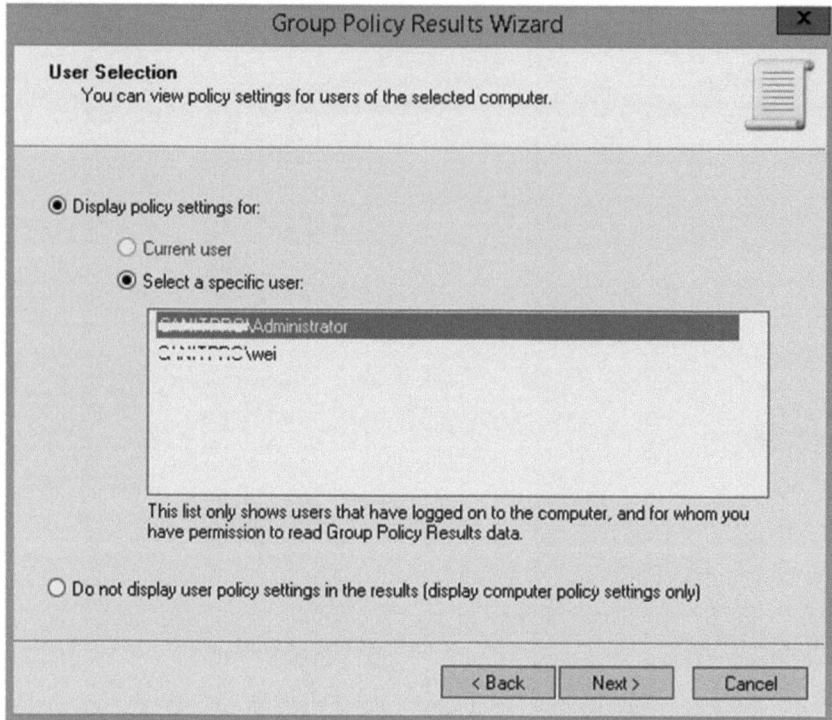

Figure 2-34. *The User Selection screen*

4. Now you will see *Summary of selections* (Figure 2-35) depending upon what you selected in step 2 and 3. Click **Next**. Then click **Finish** to close the Group Policy Results Wizard.

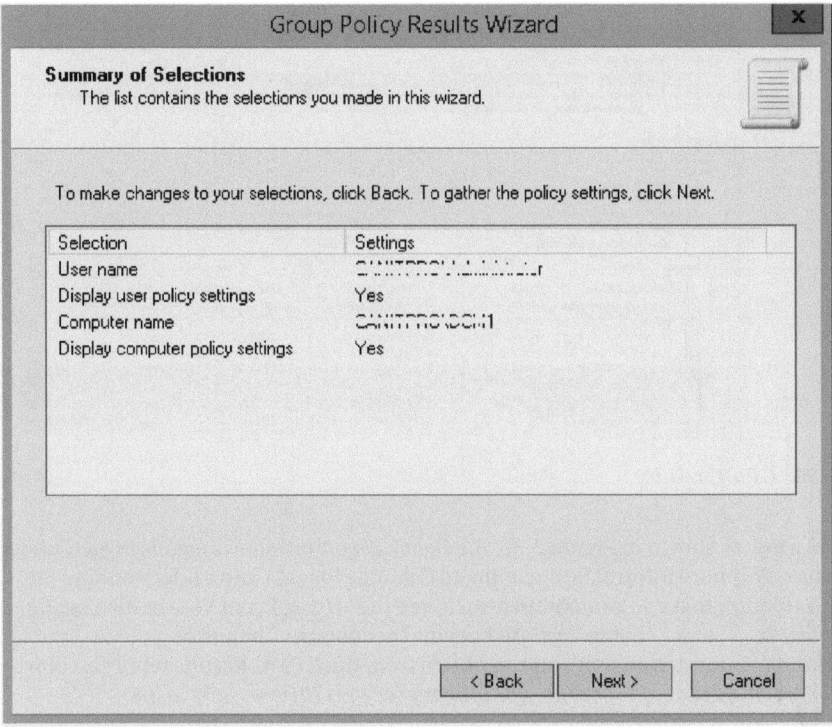

Figure 2-35. *Summary of selections*

5. In the GPMC window, expand the Group Policy Objects and you can see the report with the name of the user/computer you selected in the wizard. The report that appears in the Details pane provides information about how the Group Policy has been applied to that user/computer (see Figure 2-36).

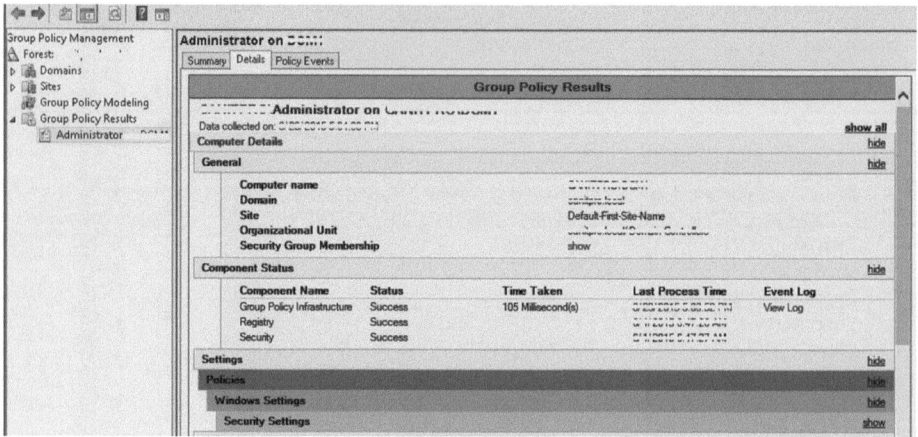

Figure 2-36. *GPMC results*

In the window shown in Figure 2-36, the *Policy Events* tab shows events logged under *Event Viewer*. For more information relating to enabling logging and understanding the type of information that you can obtain from it, see the "Using Event Viewer for Tracing Group Policy Logs" and "Enable Verbose Logging" sections in Chapter 5.

The kind of information that you can obtain from the GPMC Results report is shown at `https://msdn.microsoft.com/en-us/library/cc759170(v=ws.10).aspx`.

GPMC Scripts

Using GPMC, various troubleshooting tasks can be quickly carried out by running one or more of the provided sample scripts. The sample scripts available are shown at `https://msdn.microsoft.com/en-us/library/cc759170(v=ws.10).aspx` and may be helpful when you need to troubleshoot various issues.

These samples are located in the `%programfiles%\GPMC\Scripts` folder. To execute a script, use the script filename and run it in command prompt.

If you cannot find a sample script that fits your needs, you can easily modify a sample script, or create your own script, or locate additional scripts online.

■ **Info** For more sample scripts, go to `https://msdn.microsoft.com/en-us/library/aa814151.aspx`.

Group Policy Preferences

Group Policy preferences (shown in Figure 2-37) are a simplified method of configuring settings within a GPO. They are basically a collection of client-side extensions (CSEs) that are used to deliver preference settings onto client machines that are members of the domain. You will read about CSEs in detail in Chapter 6.

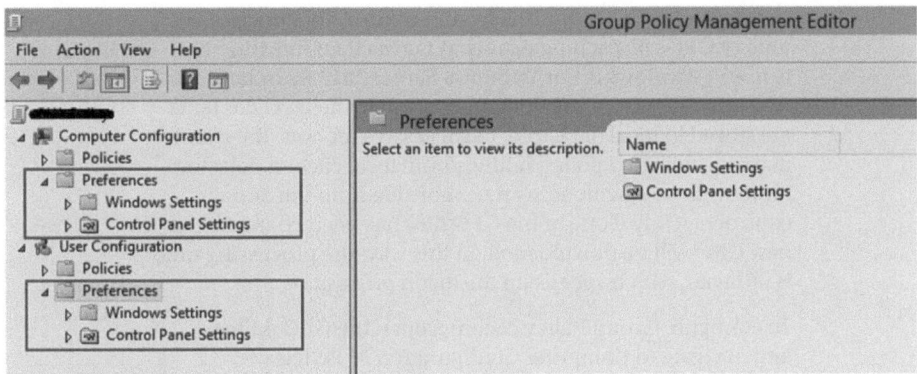

Figure 2-37. *Group Policy preferences*

Occasionally, GPO preferences may not work as expected. In such a case, you can troubleshoot them with the help of a special feature called Group Policy Preferences Tracing. This feature is disabled by default. Here are the steps to enable and use it:

1. Create a new GPO and link it where GPO Preferences are not working.

2. Next, navigate here to Computer Configuration ➤ Policies ➤ Administrative Templates ➤ Group Policy ➤ Logging and tracing.

3. Then configure the *Shortcut preferences logging and tracing policy* and set it to **Enabled**. Make sure you set the *Tracing* option to **On** in the policy configuration window. Click **Apply**, followed by **OK**. Restart the machine or refresh the GPOs.

When this policy is in effect, a log file will be generated. The log will be called a Group Policy Preferences trace file, located under `<System Root Drive>\ProgramData\GroupPolicy\Preference`. You can read the log file to find out how GPO preferences look to the Group Policy management. If you find the return error code 0x0000000 at the end of this log, it means that there is no error. If you obtain any other error code, you need to troubleshoot it accordingly.

What's New in Group Policy for Windows Server 2012 R2

At the time of writing this book, Windows Server 2012 R2 is the current version of Windows Server. This section highlights what is new in Group Policy for Windows Server 2012 R2.

1. **Group Policy Caching**: This feature reduces the processing time of GPOs by caching results. When a client machine running Windows 8.1 or Windows Server 2012 R2 or later receives GPOs from the domain controller, the GPO contents are stored in local datastore. In successive reboots, the client machine will load policy settings from local cached datastore, rather than redownloading the whole file from the domain controller. Only if one of the GPO files has been changed, the new GPO will be downloaded. In this way, the processing time is reduced, which speeds up the logon process.

    To configure Group Policy caching, open the GPO editor and navigate to Computer Configuration ➤ Policies ➤ Administrative Templates ➤ System ➤ Group Policy.

    Now set *Configure Group Policy Caching* to **Enabled**.

2. **IPv6 Support:** Microsoft has included support for IPv6 settings within GPOs. For example, you can now choose IPv6 settings for configuring TCP/IP printers and using IPv6 VPN networks.

3. **Updated GPO Event Logging:** Server 2012 R2 provides greater detail in the events generated by Group Policy. Detailed logging can help administrators when analyzing GPOs and helps in troubleshooting GPO issues such as long logon times.

■ **Info**   A comprehensive list of the improvements to Group Policy in Windows Server 2012 R2 can be found at `https://technet.microsoft.com/en-us/library/dn265973.aspx#BKMK_gpinfra`.

Key Points

-   GPMC is very robust and useful tool for manipulating GPOs in the domain environment.

-   In Windows Server, you can enable GPMC via Server Manager, while in Windows desktop editions, you can enable GPMC using RSAT, which connects to a domain-joined server.

-   Deleting a GPO will delete the GPO. Deleting a *GPO link* will delete the *link* only, but will leave the GPO in place.

-   GPMC Modelling allows simulation before changes are made, like a user logging into a particular machine or moving to a different OU, while GPMC Results is a tool for generating information about policies that are currently applied.

- Group Policy preferences are not GPO settings, but instead they use GPOs to deploy system preferences to domain-joined computers.

- Group Policy caching helps to reduce overall processing time by loading GPOs from a local data store for successive reboots.

Summary

When administrators are managing GPOs, the GPMC is normally the tool of choice. You have seen how to install, configure, and use the GPMC for your day-to-day work. The GPMC is a great tool for troubleshooting Group Policy issues as well, and we discussed GPMC reports and their usefulness in solving client and machine problems. Nowadays other equivalent tools to manage Group Policies are also available. Advanced Group Policy Management (AGPM) is one of those tools, and it is discussed later in this book. We hope this dedicated chapter on the GPMC has enabled you to explore it thoroughly and has provided enough guidance to make efficient use of this essential tool. In the next chapter, you will learn how to use LGPO and GPMC tools to configure Group Policy on Windows devices.

CHAPTER 3

■ ■ ■

Managing the Windows Environment with Group Policy

In this chapter, we will explain how to use Group Policy for managing and configuring Windows for end users. Our aim is to help you understand why Group Policy is commonly used and why it is an essential tool, especially in a corporate environment where you may need to configure hundreds or thousands of domain-joined devices. It is therefore important that how you can use Group Policy effectively and efficiently.

In Chapter 2, you saw how to use GPMC to manage GPOs. Now, you will discover how to configure and apply Group Policy properly to customize and secure a Windows machine. The first part of this lesson starts by using GPOs to customize Windows. We will then show you how to use GPOs to turn off unnecessary features. GPOs are also an excellent method of securing Windows machines, which you will see in the final section.

So strap in and get ready to launch as we lift the lid off the art of Group Policy. We will show you how Group Policy can help you take your Windows administration to another level.

Using GPOs for Windows Customization

When it comes to Windows customization, the registry and Group Policy should be the first tools that come to your mind. If you are an IT professional or system administrator, you probably work in domain environment. You will need to become very familiar with GPOs as a tool for Windows to ensure that users have a consistent and controlled experience. Of course, you do not need a domain to customize and tweak Windows extensively; the domain simply allows you to distribute and control the settings across your domain-connected devices easily and with minimal administrative effort. Customizing Windows with the help of GPOs can provide you with many benefits, including:

- An easy-to-use user interface (UI) with no complex manipulation required, as compared to registry editing.

© Kapil Arya 2016
K. Arya, *Windows Group Policy Troubleshooting*, DOI 10.1007/978-1-4842-1886-0_3

- The ability to apply Windows customizations to selected (or all) devices on your corporate environment within a domain from a centralized location.

- GPOs provide policy explanations and help for every setting, helping you to learn, understand, and configure the policy accordingly.

Group Policy can be extremely useful, and in this section we will illustrate this with some examples. You can try these examples on a local computer or within a domain environment.

Customizing the Start Menu or Start Screen Layout

Group Policy allows you to customize Windows. The Start Menu and Start Screen can be two of most crucial (and potentially confusing) components for a Windows user. The Start Screen (introduced in Windows 8) beautifully displays many default tiles, including Live Tiles, which can be pinned to the Start Screen. These Live Tiles provide real-time notifications to users.

For users more familiar with Windows 7 or Windows XP, the Start Menu is welcomed back in Windows 10. The new Start Menu in Windows 10 allows both classic as well as Universal App/Live Tiles.

When deploying or refreshing a desktop client to your users, you should be careful not to confuse or disrupt their normal computing habits. By way of example, Windows 8 was pretty radical in design, and this created a significant negative impact on user productivity. Providing users with a custom or predefined Start Screen or Start Menu can reduce initial confusion, increase productivity, and cut down the number of help desk incidents relating to users not being able to locate app icons that they need to perform their work. Many end users are unaware that tiles can be pinned, moved, or removed from the Start Screen/Menu. In this scenario, it is beneficial to provide corporate users with preconfigured settings that include tiles for common apps such as Microsoft Office Word and Excel and also to remove unnecessary tiles that are unlikely to be used such as News, Microsoft Solitaire, Money, and the like.

In addition to configuring the Start Screen used by the default user profile (which then allows users to modify it), you may want to prevent users from customizing the Start Screen or Start Menu at all and force users to only use your precustomized Start Screen/Menu. Here, you can configure a policy that restricts users from customizing the Start Screen/Menu; this especially useful in a highly controlled environment such as a kiosk or call center or for a multiple-user system.

To restrict users from modifying the Start Screen/Menu, you first customise the Start Screen/Menu and then export the settings using PowerShell. These settings are then added to a Group Policy that is used to configure the Windows device during logon. The detailed steps are as follows:

1. Customize and rearrange the Start Screen/Menu that you want for your users.

2. Open an Administrative Windows PowerShell command prompt.

3. To export the Start Menu layout to the F: drive (you can use any other drive/location on your system) with "MyStartMenu" as the filename, run the following cmdlet (also shown in Figure 3-1):

Export-StartLayout -path **F:\MyStartMenu.xml** *-As XML*

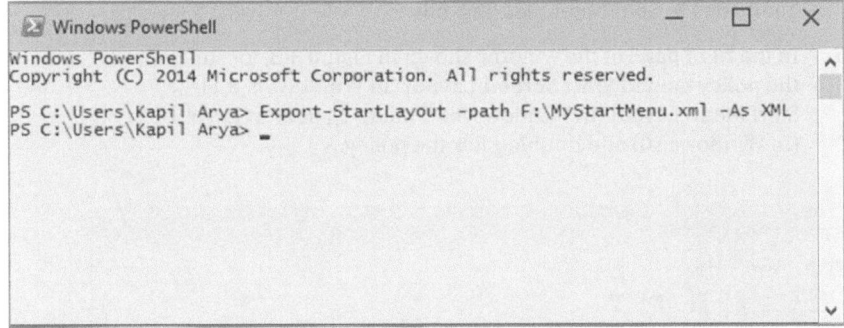

Figure 3-1. *Exporting Start Screen/Menu as an XML file using Windows PowerShell*

The exported XML file can be located using File Explorer. You can open this file with any XML handler such as Internet Explorer and see the exported code. This is shown in Figure 3-2.

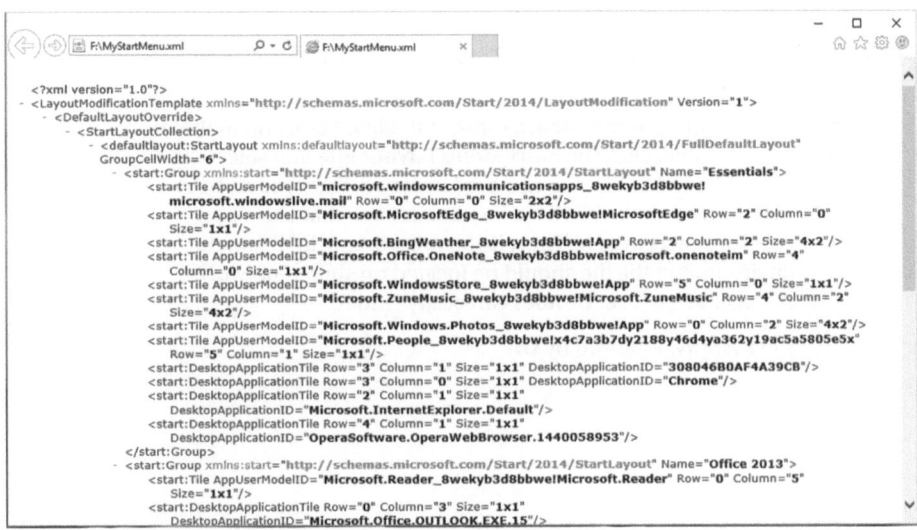

Figure 3-2. *Exported Start Screen/Menu configuration XML file*

4. Open Run by pressing **Windows Key + R**, type **gpedit.msc**, launch the Local Group Policy Editor (LGPO), and navigate to User Configuration ➤ Administrative Templates ➤ Start Menu and Taskbar. If you are using Group Policy Management Console (GPMC), open it using the **gpmc.msc** command and go to User Configuration ➤ Policies ➤ Administrative Templates ➤ Start Menu and Taskbar.

5. In the right pane of the window shown in Figure 3-3, locate the policy named **Start Screen Layout** (in Windows 8, 8.1), Start Menu Layout (in Windows 8.1 Update 2), or Start Layout (in Windows 10) and double-click the policy.

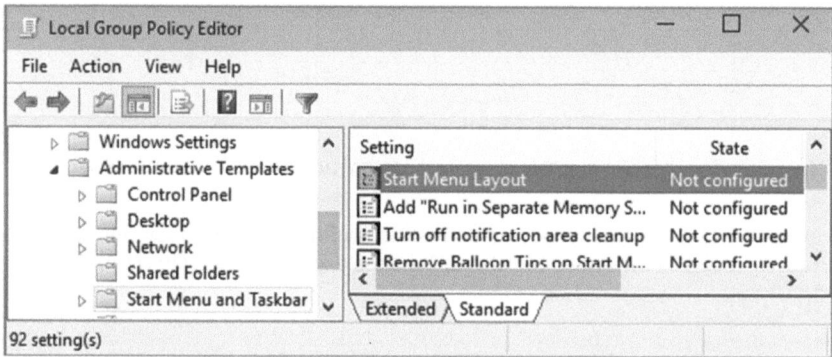

Figure 3-3. *Locating the Start (Screen/Menu) layout policy setting in GPO*

6. Set the policy to **Enabled**, as shown in Figure 3-4, and in the Options area, click the **Start Menu Layout File** and select the location of XML file you obtained in step *3*. Here you need to make sure that the XML file location is such that users have read-only access to it. Thus, if you are working in a domain environment, the file should be located on shared network storage, where user profiles can easily read it.

7. Click **Apply**, followed by **OK**.

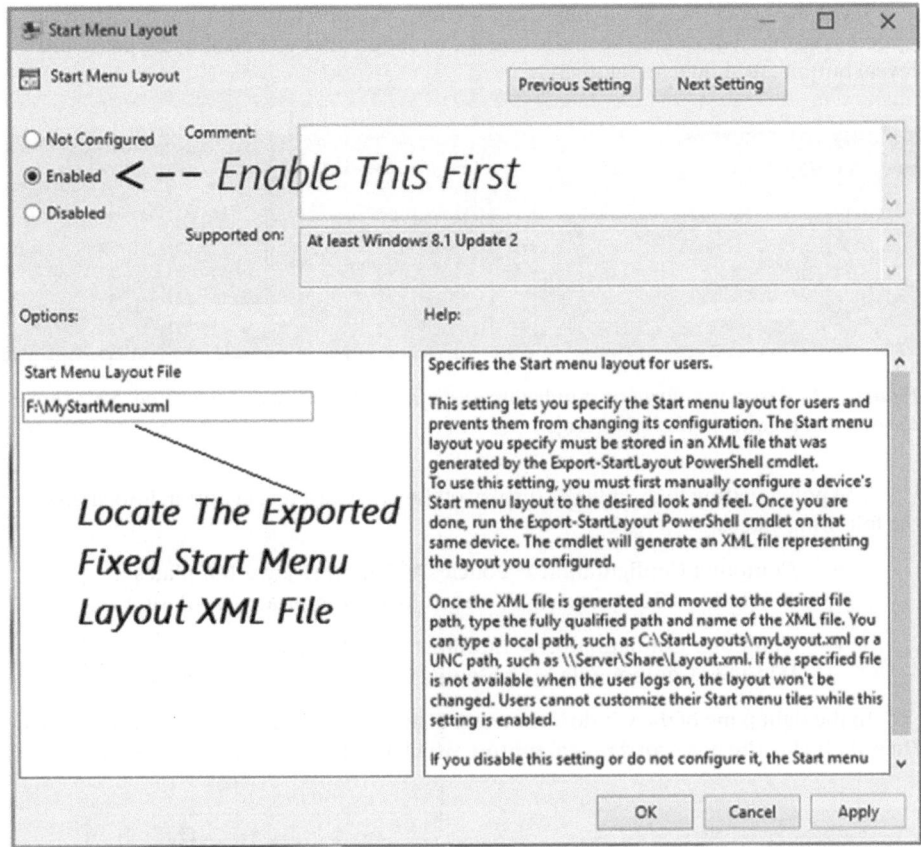

Figure 3-4. *Start (Screen/Menu) Layout policy setting configure window*

8. Close LGPO and restart your device to make the policy setting effective. In the GPMC, you can run the **gpupdate /force** command to get the setting applied.

After rebooting the device, the Start Screen/Menu tiles are fixed and users can't customize them. You just used a GPO to customize Windows the way you want it.

Enabling or Disabling the Password Reveal Button from Appearing

In Windows 8 or later, there is a password reveal button that appears next to the typed password on an input form. Clicking this button displays the typed password. You can use GPOs to customize this feature and configure how Windows should display or hide passwords.

If you are concerned about password security, you don't want the password reveal option available. The default scenario and the situation after you disable the password reveal button are shown in Figure 3-5.

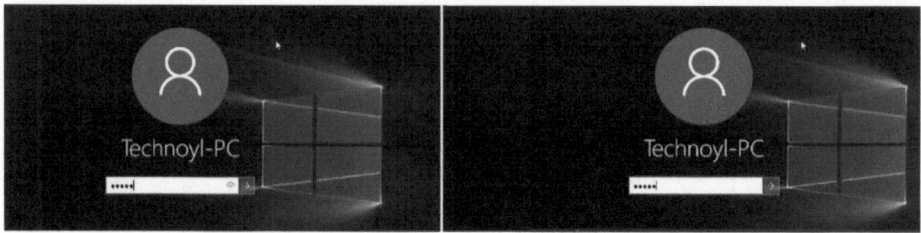

Figure 3-5. *Password reveal button before and after configuring policy setting. Note that the eye icon is gone in the right image*

The policy setting to disable the display of the password reveal button is located at the following places:

- Computer Configuration ➤ Policies ➤ Administrative Templates ➤ Windows Components ➤ Credential User Interface (in GPMC)

- Computer Configuration ➤ Administrative Templates ➤ Windows Components ➤ Credential User Interface (in LGPO)

In the right pane of the window shown in Figure 3-6, double-click the setting named **Do not display the password reveal button**, which is set to *Not Configured* by default.

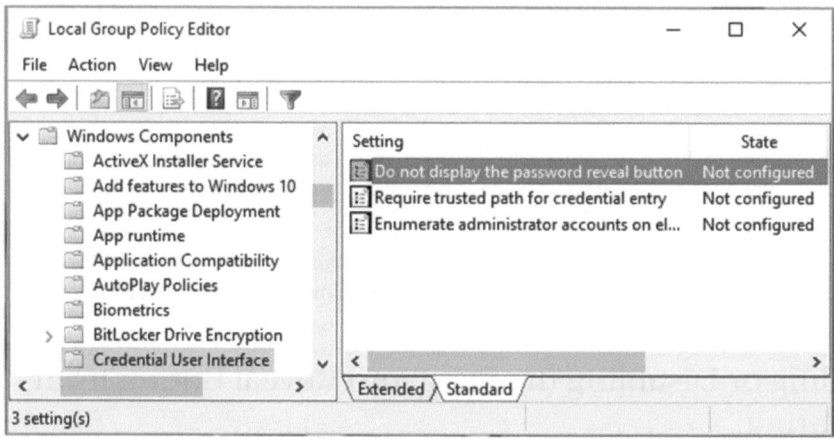

Figure 3-6. *Locating the **Do not display the password reveal button** policy setting*

In the policy setting configuration window shown in Figure 3-7, set the policy to **Enabled**. Click **Apply** and click **OK**. Close the GPO, and reboot or update Group Policy to make the setting effective.

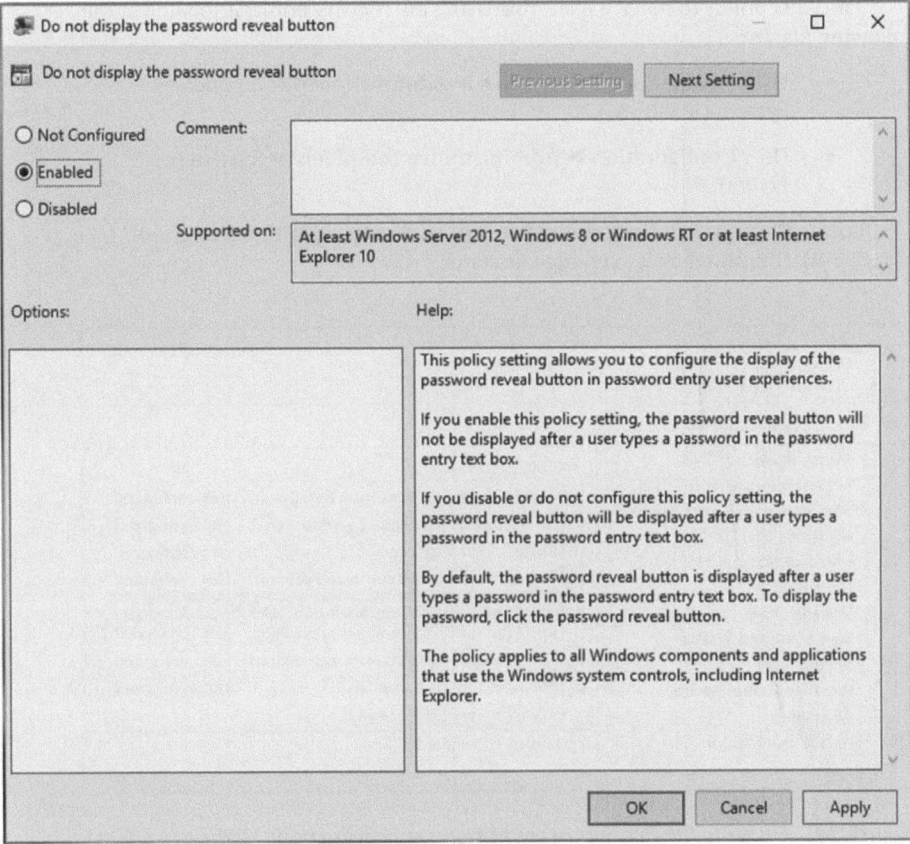

Figure 3-7. *Configuring the **Do not display the password reveal button** policy setting*

Hiding the password reveal button from credential forms should provide enhanced security.

Preventing Users from Customizing Windows Using Registry Manipulation

The registry editor is available in all Windows editions. You have already seen that changing a policy setting can be equivalent to changing the corresponding registry values for that setting, in Chapter 1. To disable the ability to edit the registry, you need to configure the **Prevent access to registry editing tools** GPO.

The GPO policy to block a user from using the registry editor is located at the following places:

- User Configuration ➤ Policies ➤ Administrative Templates ➤ System (in GPMC)

- User Configuration ➤ Administrative Templates ➤ System (in LGPO)

Locate the policy setting named **Prevent access to registry editing tools** (see Figure 3-8). Double-click it to change its status.

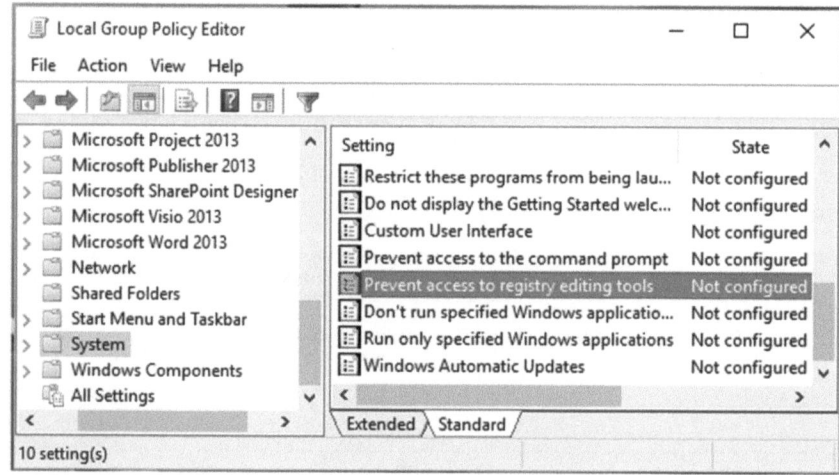

Figure 3-8. *Locating the **Prevent acces to registry editing** policy setting in a GPO*

Next, in the policy setting configuration window (Figure 3-9), change the setting status to **Enabled**. You can also choose whether you want to run the registry silently or not.

■ **Note**   To allow RegEdit to run silently, you can use Registry Editor in silent mode using the switch **/s**. Silent means that if you type **RegEdit /s filename.reg** at the command prompt, you can import the filename.reg registry file directly into the registry without the user being prompted. This is useful for scripting registry actions and automation scenarios.

Click **Apply** and then **OK**. Close the GPO, and update Group Policy. In case of LGPO, no restart is required for this policy.

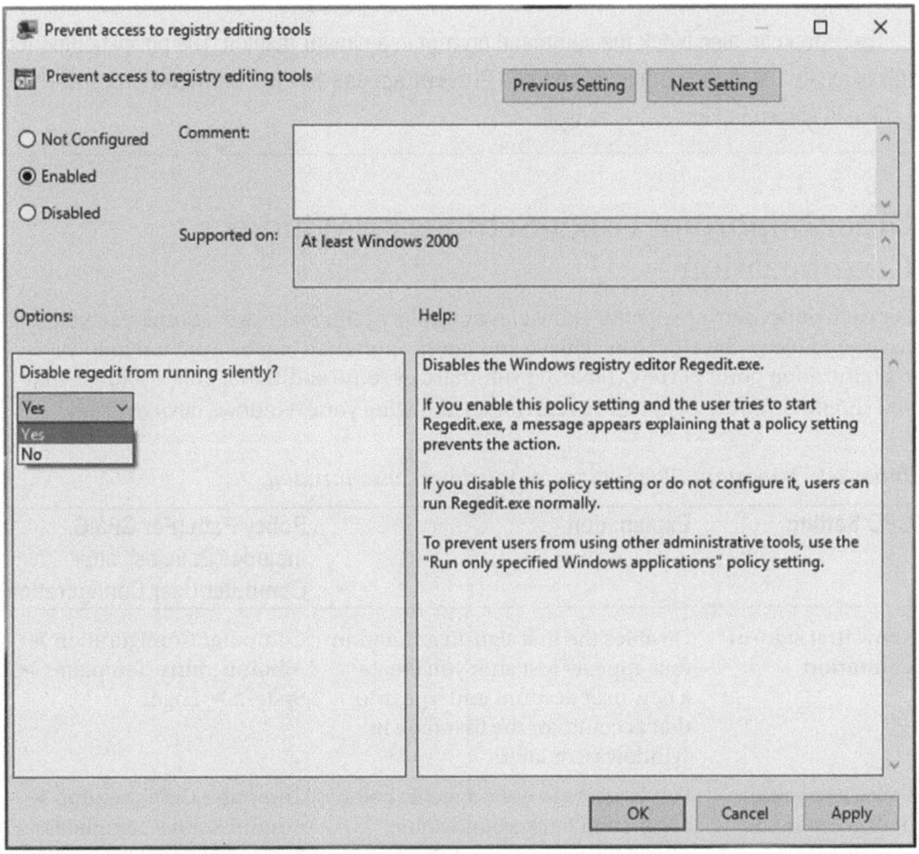

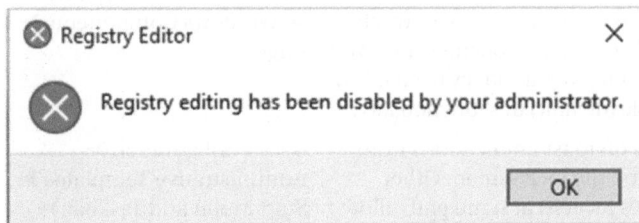

Figure 3-9. *Configuring the* **Prevent access to registry editing** *policy setting*

Once configured, when users try to access the registry editor, they will see the error message shown in Figure 3-10.

Figure 3-10. *Registry editor is blocked when the* **Prevent access to registry editing** *GPO is enabled*

■ **Tip**   You can also block the command prompt in a similar fashion. The policy setting for this is located at same path and is named **Prevent access to the command prompt**. This setting is shown in Figure 3-8 as well.

Other Important Policy Settings for Windows Customization

For each policy setting we have shown an example. At this stage, we assume that you have good idea what GPO can achieve and how important it can be from a Windows customization point of view. Table 3-1 summarizes some additional policy settings that you should be aware of that are useful for customizing your Windows devices.

Table 3-1. *Important GPO Settings for Windows Customization*

GPO Setting	Explanation	Policy Path (For GPMC, include "Policies" after Computer/User Configuration)
Show first sign-in animation	Disables the first sign-in animation that appears just after you create a new user account and sign into that account for the first time in Windows 8 or later.	Computer Configuration ➤ Administrative Templates ➤ System ➤ Logon
Force a specific background and accent color	Forces users to use a specific color accent and background color, especially for the Start Screen in Windows 8 and 8.1. For this, you must enable the policy setting and define a HTML color code in the available color option.	Computer Configuration ➤ Administrative Templates ➤ Control Panel ➤ Personalization
Turn off switching between recent apps	In Windows 8 and 8.1, you can move cursor/pointer to top left corner of screen, which lets you to switch between currently opened apps. You can configure this policy to enable or disable (default) this functionality.	User Configuration ➤ Administrative Templates ➤ Windows Components ➤ Edge UI
Turn off toast notifications on the lock screen	Turns off toast notifications from apps on the lock screen. Other polices located at same path allow you to customize the amount of notifications you receive. Applicable to Windows 8, Windows Server 2012, or later.	User Configuration ➤ Administrative Templates ➤ Start Menu and Taskbar ➤ Notifications

(continued)

Table 3-1. (*continued*)

GPO Setting	Explanation	Policy Path (For GPMC, include "Policies" after Computer/User Configuration)
Turn off automatic download and install of updates	Turns off automatic updates to installed Store apps on your system. Applicable to Windows 8.1, Windows Server 2012 R2, or later. You can locate the policy to turn off the Store app itself at this same path.	Computer Configuration ➤ Administrative Templates ➤ Windows Components ➤ Store
Allow telemetry	In Windows 10, Microsoft collects data such as crash logs, usage of features, etc. to improve the OS in successive builds. This policy helps you limit how much data Microsoft can take from your system. In Enterprise-based editions, you can completely block telemetry. In other editions, it is possible to prevent telemetry partially with this setting.	**Computer Configuration ➤ Administrative Templates ➤ Windows Components ➤ Data Collection and Preview Builds**
Disable user control over preview builds	Microsoft offers preview builds of Windows 10 to *Windows Insiders,* people who test these previews and provide feedback to the company. Using this policy setting, you can customize the way users receive newer preview builds on their system. If you turn on or enable the policy, users won't be able to change their settings for the *Choose how preview builds are installed* section under Settings app ➤ Windows Updates.	**Computer Configuration ➤ Administrative Templates ➤ Windows Components ➤ Data Collection and Preview Builds**
Low battery notification level	By default, Windows triggers low battery notification at 10% battery left; you can customize this setting to enter your desired percentage. It works for Windows Vista and later.	Computer Configuration ➤ Administrative Templates ➤ System ➤ Power Management ➤ Notification Settings
Untrusted font blocking	Using this security-based policy, you can prevent programs from loading untrusted fonts, or fonts that have not been verified, to your Windows 10 system. You can also customize this policy to unblock untrusted fonts but create a log of events they make.	Computer Configuration ➤ Administrative Templates ➤ System ➤ Mitigation Options

(*continued*)

Table 3-1. (*continued*)

GPO Setting	Explanation	Policy Path (For GPMC, include "Policies" after Computer/User Configuration)
Items displayed in Places bar	The Places bar is basically the items linked under Favorites in File/Windows Explorer. To add your desired folder manually to the Places bar, you must browse to the folder, right-click it, and select **Add current location to Favorites**. Using this setting, you can customize the Places bar and forcefully add your desired items for users in your environment.	User Configuration ➤ Administrative Templates ➤ Windows Components ➤ File Explorer ➤ Common Open File Dialog
Show the Apps view automatically when the user goes to the Start Screen	With this setting, you can configure Windows 8.1 such that when a user tries to go to Start Screen, he/she sees the Apps view instead of the app tiles.	User Configuration ➤ Administrative Templates ➤ Start Menu and Taskbar
Prevent users from uninstalling applications from the Start Screen	In Windows 8, Windows Server 2012 and later, users are able to uninstall apps straight from the Start Screen. You can prevent this from happening via this setting.	User Configuration ➤ Administrative Templates ➤ Start Menu and Taskbar
Allow all trusted apps to install	Generally, you can't install apps in Windows 8 or later unless they are installed via the Windows Store. To allow Windows to install apps from a trusted source other than from the Store, you may configure this policy and apply it on user systems.	Computer Configuration ➤ Administrative Templates ➤ Windows Components ➤ App Package Deployment
No auto-restart with logged-on users for scheduled automatic updates installation	This policy setting helps you to decide whether you want to have automatic restart after you make scheduled installation of Windows Updates or not. When this setting is Enabled, users are asked to reboot manually and the system does not automatically reboot. You can also configure various Window Update settings at this policy path.	Computer Configuration ➤ Administrative Templates ➤ Windows Components ➤ Windows Update

(*continued*)

Table 3-1. (*continued*)

GPO Setting	Explanation	Policy Path (For GPMC, include "Policies" after Computer/User Configuration)
Force a specific default lock screen image	Forces users to have a particular lock screen wallpaper. In the policy configuration options, you can specify the wallpaper path. You can type a local path, such as *C:\ windows\web\screen\lockscreen. jpg* or a UNC path, such as *\\Server\ Share\Corp.jpg*. This setting only applies to domain-joined machines. On this same path, you can also locate the lock screen settings to not display it at all, prevent enabling slide show on it, and prevent users from changing its image. These settings work for Windows 8 and later.	Computer Configuration ➤ Administrative Templates ➤ Control Panel ➤ Personalization
Show a "Run as different user" command on Start	Generally, when we right-click a program within File Explorer or at the Start Screen, we see the option to *Run as administrator* using which program can be opened in elevated mode. Via this policy, you can modify the behavior to allow the **Run as different user** option. You can then run programs as the other users that are available on your system. This is especially helpful to administrators while troubleshooting issues for a specific user account and to observe problems on it. This works well with a domain as well as on a local machine. This policy is available on Windows 8 or later.	User Configuration ➤ Administrative Templates ➤ Start Menu and Taskbar

■ **Tip** To configure Startup/Logon and Shutdown/Logoff scripts in GPO, navigate to GPO ➤ Computer/User Configuration ➤ Windows Settings ➤ Scripts. The configured scripts are stored in the registry database at HKEY_LOCAL_MACHINE\SOFTWARE\Policies\Windows\ System\Scripts for the computer side and HKEY_LOCAL_MACHINE\SOFTWARE\Policies\ Windows\System\Scripts at the user side.

Managing Windows Features with GPOs

As you have seen, GPOs provide extended possibilities, and they can be used to configure hundreds of settings in Windows. GPOs are equally beneficial in dealing with features available in the Windows operating systems. For example, if you don't want to store your files in the cloud, you can use a GPO to turn off OneDrive. Similarly, if you don't want to use online search in conjunction with localized search, you can turn off Cortana with the help of GPOs.

Table 3-2 summarizes the policy settings that you can configure to enable or disable a specific Windows feature. Using Group Policy, these customizations can then be applied to users and computers.

Table 3-2. *Important GPO Settings to Enable or Disable Windows Features*

GPO Setting	Importance	Policy Path (For GPMC, include "Policies" after Computer/User Configuration)
Allow Cortana	Cortana offers web search integration with an offline search feature in Windows 10. It can provide additional assistance, such as real-time updates on weather forecast, news, reminders and local information. It can also accept multiple inputs such as ink, voice, and gestures. To avoid extra or unnecessary data consumption on mobile devices, you may want to block Cortana completely.	Computer Configuration ➤ Administrative Templates ➤ Windows Components ➤ Searches
Prevent the usage of OneDrive for file storage	In Windows 8 or later, OneDrive (formerly SkyDrive) helps you to store and synchronize your files between the cloud server and your machine. In Windows 8.1 and later, Microsoft made an in-depth integration of OneDrive with File Explorer. With this policy, you may block usage of OneDrive completely. Other OneDrive-dedicated settings are at this policy path.	Computer Configuration ➤ Administrative Templates ➤ Windows Components ➤ OneDrive
Turn off Windows Defender	Windows Defender has been part of the Windows family since Windows Vista. It is the first line of defense against malware. This policy can be used to disable Windows Defender if you plan to use a third-party security suite (although most third-party anti-malware tools will disable Windows Defender during installation).	Computer Configuration ➤ Administrative Templates ➤ Windows Components ➤ Windows Defender

(continued)

Table 3-2. (*continued*)

GPO Setting	Importance	Policy Path (For GPMC, include "Policies" after Computer/User Configuration)
Prevent the computer from joining a HomeGroup	Specifies whether users can add computers to a HomeGroup. By default, users can add their computer to a HomeGroup on a private network. Enabling this policy will result in users losing the ability to add their machine to a HomeGroup. This works with Windows 7 or later.	Computer Configuration ➤ Administrative Templates ➤ Windows Components ➤ HomeGroup
Turn off Windows Mail application	Blocks the Windows Mail application in Windows Vista or later.	Computer Configuration ➤ Administrative Templates ➤ Windows Components ➤ Windows Mail
Do not allow Windows Media Center to run	Windows Media Center is a digital media player and video recorder that allows users to organize and play music and videos, and to view and record live television. However, it is not included with Windows 10 but it was a highlighted feature in previous editions. Altering this policy may help to block access to Windows Media Center.	Computer Configuration ➤ Administrative Templates ➤ Windows Components ➤ Windows Media Center
Turn off location	For today's users, location is one of the most important features in Windows. Most of the apps available nowadays require a location setting to provide the full user experience. From a security point of view, location is a prime concern, especially for apps like banking. This policy allows you to control whether you want to share your location with programs and settings or not. Applicable to Windows 7 and later.	User Configuration ➤ Administrative Templates ➤ Windows Components ➤ Location and Sensors
Disable Windows error reporting	Whenever something unexpected occurs on your Windows machine, such as crash or freezing of programs, a log file is created. The Windows Error Reporting Service running in the background collects these logs and may send them to Microsoft or an internal server in your organization. Enabling this policy will completely disable the error reporting feature. It is applicable to Windows Vista or later.	User Configuration ➤ Administrative Templates ➤ Windows Components ➤ Windows Error Reporting

(*continued*)

Table 3-2. (*continued*)

GPO Setting	Importance	Policy Path (For GPMC, include "Policies" after Computer/User Configuration)
Allow the use of biometrics	Biometrics allows you to log in using fingerprint or facial recognition. If your system supports biometrics, then this policy lets you disable this feature. This setting works well in Windows 7, Windows Server 2008 R2 systems, or later.	Computer Configuration ➤ Administrative Templates ➤ Windows Components ➤ Biometrics
Disable Wi-Fi Sense	Wi-Fi Sense is one of many new features introduced in Windows 10. It automatically locates and connects to Wi-Fi hotspots. Wi-Fi Sense allows you to join networks that your contacts in Skype, Outlook, and Facebook share. The feature is also available with Windows Phone since version 8. This policy can be configured to enable or disable Wi-Fi Sense. It is applicable to Windows 10 Build 10586 (Version 1511) or later.	Computer Configuration ➤ Administrative Templates ➤ SCM: Wi-Fi Sense
Remove Task Manager	Task Manager (taskmgr.exe) lets you view running processes and CPU memory usage, and manage services. Using this policy, you can configure whether users can access Task Manager. When this policy is enabled, users can't open Task Manager. Within the policy path, you can configure other policies such preventing users from changing password on demand, locking their system. You can remove all buttons that can contribute to logging off users.	User Configuration ➤ Administrative Templates ➤ System ➤ Ctrl+Alt+Del Options
Turn off Autoplay	Autoplay allows Windows to begin reading data when you plug in a drive such as USB, DVD, floppy etc. Though you can manage Autoplay options in the Settings app, with this policy you can configure the setting via a GPO. When this policy is *Enabled*, Autoplay won't work on CD-ROM and removable media drives, or it can be disabled on all drives. You can find other Autoplay customization policies on this setting path.	Computer Configuration ➤ Administrative Templates ➤ Windows Components ➤ Autoplay Policies

Enhancing System Security by Using Security Policies (GPO Subset)

Security policy settings are another extension of Group Policy settings that can help you to enhance the security of your Windows operating systems. They help administrators audit user account activities, maintain network profiles, manage Windows Firewall settings, etc. You can locate security policies inside a GPO under Computer/User Configuration ➤ Windows Settings ➤ Security Settings, as shown in Figure 3-11.

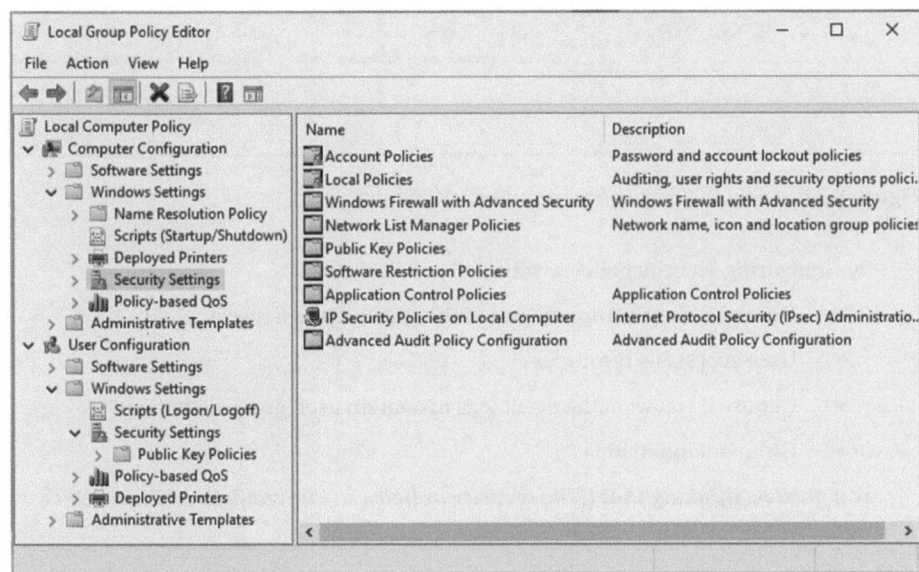

Figure 3-11. *Locating security policy settings inside a GPO*

Another way to open security settings is to type the **secpol.msc** command to open the *Local Security Policy* console/snap-in. This opens a standalone *Microsoft Management Console* (MMC) window, as shown in Figure 3-12. After reading this section you should be familiar with accessing the security settings using either method.

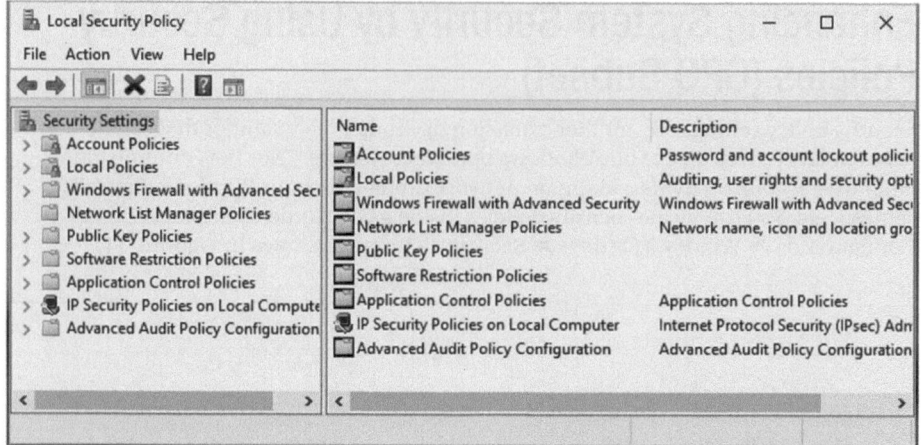

Figure 3-12. *Local Security Policy snap-in for Windows*

By configuring security policies, you can broadly control

- How an user or computer gets authenticated by a network

- User-accessible resources

- Choose if you want the event logs to contain user/group activities.

- Group membership

You must be thinking that if the security policies can be configured inside GPO, then why there is a separate snap-in for it?

■ **Answer**   Security policies within GPOs can be configured for a domain environment, potentially affecting hundreds or thousands of devices, whereas the security policies available inside the standalone snap-in can be used to apply settings for local machines only.

A standalone snap-in also allows administrators to delegate control of just the security settings rather than all Group Policy settings.

As per Microsoft (*https://technet.microsoft.com/en-us/library/ jj966254(v=ws.11).aspx*), the Local Security Policy snap-in restricts the view of local policy objects to the following policies and features:

- Account Policies

- Local Policies

- Windows Firewall with Advanced Security

- Network List Manager Policies

- Public Key Policies

- Software Restriction Policies

- Application Control Policies

- IP Security Policies on Local Computer

- Advanced Audit Policy Configuration

Remember that local policies are overridden if the computer is joined to the domain.

■ **Note**   In Local Security Policy snap-in, if you have a more than one policy configuration window open, you won't be able to quit from the console directly until you close each of the policy configuration windows, as shown in Figure 3-13.

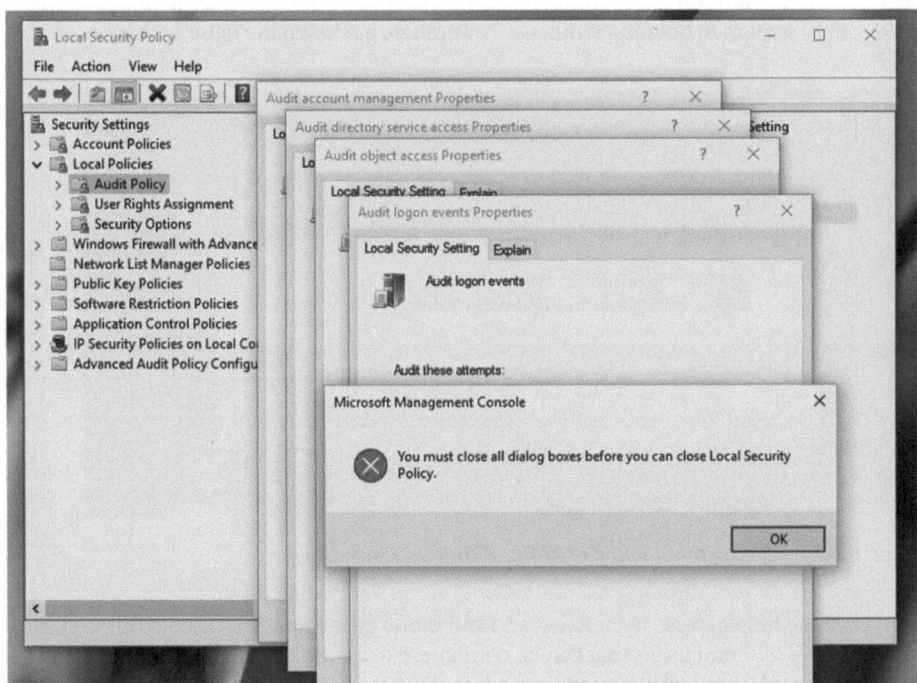

Figure 3-13. *You can't close the Local Security Policy snap-in when policy windows are open*

Configuring a security policy is quite simple and similar to configuring a Group Policy setting. GPO settings can be either set to Enabled, Disabled, or Not Configured, but security policies in the Local Security Policy snap-in can be set to a specific acceptable value or any numerical value. These are conditional arguments and can be configured according to your requirement.

To reinforce security settings, let's look at some important security policy examples that make the Local Security Policy tool extremely useful in system administration.

Changing the Impact of User Account Control (UAC) Prompts

User Account Control (UAC) settings were implemented in Windows since Windows Vista and UAC continue to protect systems on later editions of Windows. The main aim of UAC is to block unauthorized, harmful, or malicious activities on a system that are not approved by an administrator. The UAC prompt will also appear when a user tries to carry out a task that they are not authorized to complete and thus requires them to enter their appropriate credentials, such as in opening Windows PowerShell, as shown in Figure 3-14.

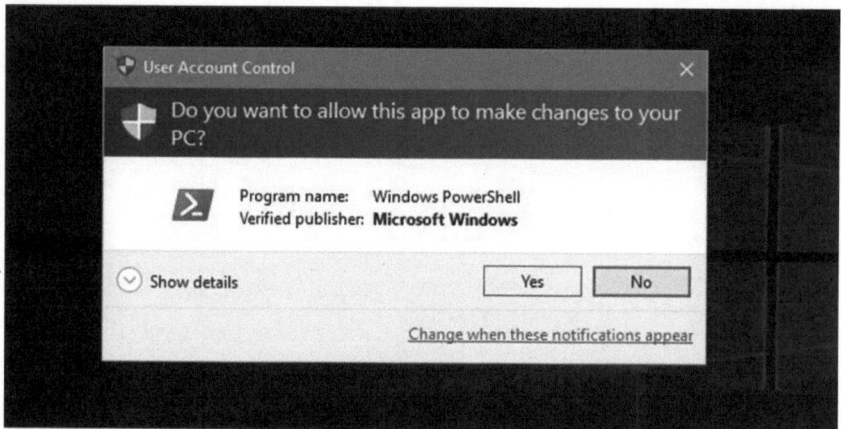

Figure 3-14. UAC prompt when opening Windows PowerShell

With the help of security policies, you can modify the impact of UAC settings. These settings have different levels that can be configured to assure the security of your device. To configure UAC settings manually, search for UAC using Windows Search. From the results, click the *Change User Account Control Settings* entry. Then you should be able to change the UAC notification level settings, as shown in Figure 3-15.

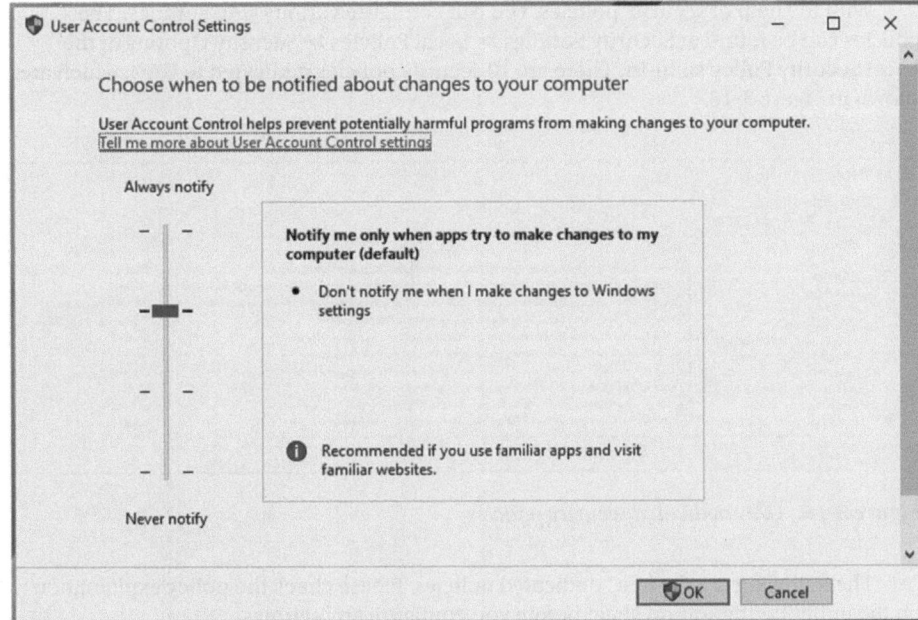

Figure 3-15. *Configuring UAC settings in the control panel*

There are four levels for UAC settings, which are as follows:

- **Always notify**: The UAC prompt appears when software/apps try to make a change to the system or when you make changes Windows settings. The screen will be dimmed and you need to read the content of the prompt and provide your approval/denial, if you are an administrator (see Figure 3-14). If you are standard user, you need to enter the administrator's password. This is a highly secure UAC level.

- **Notify only when apps try to make changes to the system (default)**: Get notified only when apps/programs try to make changes to your system and you accept/reject these operations. The desktop will be dimmed when the UAC prompt appears. No notification/prompt will be sent when you're changing settings.

- **Notify only when apps try to make changes to system (but don't dim desktop)**: This level has the same effect as the previous one. The only difference is that the desktop is not dimmed when the UAC prompt appears.

- **Never notify**: This level disables UAC, and no notification/prompt appears when either you or any app makes changes to the system. This setting is not recommended due to the reduced security.

With the help of security policies, you can configure various UAC settings. These policies can be found at Security Settings ➤ Local Policies ➤ Security Options in the Local Security Policy snap-in. There are 10 security policies dedicated to UAC, which are shown in Figure 3-16.

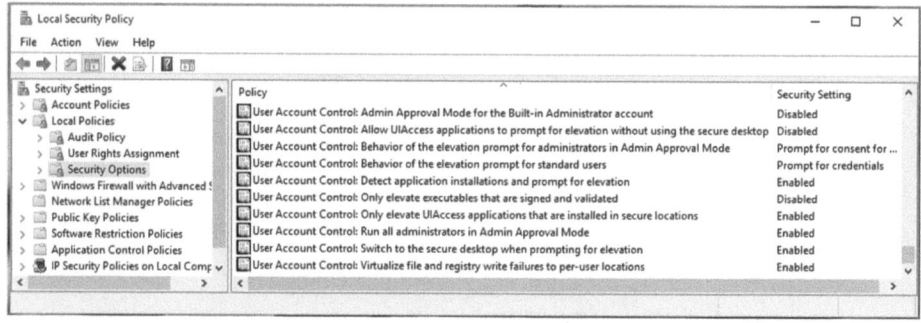

Figure 3-16. *UAC dedicated security policies*

The following are the UAC dedicated policies. Please check the policy explaination on the policy configuration sheet before you configure any settings.

1. **Admin Approval Mode for the Built-In Administrator account**

2. **Allow UIAccess applications to prompt for elevation without using the secure desktop**

3. **Behavior of the elevation prompt for administrators in Admin Approval Mode**

4. **Behavior of the elevation prompt for standard users**

5. **Detect application installations and prompt for elevation**

6. **Only elevate executables that are signed and validated**

7. **Only elevate UIAccess applications that are installed in secure locations**

8. **Run all administrators in Admin Approval Mode**

9. **Switch to the secure desktop when prompting for elevation**

10. **Virtualize file and registry write failures to per-user locations**

■ **Note**   You can explore details about these UAC dedicated policies and their corresponding registry manipulation on *TechNet* library at `https://technet.microsoft.com/en-us/library/dd835564.aspx`.

Customize Password Policies

Let's talk about passwords in detail. Local Security Policy contains six power-packed, dedicated password policies to help you to customize the usage of password on your system.

The password policies can be located at Security Settings ➤ Account Policies ➤ Password Policy in the local snap-in (as shown in Figure 3-17), and at Computer Configuration ➤ Windows Settings ➤ Account Policies ➤ Password Policy in a LGPO, and at Computer Configuration ➤ Policies ➤ Windows Settings ➤ Account Policies ➤ Password Policy in the GPMC.

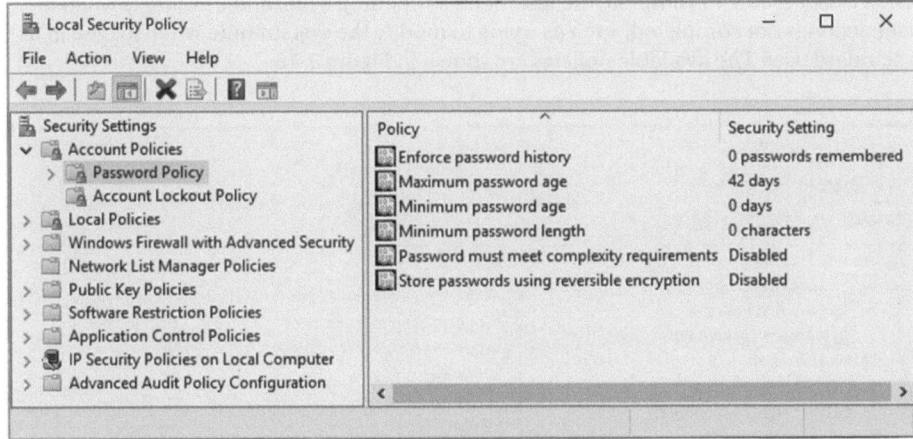

Figure 3-17. *Password policies in Local Security Policy snap-in*

The following password policies are available. It is highly recommended that you read the complete policy explanation (double-click a policy and click **Explain**) before changing any setting.

1. **Enforce password history**

2. **Maximum password age**

3. **Minimum password age**

4. **Minimum password length**

5. **Password must meet complexity requirements**

6. **Store passwords using reversible encryption**

■ **Note**   You can additionally refer to the following article to get more details on these security settings: *https://technet.microsoft.com/en-in/library/cc786468.aspx.*

Auditing User Activities Using Security Policies

With the help of audit policies, you can trace the activities on your client systems. As far as local audit policies are concerned, there are nine policies available in total. For advanced and forensic level audit policies, you can configure a total of 53 policies. This section gives you the overview of the architecture of the nine local audit policies available.

Local Audit Policies

The local audit policies are available under Security Settings ➤ Local Policies ➤ Audit Policy. You can configure them with *Success* or *Failure* options. A success criterion is when a user is able to complete the task, such as opening a file, and a failure is when a user action is not completed, such as trying to modify the system time when logged in as a standard user. The available policies are shown in Figure 3-18.

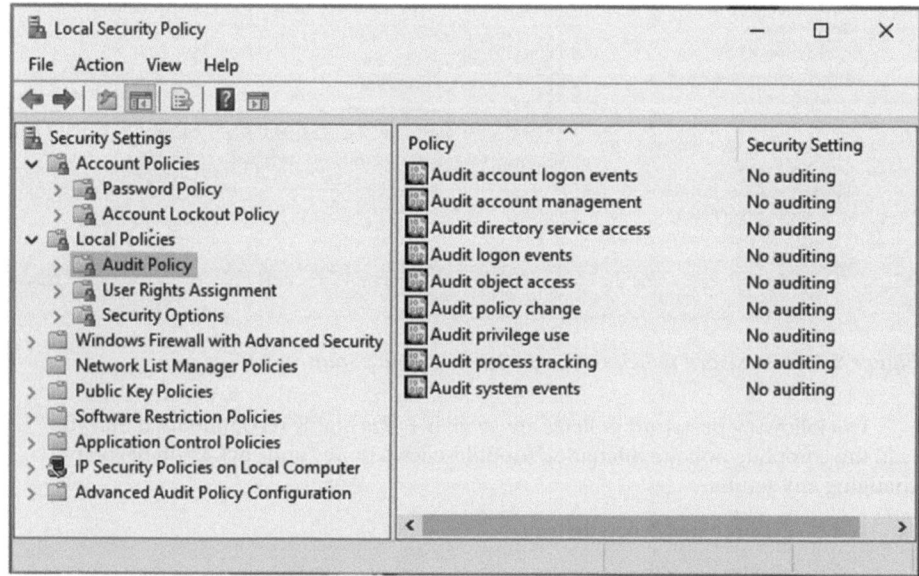

Figure 3-18. *Local auditing policies in the Local Security Policy snap-in*

The following are the policies you can alter here:

1. **Audit account logon events**

2. **Audit account management**

3. **Audit directory service access**

4. **Audit logon events**

5. **Audit object access**

6.   **Audit policy change**

7.   **Audit privilege use**

8.   **Audit process tracking**

9.   **Audit system events**

We highly recommend that you read through the policy explanations before configuring a particular setting. If you configure a setting incorrectly, it may result in overheading the system, more resources consumption in event logging, etc.

Advanced Auditing Policies

These advanced auditing policies apply to Windows Vista and later. They can be located at Security Settings ➤ Advanced Audit Policy Configuration inside the snap-in. This is shown in Figure 3-19.

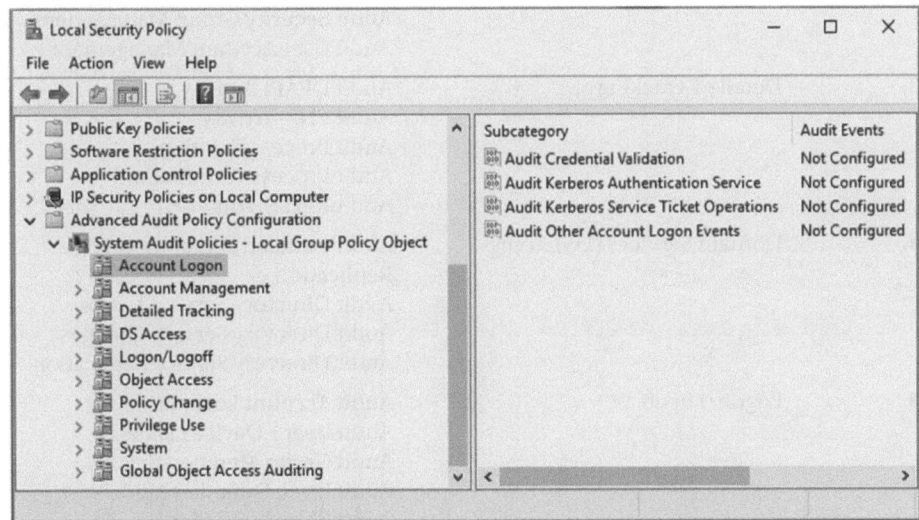

Figure 3-19. *Advanced auditing policies located in Local Security Policy snap-in*

These 50+ policies are classified into 10 dedicated categories. All of these policies are mentioned in Table 3-3. It is highly recommended that you read the complete policy explanation (double-click the policy and click **Explain**) before changing any settings.

Table 3-3. *List of System/Advanced Audit Policies in Windows*

S.no.	Audit Policy Category	Audit Policy Subcategories
1.	Account Logon	Audit Credential Validation Audit Kerberos Authentication Service Audit Kerberos Service Ticket Operations Audit Other Logon Events
2.	Account Management	Audit Application Group Management Audit Computer Account Management Audit Distribution Group Management Audit Other Account Management Events Audit Security Group Management Audit User Account Management
3.	Detailed Tracking	Audit DPAPI Activity Audit PNP Activity Audit Process Creation Audit Process Termination Audit RPC Events
4.	Domain Services (DS) Access	Audit Detailed Directory Service Replication Audit Directory Service Access Audit Directory Service Changes Audit Directory Service Replication
5.	Logon/Logoff	Audit Account Lockout Audit User / Device claims Audit Group Membership Audit IPsec Extended Mode Audit IPsec Main Mode Audit IPsec Quick Mode Audit Logoff Audit Logon Audit Network Policy Server Audit Other Logon/Logoff Events Audit Special Logon

(*continued*)

Table 3-3. (*continued*)

S.no.	Audit Policy Category	Audit Policy Subcategories
6.	Object Access	Audit Application Generated Audit Certification Services Audit Detailed File Share Audit File Share Audit File System Audit Filtering Platform Connection Audit Filtering Platform Packet Drop Audit Handle Manipulation Audit Kernel Object Audit Other Object Access Events Audit Registry Audit Removable Storage Audit SAM Audit Central Access Policy Staging
7.	Policy Change	Audit Policy Change Audit Authentication Policy Change Audit Authorization Policy Change Audit Filtering Platform Policy Change Audit MPSSVC Rule-Level Policy Change Audit Other Policy Change Events
8.	Privilege Use	Audit Non-Sensitive Privilege Use Audit Sensitive Privilege Use Audit Other Privilege Use Events
9.	System	Audit IPsec Driver Audit Other System Events Audit Security State Change Audit Security System Extension Audit System Integrity
10.	Global Access Object Auditing	File System Registry

■ **Note** To explore each of these security policies individually, you can read about them on the TechNet library at the following link: `https://technet.microsoft.com/en-in/library/dn319056.aspx`.

Managing Windows Firewall with Security Policies in GPO

Windows Firewall with its advanced security is helpful to system administrators and IT professionals for managing both Windows Firewall and Internet Protocol Security (IPsec) settings. These settings inside the GP editor are shown in Figure 3-20. Windows Firewall with Advanced Security provides more fine-grained control over firewall rules and requires a deeper level of understanding of the implications. The Windows Firewall applet found in the Control Panel/Settings app is simpler to use and appropriate for most users.

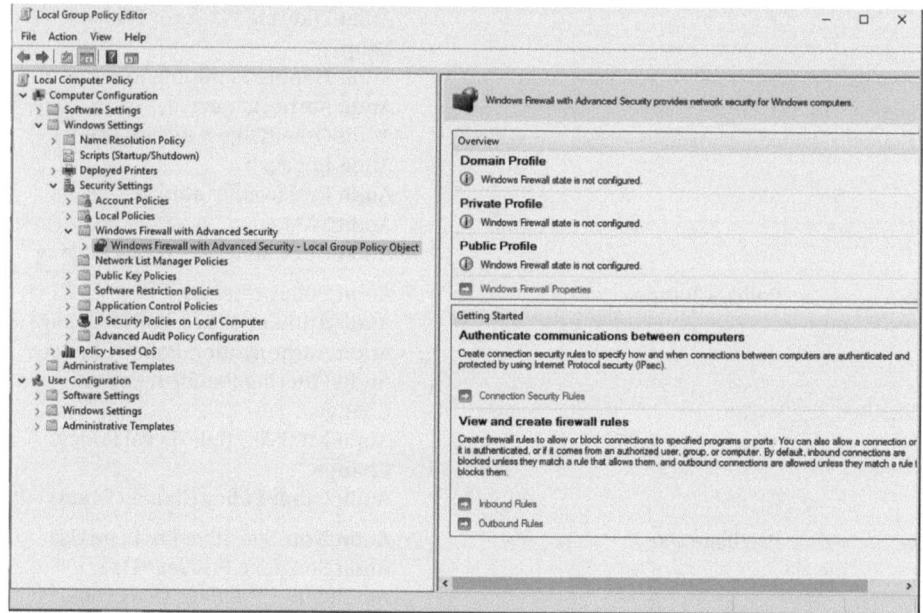

Figure 3-20. *Locating Windows Firewall with advanced security policies*

To manage advanced Windows Firewall by using a GPO, you should open Group Policy and navigate to the following path in LGPO: Computer Configuration ➤ Windows Settings ➤ Security Settings ➤ Local Policies ➤ Security Options.

For GPMC, go here: Computer Configuration ➤ Policies ➤ Windows Settings ➤ Security Settings ➤ Local Policies ➤ Security Options. Windows also includes Windows Firewall with Advanced Security as Desktop tool. To access it, you can directly search for this tool in system search. Or you can go to Control Panel ➤ Windows Firewall ➤ Advanced Settings to open the tool.

You can directly configure Windows Firewall rules by clicking the **Windows Firewall Properties** link in the right pane of the window shown in Figure 3-20. You can also manage Inbound and Outbound rules from here. With the help of the property sheet shown in Figure 3-21, you can

- Specify the behavior of Windows Firewall when connected to the Domain, Public, and Private Profiles.

- Specify settings for behavior and logging settings for troubleshooting.

- Specify and configure IPsec settings.

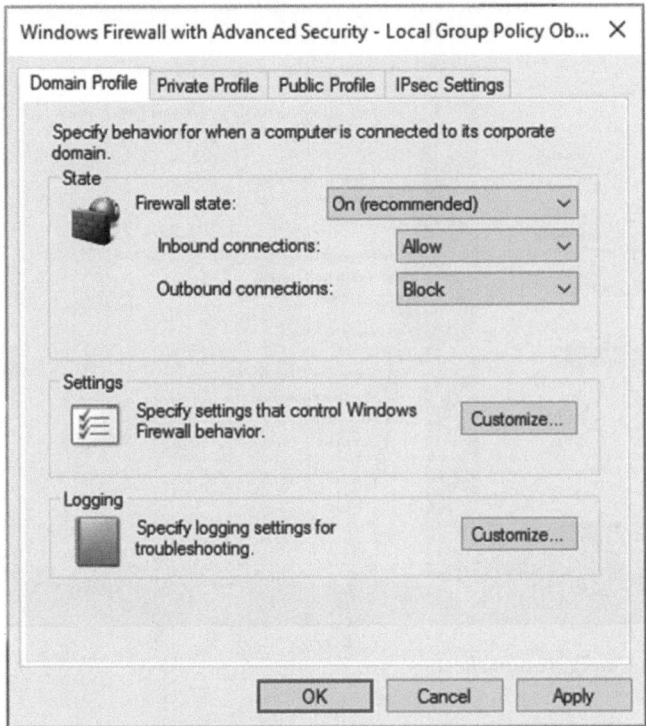

Figure 3-21. *Windows Firewall with advanced security property sheet*

Internet Protocol Security (IPsec) is basically a protocol suite for securing IP communications by authenticating and encrypting each IP packet of a communication session. IPsec is used when very secure communications are required, such as between banks or government departments or between multi-tier applications like web servers and databases.

Within the *IPsec Settings* available on the advanced Windows Firewall property sheet, you can:

- Specify settings that are used by IPsec to establish secured connections.

- Exempt Internet Control Message Protocol (ICMP) from IPsec. ICMP is used by network devices, like routers, to send error messages indicating, for example, that a requested service is not available or that a host or router could not be reached.

- Configure IPsec tunnel authorization.

99

Thus, in this way security policies can help you manage firewall settings very easily in a complex environment. Figure 3-22 shows the IPsec settings available in the Windows Firewall property sheet. It also shows the sheet to customize IPsec defaults.

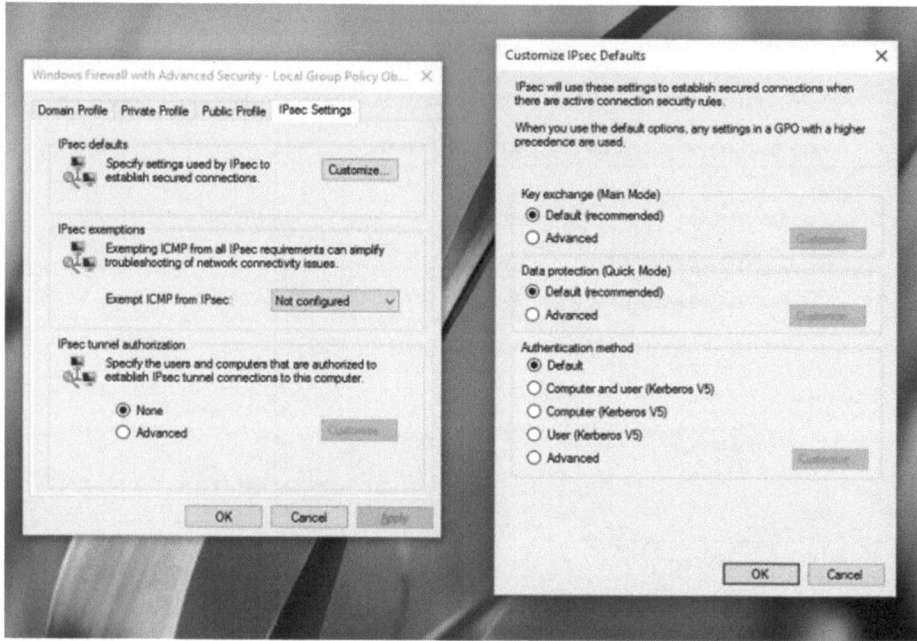

Figure 3-22. *IPSec Settings Configuration sheet*

Working with Network Lists via Security Policies

You can maintain network profiles using the Local Security Policy snap-in, which we are going to discuss here. These settings are found at Security Settings ➤ Network List Manager Policies, as shown in Figure 3-23.

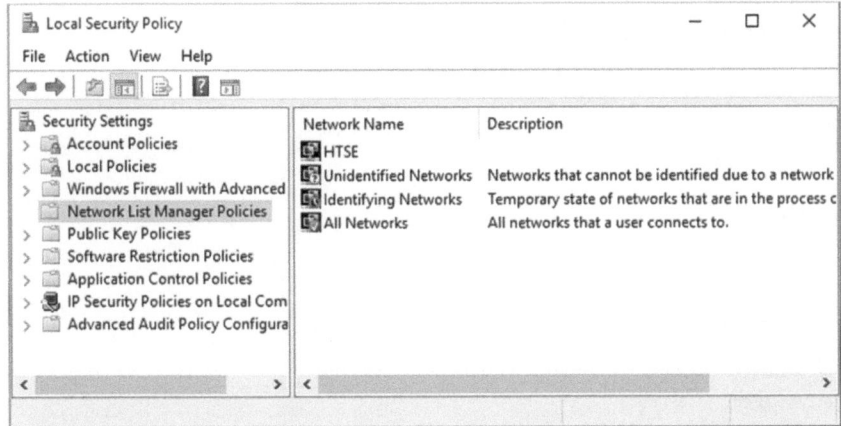

Figure 3-23. *Network List Manager Policies in Local Security Policy snap-in*

With the help of the network settings available under security policies, you can perform following operations:

- Set a network name and allow/prevent users from customizing it.

- Set a network icon and allow/prevent users from customizing it.

- Set a network location and allow/prevent users from customizing it. The network location can be public or private.

All of these settings can be configured on the All Network Properties sheet, shown in Figure 3-24.

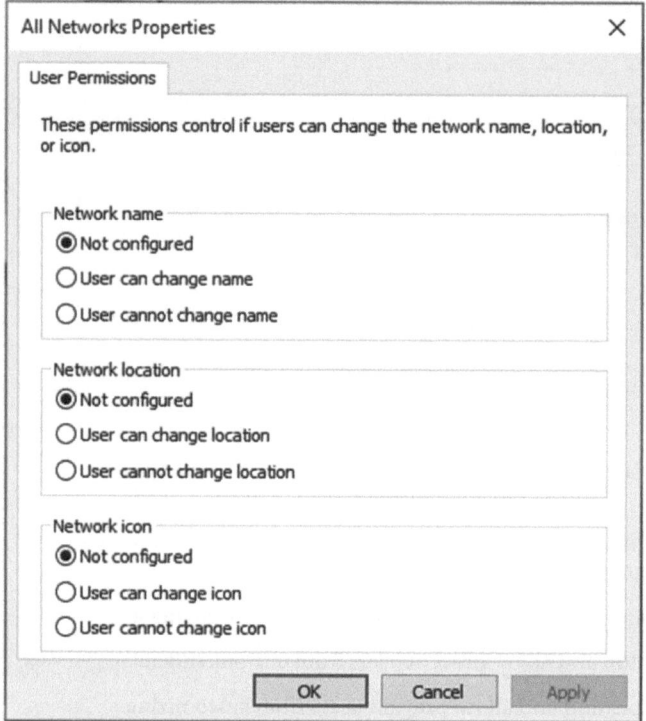

Figure 3-24. *All Network properties sheet for Network List Manager Policies*

As you can see in the All Network Properties window, it is really handy to manage restrictions for users from customized network settings.

Other Important Security Policies

We will summarize some of the other important security policies that are often configured and applied by administrators. Table 3-4 outlines these policies and their roles.

Table 3-4. *List of Important Security Policies in Windows*

Security Policy	Importance	Policy Path
Accounts: Guest account status	If someone wants to use your Windows machine but they do not have a permanent account, they will need use a Guest account. While users are on Guest account, they can't install new programs to your machine and they don't have any access to user data of permanent account profiles. This security setting determines if the Guest account is enabled or disabled. By default, the policy is Disabled. Guest accounts are seldom used in practice.	Security Settings ➤ Local Policies ➤ Security Options
Interactive logon: Do not require CTRL+ALT+DEL	If this policy is enabled on a computer, a user is not required to press the CTRL+ALT+DEL key combination to log on. You should note that not having to press CTRL+ALT+DEL leaves users susceptible to attacks that attempt to intercept the user's passwords as the attack can be initiated remotely. Requiring CTRL+ALT+DEL before users log on ensures that users are physically present when entering their passwords. By default, on domain-connected computers, this setting is enabled for at least Windows 8 or later and disabled for Windows 7 or earlier. On stand-alone computers, the default setting is Enabled.	Security Settings ➤ Local Policies ➤ Security Options
Take ownership of files or other objects	In many cases, we need to take ownership of items such files, folders, and Active Directory Objects (ADOs). This security policy helps you decide who can take ownership of these objects from you are the user group under your administration. You can also discover other security policies regarding user rights at this same policy path.	Security Settings ➤ Local Policies ➤ User Rights Assignment

(continued)

Table 3-4. (*continued*)

Security Policy	Importance	Policy Path
Account Lockout Threshold	If this policy is appropriately defined, and a user login fails due to incorrect credentials, the user will be blocked from entering further login details for a specific amount of time. You can modify the number of failed attempts and also the amount of time (using Account Lockout Duration policy) that the user is locked out of the system. The default value is 0, which means the user will not be blocked, even after entering incorrect credentials an infinite number of times.	Security Settings ➤ Account Policies ➤ Account Lockout Policy

Key Points

- Group Policy is used as a robust tool when customizing and maintaining core features of Windows.

- You can force users to adopt specific settings and deploy a fixed layout of the Start Menu/Screen with the help of a GPO.

- It is easy to disable Windows features, such as access to the registry, or the ability to run the command prompt, or to open Windows Firewall, via Advanced Security.

- The whole Control Panel, or access to selected applets in the Control Panel, can be disabled from users with Group Policy.

- You can easily change your network name or alter its visibility using the Network List Manager Policies within Group Policy.

Summary

In this chapter, you learned some useful ways to customize Windows using GPOs. You should now understand how GPOs are applied within various scenarios including managing and configuring Windows features, Control Panel access, and security settings. In the next chapter, you will discover how to employ basic troubleshooting approaches to resolve problems that can affect Group Policy.

CHAPTER 4

■ ■ ■

Managing Microsoft Office with Group Policy

One of the most versatile applications of Group Policy is to manage Microsoft Office, which you will explore in detail in this chapter. There are more than 2,000 Group Policy Settings (including both User and Machine configurations) for Office applications.

This chapter has three parts and each part has a special importance. The first part provides an overview of the dedicated Microsoft Office group policies; you will learn how to add the necessary administrative templates for Microsoft Office to your system. Next, you will learn about key policy settings related to Office. The chapter ends with some common Office application issues and resolutions using GPOs. So let's get started.

Introduction to Managing Microsoft Office with Group Policy

Microsoft Office applications are generally very well maintained for the single, standalone user. However, in a workgroup or domain environment, your investment in learning how to manage the Office features and settings that can be manipulated using Group Policy will bring significant benefits to any organization. These benefits include streamlined rollout, simplified configuration, and better integration with existing network and cloud storage locations. Most organizations should gain a reduction in the total cost of ownership (TCO) of using Microsoft Office if they use some of the GPOs explored in this chapter.

The Microsoft Office package has many applications and there are Group Policy settings for each of these components to manage their specific features. Table 4-1 lists all of the applications and the corresponding administrative templates (admx and adml) required for configuring Group Policy settings for these applications.

© Kapil Arya 2016

K. Arya, *Windows Group Policy Troubleshooting*, DOI 10.1007/978-1-4842-1886-0_4

Table 4-1. *Microsoft Office Administrative Template Files*

Application	ADMX File Name*	ADML File Name*
Microsoft Access <Edition>	accessXX.admx	accessXX.adml
Microsoft Excel <Edition>	excelXX.admx	excelXX.adml
Microsoft InfoPath <Edition>	infXX.admx	infXX.adml
Microsoft OneNote <Edition>	onentXX.admx	onentXX.adml
Microsoft Outlook <Edition>	outlkXX.admx	outlkXX.adml
Microsoft PowerPoint <Edition>	pptXX.admx	pptXX.adm
Microsoft Publisher <Edition>	pubXX.admx	pubXX.adml
Microsoft Project <Edition>	projXX.admx	projXX.adml
Microsoft SharePoint Designer <Edition>	spdXX.admx	spdXX.adm
Microsoft SharePoint WorkSpace <Edition>	spwXX.admx	spwXX.adml
Microsoft Visio <Edition>	visioXX.admx	visioXX.adml
Microsoft Word <Edition>	wordXX.admx	wordXX.adml
Microsoft Office <Edition> System	officeXX.admx	officeXX.adml

* Replace XX with 12 for Office 2007, 14 for Office 2010, 15 for Office 2013, 16 for Office 2016 editions.

■ **Note**   If you're using Office 365, keep in mind that only these versions of Office 365 support Group Policy: Office 365 Enterprise E3, Office 365 Enterprise E4, Office 365 Enterprise E5, Office 365 Pro Plus, Office 365 Government E3, Office 365 Government E4, and Office 365 Nonprofit E3.

There are some common GPO settings that can act as global settings for an Office installation. The administrative template file named *OfficeXX.admx* contains these common settings. The Microsoft Office GPOs are not included in Windows or installed when you install Microsoft Office. In order to enable the Office-specific GPOs, you must install the relevant administrative templates. As discussed in Chapter 1, Administrative Templates are XML representations of registry-based settings that, once installed, will appear in the Group Policy editor under the Administrative Templates node of both the Computer and User Configuration nodes.

▓ **Info**   Microsoft Office GPOs can be added to a system by installing Administrative Templates. These Administrative Templates are downloaded from the Microsoft Download Center. Here are the links for the different editions:

Office 2007: `www.microsoft.com/en-us/download/details.aspx?id=22666`

Office 2010: `www.microsoft.com/en-us/download/details.aspx?id=18968`

Office 2013: `www.microsoft.com/en-us/download/details.aspx?id=35554`

Office 2016: `www.microsoft.com/en-us/download/details.aspx?id=49030`

Installing Microsoft Office Group Policy Administrative Templates

Here are the instructions to install and enable Microsoft Office Administrative Templates, which you will use later in this chapter to configure specific GPOs:

1. Download the official Microsoft Office Administrative Templates from the Microsoft Download Center (using links provided in Note) that relate to your system architecture.

2. After you download the executable file, double-click to run it. You may be asked for UAC permissions, which you should provide. Accept the *Microsoft Software License Terms* option in the window shown in Figure 4-1. Once you accept the agreement, you can extract the required GPO templates.

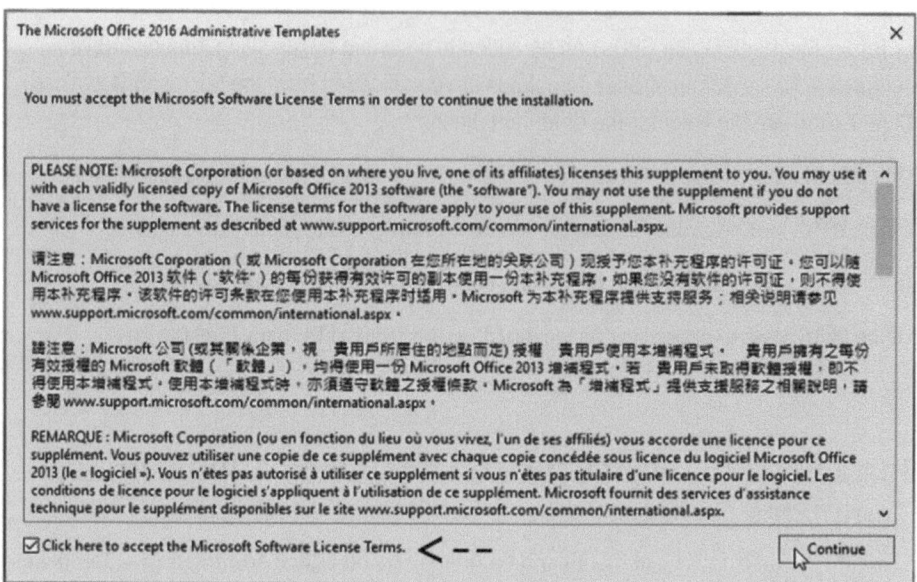

Figure 4-1. *The Microsoft Office <Edition> Administrative Templates license agreement*

3. The folder in which the files are extracted contains two folders: admin and admx. The admx folder is of interest because it contains GPO-based administrative templates (.admx files) for Office. The admin folder contains GPO templates (.opax files) for the Office Customization Tool. There is an Excel spreadsheet for each version in the folder, which gives you a list referencing all the GPO settings for which templates are available in the admin and admx folders. It also provides other useful information like the corresponding registry path for a GPO and the policy setting path within the GPO editor. Administrators can use this spreadsheet as a reference to edit GPOs.

4. Within the folder, the extracted admx files shown in Figure 4-2 will be present. You should also find some language-specific folders together with the Office application's specific admx files. On a standalone device, select all of the admx files and move them into the C:\Windows\PolicyDefintions folder (we're assuming Windows is installed on C: drive). If you are configuring the GPOs as part of a domain, then the files should be copied to %systemroot%\sysvol\domain\policies\PolicyDefinitions. If the PolicyDefinitions folder does not exist, create it. The copying operation requires administrative privileges.

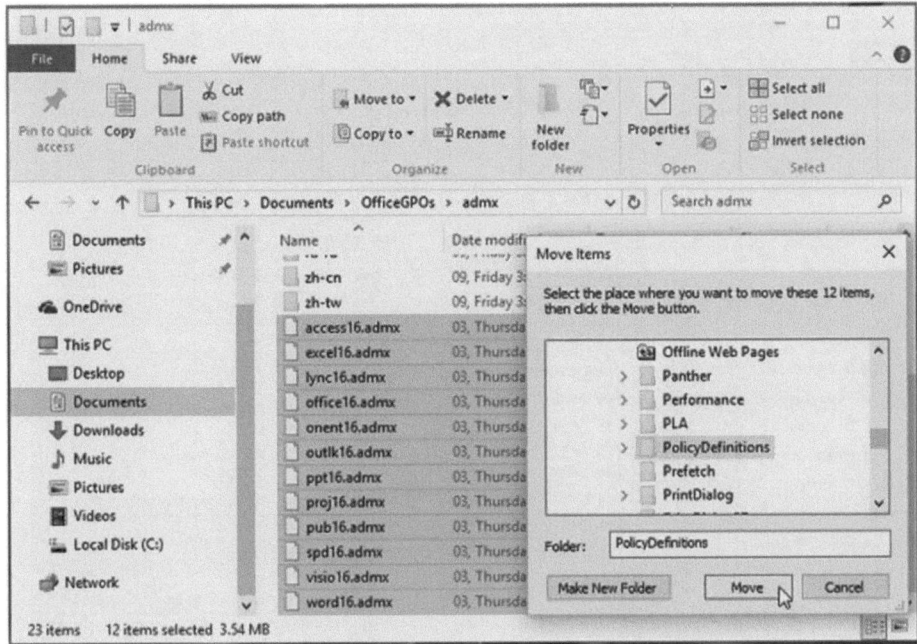

Figure 4-2. *Moving Office 2016 Administrative Templates (admx files)*

5. Now open the language specific folder, for example en-us, inside the admx folder, as shown in Figure 4-3. Here you will be able to locate specific Office application-based adml files. You have to move them in a similar fashion as you did with the admx files, but to a different location. The adml files should be moved to C:\Windows\PolicyDefintions\<same language folder> (such as C:\Windows\PolicyDefintions\ en-us). In a domain environment, they should be moved to %systemroot%\sysvol\domain\policies\ PolicyDefinitions\<same language folder>.

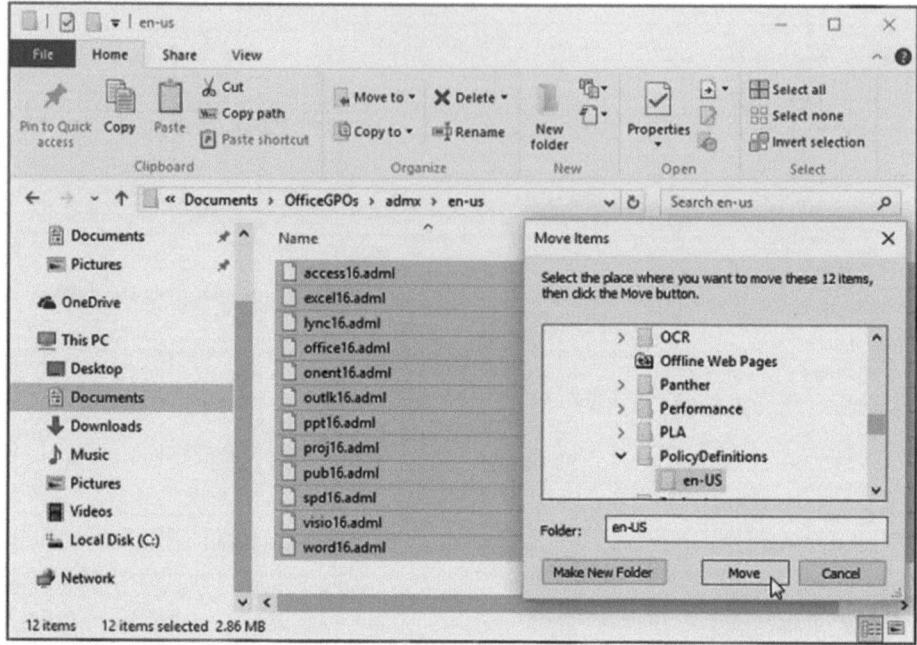

Figure 4-3. *Moving Office <Edition> Administrative Templates (adml files)*

■ **Note**   Care should be taken to ensure the files are moved to the correct location. Often users will move both admx and adml files to same `PolicyDefintions` folder, which generates the error shown in Figure 4-4.

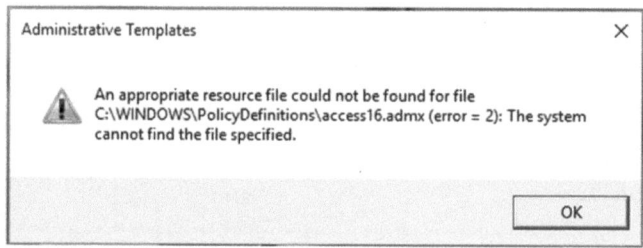

Figure 4-4. *If you move both admx and adml files to same folder, this error appears:*

6.   Open an administrative command prompt and run **gpupdate /force** to refresh the GP engine and load the administrative templates in the GP editor snap-in.

7.   Open the Group Policy editor by typing **gpedit.msc** to verify that the templates have been loaded. Expand **Computer** or **User Configuration** ➤ **Administrative Templates**. You should now see that the Office *<Edition>* Administrative Templates have been loaded, as shown in Figure 4-5. If the templates have not loaded, you should restart Windows.

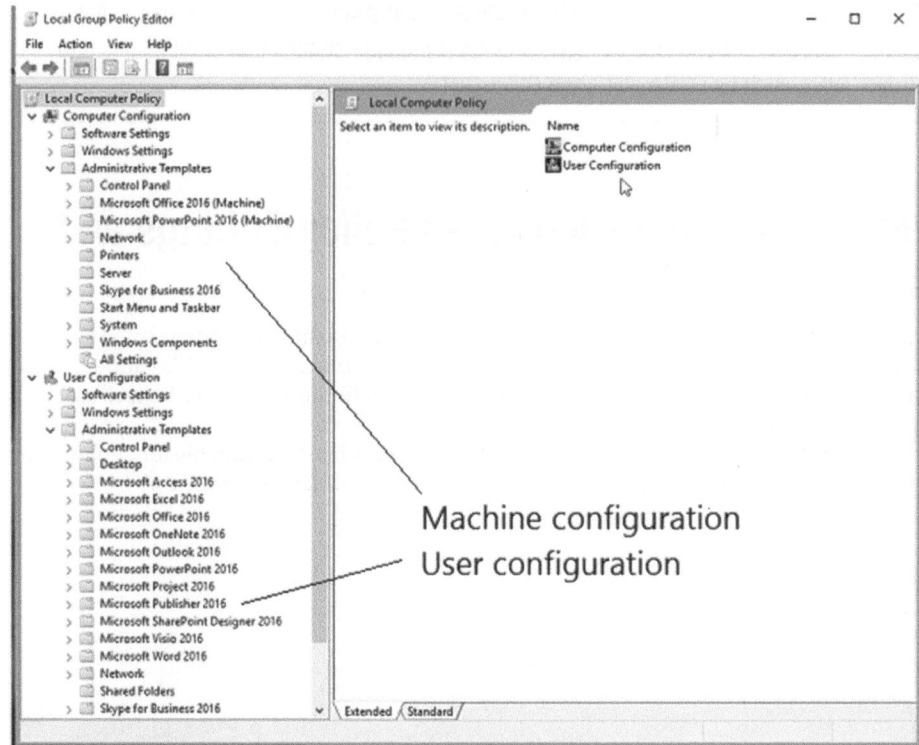

Figure 4-5. *Group Policy templates for Office installed*

You should spend a little time exploring some of the settings available within these GPOs to appreciate the level of customization possible. Within each of the Office application template folders, there are numerous individual policy settings, which you should open and review.

In the next section, you will deploy some of the Microsoft Office policy settings available to you to configure features on client machines.

■ **Note**   If you are creating Microsoft Office-related GPOs, you do not need Office to be installed on your administration PC (which could be a server). The Office GPOs will be available on your system after you import the necessary admx and adml template files. Unlike most applications on a PC, you can import multiple administrative templates into Group Policy, such as Office 2013 and Office 2016.

Important Office-Dedicated Policy Settings and Effects

There are more than 2,000 Group Policy settings (covering the user and machine side) available for the configuration of the Microsoft Office application suite. We cannot possibly explore all of these settings, but we will highlight the settings we believe are extremely useful.

All of the policies found in the Administrative Templates are suitable for deployment to Windows 7 or later operating systems. Table 4-2 lists our favorite policies.

Table 4-2. Useful Group Policy Settings Relating to Microsoft Office

Policy Setting	Explanation	Policy Path (For GPMC, include "Policies" after Computer/User Configuration)	Filename*
Online content options	This policy controls whether users can use the Internet with Microsoft Office applications. This is a universal setting that, if configured once, will be applied to all Office applications.	User Configuration ▶ Administrative Templates ▶ Microsoft Office <Edition> ▶ Tools | Options | General | Service Options… ▶ Online Content	**OfficeXX.admx**
Disable Office animations	By configuring this policy setting, you can allow or prevent animations in Office applications. Disabling animations may increase the performance of Office slightly.	User Configuration ▶ Administrative Templates ▶ Microsoft Office <Edition> ▶ Miscellaneous	**OfficeXX.admx**
Display Developer tab in the Ribbon	By default, Office applications are missing the Developer tab in their Ribbon. After enabling the Developer tab, you can make the following features available for developers or advanced users: - Create applications to use with Microsoft Office apps - Use XML commands - Use ActiveX controls - Write and run macros that you have previously recorded - Work with ShapeSheet in Microsoft Visio - Create new shapes and stencils in Microsoft Visio You can set this policy setting to **Enabled** to make the Developer tab available. This policy has to be configured individually for different apps inside the Office package.	User Configuration ▶ Administrative Templates ▶ Microsoft Office <Edition> ▶ <Application> Options ▶ Customize <Application> ▶ Customize Ribbon	**accessXX.admx** **excelXX.admx** **infXX.admx** **onentXX.dmx** **outlkXX.admx** **pptXX.admx** **projXX.admx** **pubXX.admx** **spdXX.admx** **spwXX.adx** **visioXX.admx** **wordXX.admx**

(continued)

Table 4-2. (*continued*)

Policy Setting	Explanation	Policy Path (For GPMC, include "Policies" after Computer/User Configuration)	Filename*
Turn off screen clipping	If you don't want to let users insert screenshots into their documents, you can configure this policy. When set to **Enabled**, it prevents all Office applications from offering the *Insert Screen Clipping* option to users. This could be useful to restrict data theft.	User Configuration ▶ Administrative Templates ▶ Microsoft Office <Edition> ▶ Disable items in user interface	**OfficeXX.admx**
Lock password protected sections as soon as I navigate away from them	As soon as you navigate away from a password-protected section in OneNote, it can be locked by enabling this policy. You can also specify a time interval in minutes after which the password-protected sections can be locked. This will enhance the security of OneNote.	User Configuration ▶ Administrative Templates ▶ Microsoft OneNote <Edition> ▶ OneNote Options ▶ Password	**onentXX.admx**
File previewing	This setting deactivates file previewers for Microsoft Office applications, although it won't disable the built-in file previewers in Windows. To disable a file previewer, set the policy to **Enabled** and type the **CLSID** for the previewer you want to disable (the previewer CLSID can be found at HKLM\ Software\Microsoft\Windows\CurrentVersion\ PreviewHandlers).	Computer Configuration ▶ Administrative Templates ▶ Microsoft Office 2013 (Machine) ▶ Miscellaneous	**OfficeXX.admx**
Disable Office backgrounds	Using this policy setting, you can decide whether you want to allow users to select Office backgrounds. When policy is set to **Enabled**, users won't be able to change Office background settings.	User Configuration ▶ Administrative Templates ▶ Microsoft Office <Edition> ▶ Miscellaneous	**OfficeXX.admx**

Enable Automatic Updates	This policy setting controls whether the Office automatic updates are enabled or disabled for all Office products installed via **Click-to-Run** (aka CTR technology). This policy has no effect on Office products installed via Windows Installer or a MSI setup. When enabled, the installation will check if the updates are available for the existing edition. You need to be connected to the Web for this. By default, the installation checks for updates.	Computer Configuration ➤ Administrative Templates ➤ Microsoft Office 2013 (Machine) ➤ Updates	**OfficeXX.admx**
Disable Office First Run on application boot	Generally, when you open Office apps for first time, there are some visual tutorials that guide you through new features and improvements about the app. This policy setting determines whether the *Office First Run* appears to the user when Office is first opened. You can set this policy to **Disabled** and the first run behavior will be blocked.	User Configuration ➤ Administrative Templates ➤ Microsoft Office <Edition> ➤ First Run	**OfficeXX.admx**
Block signing into Office	With the help of this policy, you can choose which ID users should use to sign in to Office. You must enable this policy and then select one of these options depending on your goal: If you select **Both IDs allowed**, users can sign in and access Office content by using either ID. If you select **Microsoft Account only**, users can sign in only by using their Microsoft Account. If you select **Organization only**, users can sign in only by using the user ID assigned by your organization for accessing Office 365. If you select **None allowed**, users cannot sign in using either ID.	User Configuration ➤ Administrative Templates ➤ Microsoft Office <Edition> ➤ Miscellaneous	**OfficeXX.admx**

(continued)

Table 4-2. (*continued*)

Policy Setting	Explanation	Policy Path (For GPMC, include "Policies" after Computer/User Configuration)	Filename*
Show OneDrive Sign in	By configuring this policy, you can prompt users to sign in to OneDrive before they save their files. In this way, you can force users to provide their Microsoft account for saving and editing Office files on the system.	User Configuration ➤ Administrative Templates ➤ Microsoft Office <Edition> ➤ Miscellaneous	**OfficeXX.admx**
Allow OneNote e-mail attachments	By enabling/disabling this policy setting, you control whether you want to let users attach files with their notes.	User Configuration ➤ Administrative Templates ➤ Microsoft Office <Edition> ➤ OneNote Options ➤ Email	**onentXX.admx**
Embedded File Size Limit	If you are worried about memory space on your SharePoint server and you want to limit the file size users can insert into their notes, this policy allows you to do so.	User Configuration ➤ Administrative Templates ➤ Microsoft Office <Edition> ➤ OneNote Options ➤ Email	**onentXX.admx**
Disable the Office Start screen for all applications	Enable this policy if you want to prevent the Office Start Screen from appearing in any of the applications of the package.	User Configuration ➤ Administrative Templates ➤ Microsoft Office <Edition> ➤ Miscellaneous	**OfficeXX.admx**

*This column shows the file name that corresponds to the administrative template. Replace XX with 12 for Office 2007, 14 for Office 2010, 15 for Office 2013, 16 for Office 2016 editions.

> ■ **Note** You can also use the Office Customization Tool (OCT) to configure and manage Office applications. This is useful for deploying a customized but consistent Office installation within your workgroup. Here's a great article that explores the possibilities: *https://technet.microsoft.com/en-in/library/cc179097.aspx.*

Troubleshooting Office Issues Using Group Policy

We demand more functionality and efficiency from our applications, and Microsoft Office is no exception. Microsoft Office is a complex package with thousands of features. It is not surprising that issues arise, but problems for users affect their productivity. You can use Group Policy to resolve many issues that occur, and you can also preconfigure your systems using Group Policy to try to eliminate problems before they reach the helpdesk.

In this section, we will discuss common issues that are often faced by administrators and some of their workarounds.

Issue: This File Can't Be Previewed Because There Is No Previewer Installed

One of the most common issues for users upgrading to Office 2016 relates to users being unable to preview one application file from within another application. For example, you may not be able to preview an *Excel* file attached to an e-mail received in *Outlook*. The error message shown in Figure 4-6 relates to incorrectly configured registry keys relating to the *PreviewHandlers* feature. You should also ensure that the corresponding Group Policy setting for *File Previewing* is set to **Not Configured** or **Enabled**.

 This file cannot be previewed because there is no previewer installed for it.

Figure 4-6. *Outlook is unable to preview an Excel file attachment*

To fix this issue, follow these steps:

1. Open the Registry Editor and navigate to registry key mentioned below if you are on a click-to-run installation. (A click-to-run installation has an Office Update section on the start page of every application.)

```
HKEY_LOCAL_MACHINE\SOFTWARE\Microsoft\Office\ClickToRun\REGISTRY\ MACHINE\
Software\Microsoft\Windows\CurrentVersion\PreviewHandlers
```

For *MSI* or setup-based installations (32-bit Office running on 64-bit Windows), go to this key:

```
HKEY_LOCAL_MACHINE\SOFTWARE\Wow6432Node\Microsoft\Windows\CurrentVersion\
PreviewHandlers
```

For *MSI* or setup-based installations (32-bit Office running on 32-bit Windows), navigate to this key (as shown in Figure 4-7):

```
HKEY_LOCAL_MACHINE\SOFTWARE\Microsoft\Windows\CurrentVersion\PreviewHandlers
```

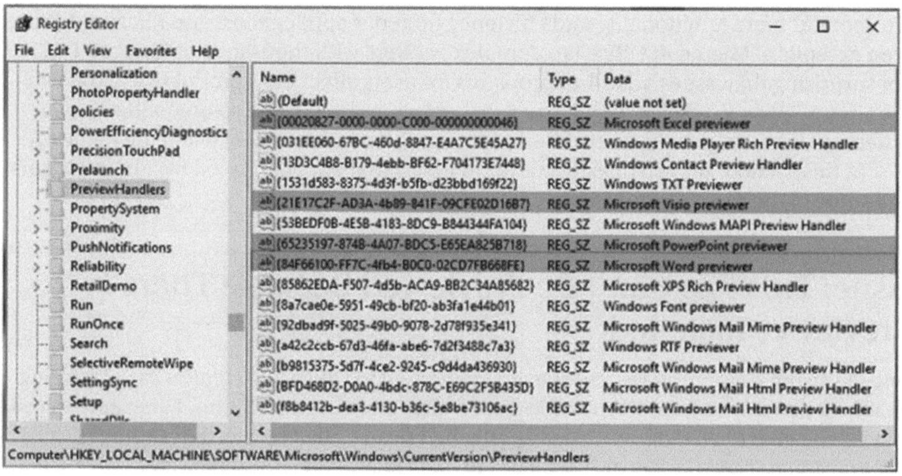

Figure 4-7. *Locating the PreviewHandlers registry keys*

2. In the right pane of the **PreviewHandlers** key, make sure following registry strings are present (they are also case sensitive), as shown in Figure 4-8, or create them as follows:

    Registry string: **{21E17C2F-AD3A-4b89-841F-09CFE02D16B7}**

    Value data: **Microsoft Visio previewer**

    Registry string: **{65235197-874B-4A07-BDC5-E65EA825B718}**

    Value data: **Microsoft PowerPoint previewer**

    Registry string: **{84F66100-FF7C-4fb4-B0C0-02CD7FB668FE}**

    Value data: **Microsoft Word previewer**

    Registry string: **{00020827-0000-0000-C000-000000000046}**

    Value data: **Microsoft Excel previewer**

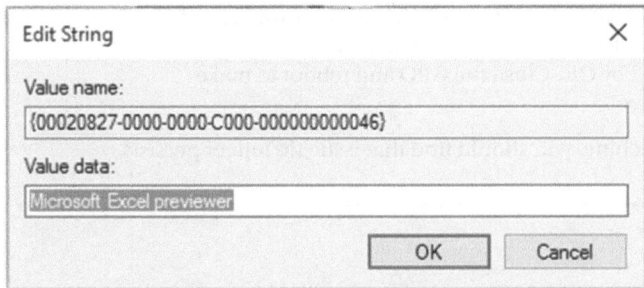

Figure 4-8. *Updating the registry string with correct data*

3. Then open GPO and navigate to following location, as shown in Figure 4-9.

For GPMC, go here:

Computer Configuration ➤ Policies ➤ Administrative Templates ➤ Microsoft Office <Edition> (Machine) ➤ Miscellaneous

For LGPO, go here:

Computer Configuration ➤ Administrative Templates ➤ Microsoft Office <Edition> (Machine) ➤ Miscellaneous

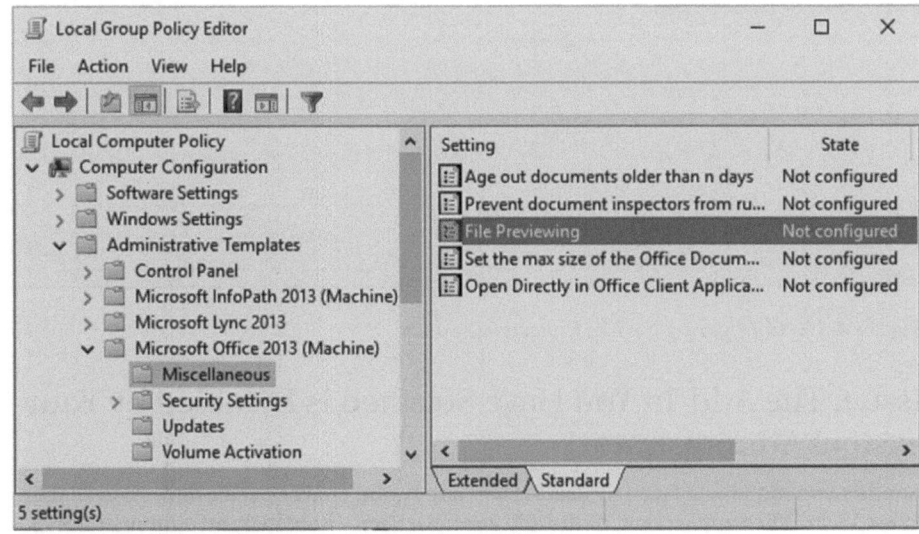

Figure 4-9. *The File Previewing policy setting in GPO*

4. Double-click this policy setting and set it to **Not Configured** rather than Enabled. This can be seen in Figure 4-10. Click **Apply**, followed by **OK**. Close the GPO and reboot to make changes effective.

After restarting the machine, you should find that issue no longer persists.

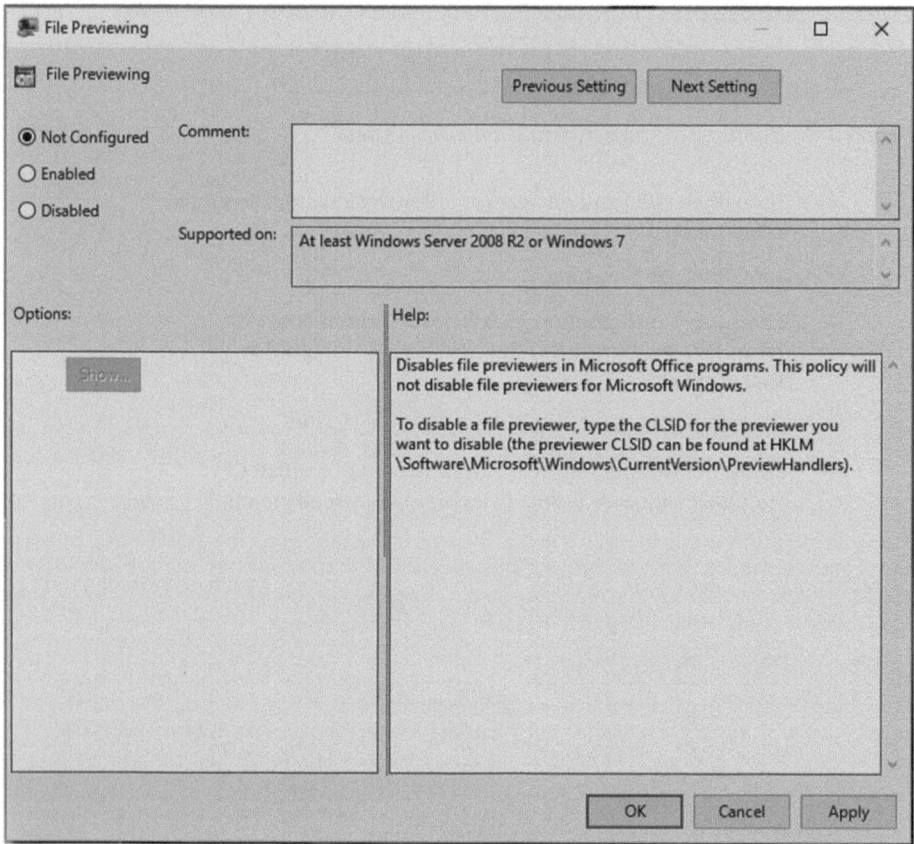

Figure 4-10. *Configuring the File Previewing policy*

Issue: The Add-In You Have Selected Is Disabled by Your System Administrator

Another common issue faced by users is when they don't have specific add-ins available to use in an Office application, or the add-ins have been disabled by an administrator or corrupted. A typical error message can be seen in Figure 4-11. Using Group Policy, you can easily resolve this problem.

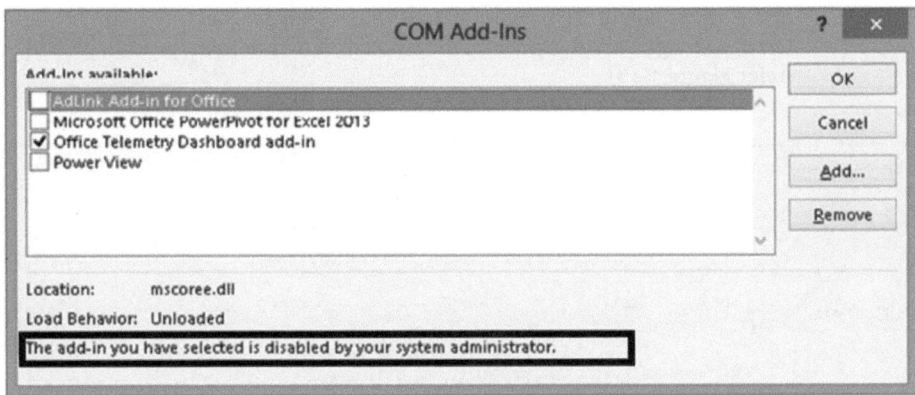

Figure 4-11. *The add-in you have selected is disabled by your system adminstrator*

Let's go on a practical walk-through:

1. Open GPO and navigate to the following path (as shown in Figure 4-12):

    For GPMC, go to User Configuration ➤ Policies ➤ Administrative Templates ➤ Microsoft <Application> <Edition> ➤ Miscellaneous

    For LGPO, go to User Configuration ➤ Administrative Templates ➤ Microsoft <Application> <Edition> ➤ Miscellaneous

    *Substitute <Application> and <Edition> with the application name and edition respectively, for which the add-in is not available; for example: Word.

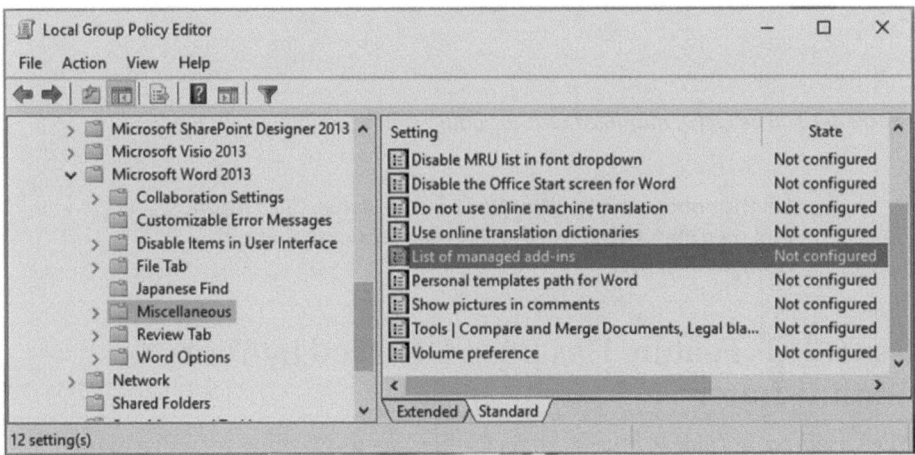

Figure 4-12. *The List of managed add-ins policy*

2.   In the right pane of the `miscellaneous` folder, look for the
     List of managed add-ins policy. Double-click it to modify
     (refer Figure 4-13).

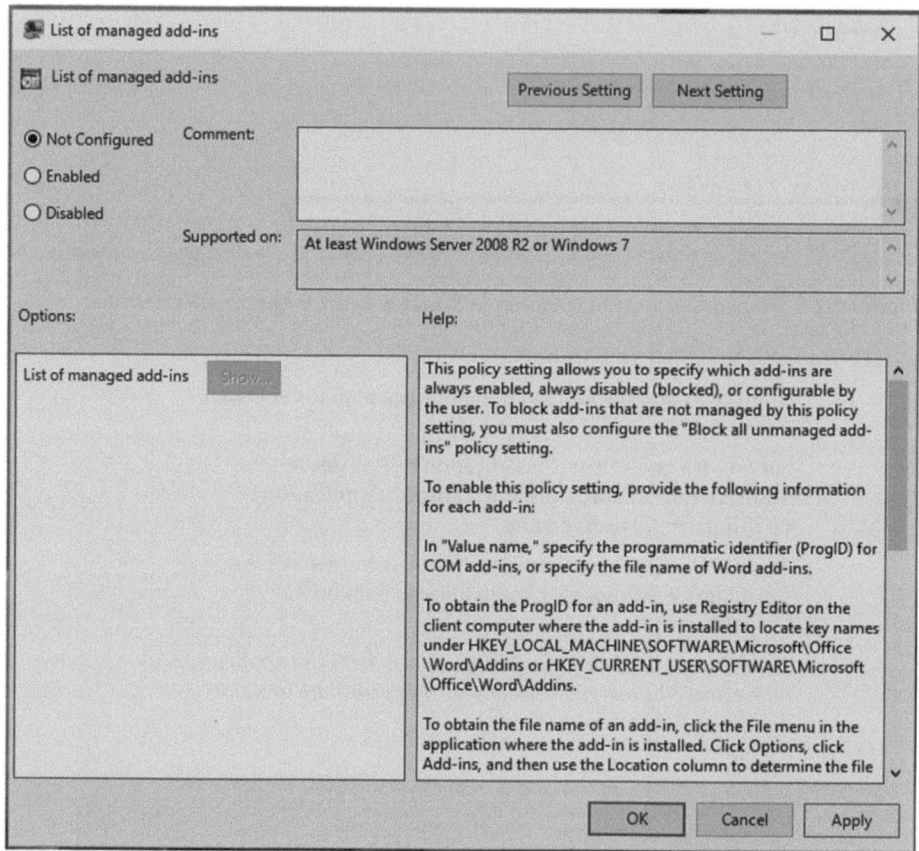

Figure 4-13. The List of managed add-ins policy setting configuration window

3.   Set the policy setting to **Not Configured** status. Click **Apply**,
     and then click **OK**. Close the GPO and reboot to make the
     changes effective.

Issue: This Feature Has Been Disabled by Your Administrator

When users are not able to access certain features, such as features requiring Internet
connectivity, they may see the *"This feature has been disabled by your administrator"*
message shown in Figure 4-14.

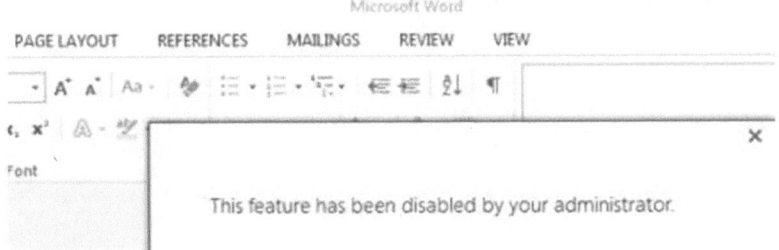

Figure 4-14. This feature has been disabled by your administrator

In such cases, an administrator may have blocked users from accessing online content from within Office applications. If you are seeing this message and you have not configured any policy to block online content, you can fix it easily via Group Policy.

To reset the offending Group Policy setting, follow these steps:

1. Open Group Policy and navigate to the following folder in the left pane:

    For GPMC, go to User Configuration ➤ Policies ➤ Administrative Templates ➤ Microsoft Office <Edition> -Tools | Options | General | Service Options... ➤ Online Content

    For LGPO, go to User Configuration ➤ Administrative Templates ➤ Microsoft Office <Edition> ➤ Tools | Options | General | Service Options... ➤ Online Content

2. Referring to the right pane of the Online Content folder, look for the setting named *Online Content Options,* as shown in Figure 4-15. If you are facing this problem, the policy is likely to exhibit the Enabled status.

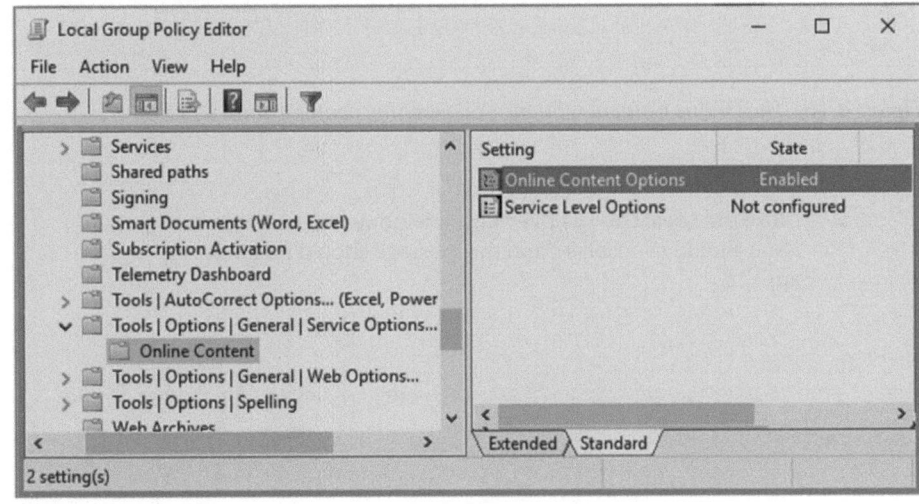

Figure 4-15. The Online Content Options policy setting in GPO

3. Double-click the policy to edit its status and set the policy status to **Not Configured**, as shown in Figure 4-16.

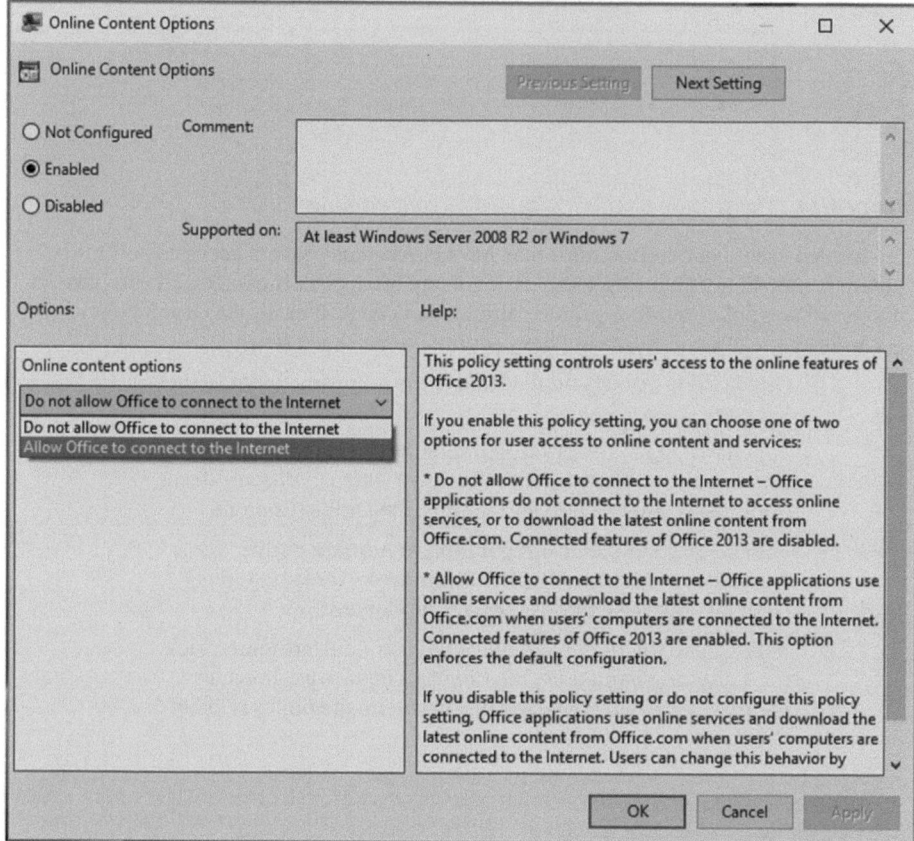

Figure 4-16. *The Online Content Options policy setting configuration window*

4. Click **Apply** and then **OK**.

5. Close the Local Group Policy Editor window. After reboot, the issue should be resolved and the message should no longer appear.

Issue: Performance and Display Problems with Office Clients

While using Office applications on different systems, you may have noticed that the display of these applications may vary from system to system. This may, of course, be related to different specifications of the different machines, but a common problem relates to how Office applications operate when deployed onto high performance or graphically advanced machines.

■ **Note** You could also attempt to diagnose this issue using the Office Configuration Analyzer Tool 2.1, which will review your installed Office suite for known configurations that cause problems. The free tool is available on the Microsoft's Download site at *www.microsoft.com/en-us/download/details.aspx?id=36852*.

Some common display issues that you may experience with Office applications are as follows:

- Office apps do not supporting the screen resolution, so text is blurry and not stable.

- The applications are not performing as you expected. You may experience crashing of apps often.

- Office apps do not distinguishes color correctly and display whites/blacks mostly.

- PowerPoint slideshows and Skype for Business video calls have poor performance.

The cause behind these problems are that in nearly all of the Office development, the application is created and tested using machines that meet the minimal specification for Windows. Thus, if you are facing an issue with some specific feature of Office, it may be possible that your machine configuration is more complex than the feature expects. The most common workaround in this scenario is to disable the hardware graphics acceleration within the application. This will be equivalent to running Office in Safe Mode. The overall system performance should not be reduced, and Office is less likely to exhibit compatibility issues.

The option to disable hardware acceleration lies individually in each application's settings. In a complex environment, you can use following steps to resolve display issues with the help of Group Policy:

1. Open the GPO and navigate to following template path:

   For GPMC, go to User Configuration ➤ Policies ➤ Administrative Templates ➤ Microsoft Office <Edition> ➤ Miscellaneous

For LGPO, go to User Configuration ➤ Administrative Templates ➤ Microsoft Office <Edition> ➤ Miscellaneous

2. In the right pane of the `Miscellaneous` folder, look for policy setting named *Do not use hardware graphics acceleration*, as shown in Figure 4-17. Double-click the policy.

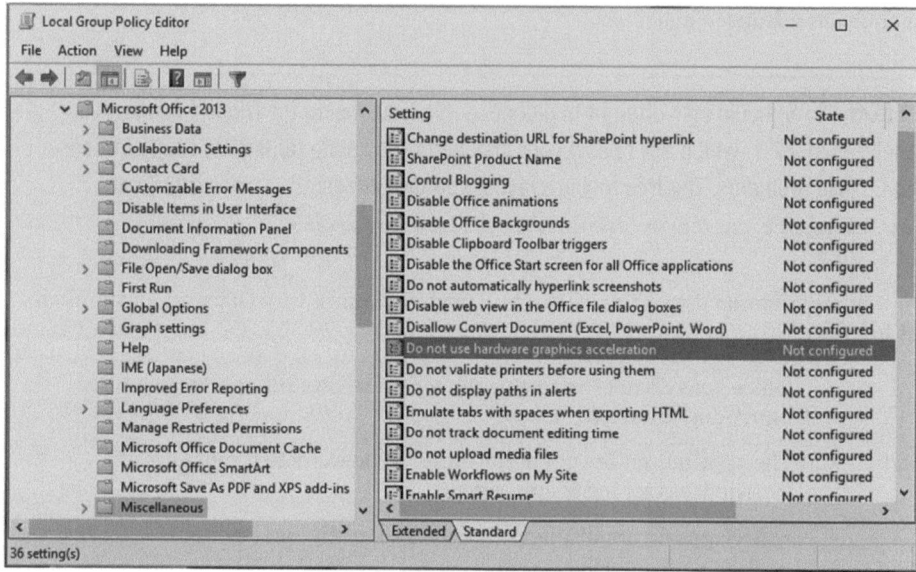

Figure 4-17. *Locating the Do not use hardware graphics acceleration policy in GPO*

3. Review the policy information and change the policy status to **Enabled** from Not Configured, as shown in Figure 4-18. Click **Apply**, and then **OK**.

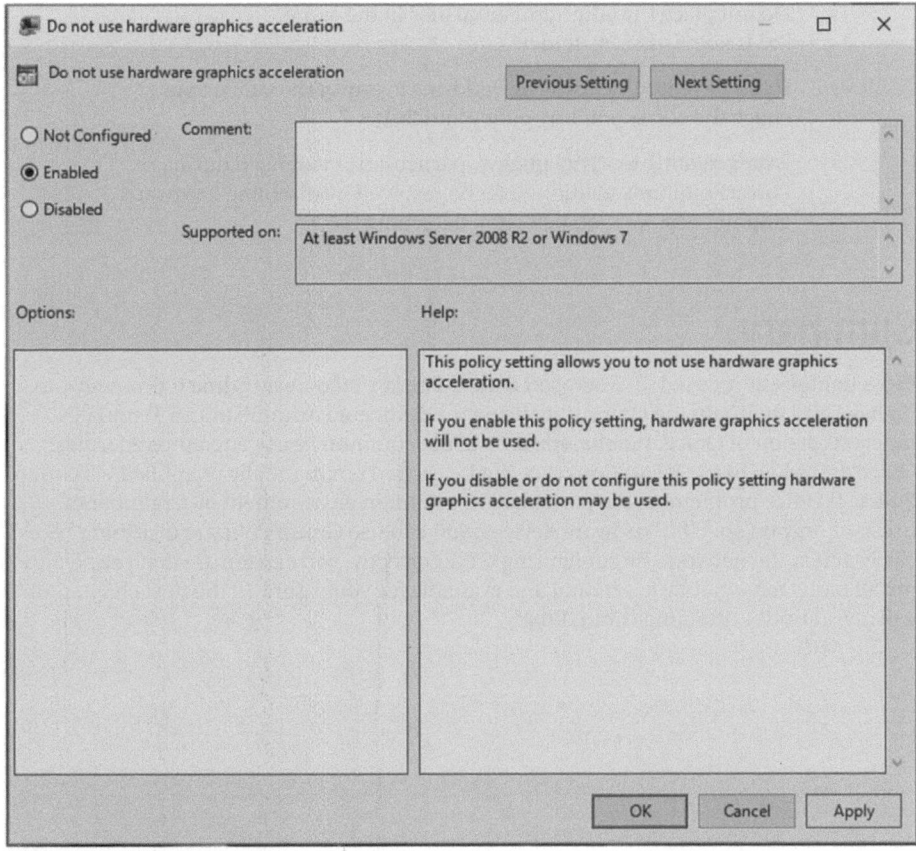

Figure 4-18. *This is the window to configure the Do not use hardware graphics acceleration policy in GPO*

4. Close the GPO and restart the system for the settings to take effect.

After a reboot, the performance and display issues you were facing should suppress.

Key Points

- The Office application suite can be configured with more than 2,000 GPOs (including both user and computer configurations).

- When adding Administrative Templates to Windows, ensure that the correct version of the template files is used. Add adml files in a language-specific folder only.

- Do not place the admx and adml files in the same `PolicyDefinitions` folder.

- If you have trouble using any add-ins in any of the Office apps, check the corresponding policy and fix it.

- Issues relating to visual quality, particularly evidenced during PowerPoint presentations, can be resolved by disabling hardware graphics acceleration using the dedicated GPO.

Summary

This chapter was focused on Microsoft Office. The key take-away is that it is possible to manage and maintain the Office suite using the dedicated Administrative Templates for each version of Office. We shared some of the common issues encountered using Office and some of the resolutions that can be carried out manually or applied via Group Policy. If Office problems are experienced in a domain environment by a number of users, or only on specific hardware devices, you can use Group Policy to distribute "fixes" easily across the network. By configuring GPO correctly, you can ensure that your Office installations remain fully functional and available for your users. In the next chapter, we will revisit troubleshooting Group Policy.

CHAPTER 5

■ ■ ■

Basics of Group Policy Troubleshooting

This chapter focuses on common Group Policy problems and their resolutions. Like all other technical disciplines, Group Policy offers the opportunity to cause you severe headaches if configured improperly. When something regarding GPO is not working as expected, you need to act quickly and troubleshoot the problem. Moreover, since GPOs can affect hundreds or thousands of users and computers, you may need to resolve policy issues quickly. In this chapter, you'll learn what troubleshooting is and the best practice approaches regarding resolving GPO issues. We will focus on specialist tools including RSoP and GPResult. The final part of this chapter will provide you with solutions to some common problems.

Getting Started with Troubleshooting

Troubleshooting is the act of fixing something that is not working as expected. Troubleshooting is also applicable to Group Policy. To effectively administrate GPOs, you should be able to analyze a system and detect when GPOs are not behaving the way they were designed. Group Policy issues mostly arise when the settings aren't configured properly or if the target for which the settings are configured is not linked correctly. Figure 5-1 shows a typical script error that you may face when something is wrong with a Group Policy structure. There are many ways to resolve Group Policy issues via different troubleshooting mechanisms. In this section, we will review various troubleshooting approaches that you will learn to apply in your environments.

© Kapil Arya 2016
K. Arya, *Windows Group Policy Troubleshooting*, DOI 10.1007/978-1-4842-1886-0_5

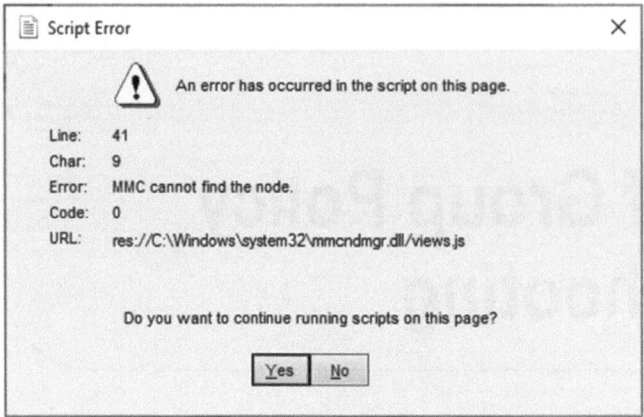

Figure 5-1. *A typical script error relating to a failing GPO*

Our journey into Group Policy troubleshooting starts with the basic approaches that you can use to fix issues arising from misconfigured policy settings.

Basic Troubleshooting Approaches

Non-critical issues may be resolved by using some basic troubleshooting steps that you can take manually. Sometimes you will see problems that can't be reproduced. If the problem is not resolved expediently, it may be obscured by a subsequent failure. As soon as you are aware of a problem, it is very important that you take corrective action to resolve the problem in order to prevent the situation from worsening. Group Policy infrastructure has many moving parts, and therefore a selective approach to fixing GPO problems must be adopted.

Here is the checklist of things to do when you initially find an issue:

1. Verify the status of the required services and tools for a GPO structure. For example, verify that the *Group Policy Client service* in the *Services* snap-in is running, as shown in Figure 5-2.

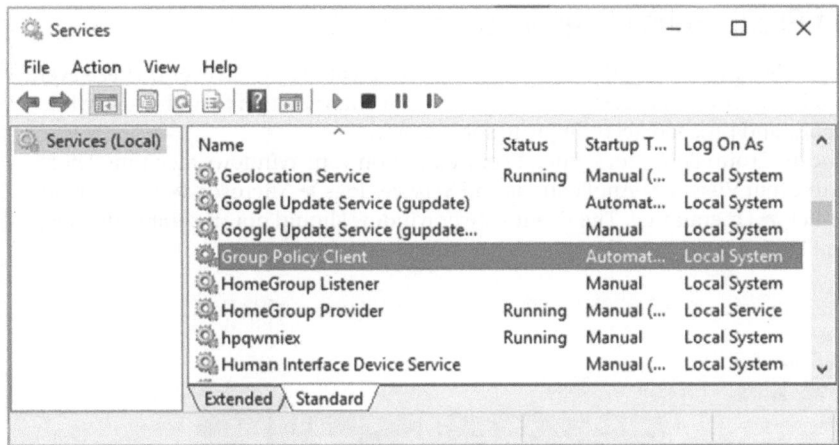

Figure 5-2. Locating the Group Policy Client service in Services

2. Verify the network connection and configuration. You can use the *Network Adapter troubleshooter* to find and fix issues automatically. The troubleshooter is available at Control Panel ➤ Troubleshooting.

3. Synchronize your network time with your machine time. For this, make sure the client system and server system are set to automatic time settings adjustment. If there is more than a 5 minute time difference, authentication issues with Active Directory can occur.

4. Review the computer and user account configurations for errors and remove any anomalies. For this, you can use the Local Auditing Policies available in the Security Policy snap-in, discussed in Chapter 3.

5. In case of domain connections, verify permissions and access to the SYSVOL shared folder. You can read this article to check the status of shared SYSVOL: *https://technet.microsoft. com/en-us/library/cc728051.aspx.*

6. Compare Group Policy results version by version and identify the differences.

Using these essential approaches, you should be able to track down the initial cause of the problem. If these steps help to resolve it, you may not need any complex solutions.

The following sections cover some other essential things you can use to fix basic issues.

Tracing Group Policy Logs in Event Viewer

For Group Policy processing, there are lots of entries created after an event. These events are logged in Event Viewer. Using these logs, you can analyze them to find issues with Group Policy and proceed accordingly to solve them.

To locate Group Policy logs, open Event Viewer on your Windows machine. Then navigate to Event Viewer ➤ Applications and Services logs ➤ Microsoft ➤ Windows ➤ Group Policy ➤ Operational. The Event Viewer window should now resemble the one shown in Figure 5-3.

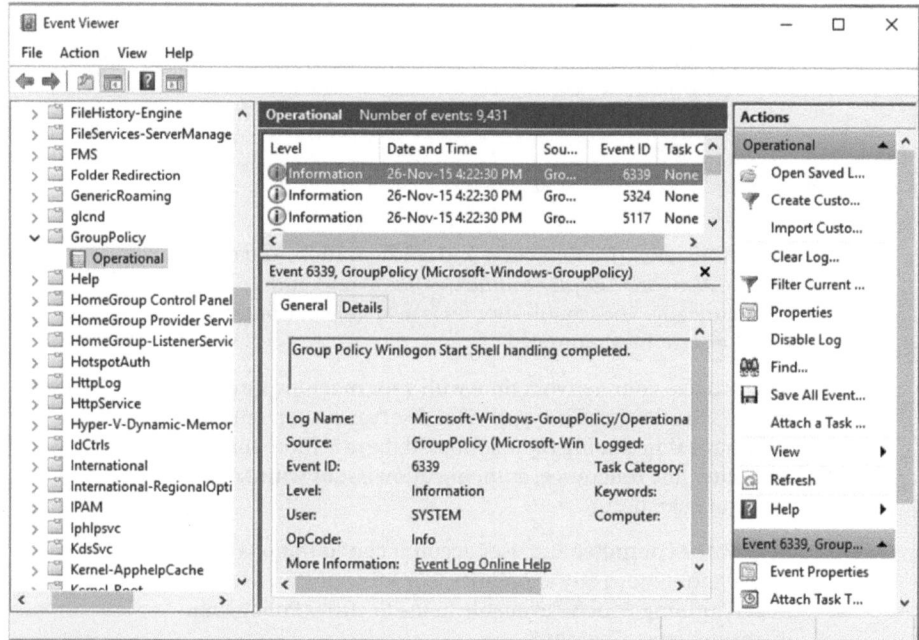

Figure 5-3. *Locating Group Policy logs in Event Viewer*

For detailed information about an event, double-click any entry in the central pane of the window shown in Figure 5-3. You can then see detailed information about the event, as shown in Figure 5-4.

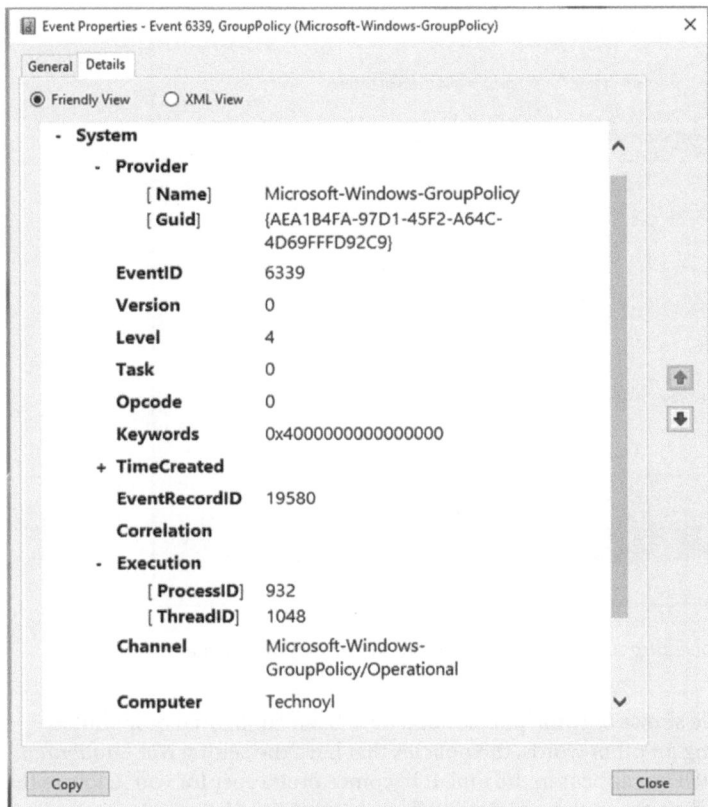

Figure 5-4. *Event log detailed information*

We are here interested in *ProcessID*, *ThreadID*, *GUID*, and *TimeCreated*. However, the other entries are sometimes useful too. These parameters will help you to analyze the event. You can read in detail about them at following article: `https://technet.` `microsoft.com/en-us/library/cc765981(v=ws.11).aspx`.

Diagnosing Problems with the Resultant Set of Policy Tool

Resultant Set of Policy (RSoP) is one of the most useful diagnostic tools available for verifying issues related to Group Policy. It is available in Windows Vista with Service Pack 1 (SP1) or later. The most common issue that occurs with Group Policies is of "GPOs not being replicated to all Domain Controllers (DCs)". With the help of RSoP, you can view the effective policy, and if the effective policy is the one that is unexpected, you can see where the unexpected policy setting is coming from.

To access RSoP, you use the **rsop.msc** command either in a command prompt or the Run utility. Once you execute this command, you'll see the RSoP processing window, as shown in Figure 5-5.

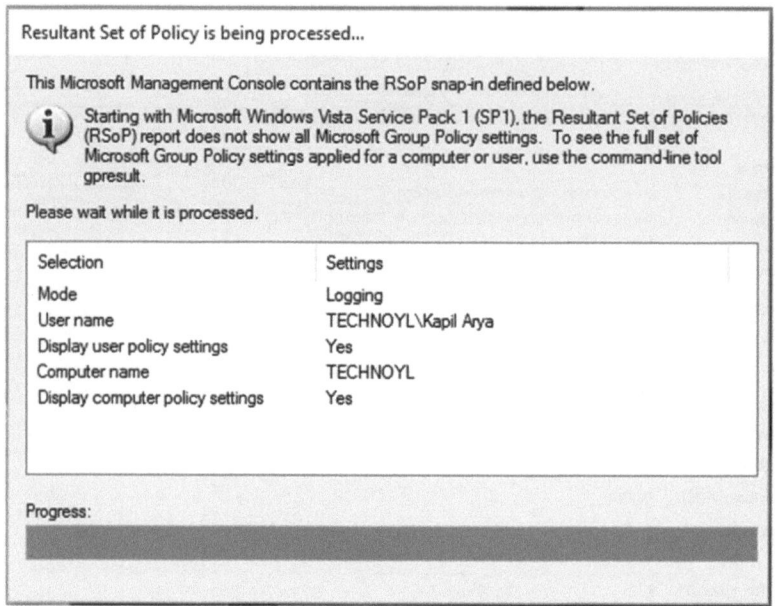

Figure 5-5. *RSoP processing window appearing before launch of console*

The RSoP console shows only the policies that have been configured or modified from the default setting. In other words, the policies that have the setting *Not Configured* or the default status will not appear in the tool. It becomes pretty easy for you to locate the faulty policy by focusing only on the policies in effect, as shown in Figure 5-6.

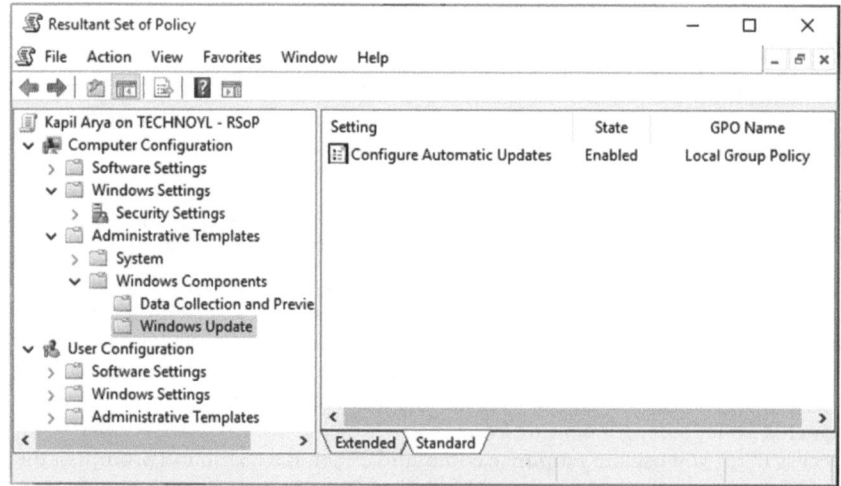

Figure 5-6. *RSoP window showing only configured policies*

Double-click these configured policies to show the window shown in Figure 5-7. You can then click the **Precedence** tab and review whether the policy is configured correctly or not.

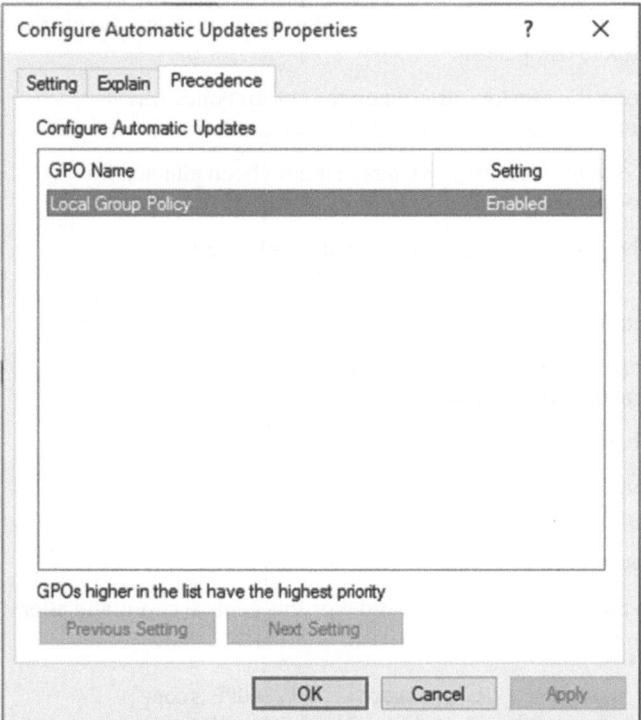

Figure 5-7. *Window to verify if the policy is configured correctly*

In this way, you can verify the policies and idenitify the validity of the GPO settings and locate entries that are not configured properly. This procedure works well with LGPO clients. If you want to use RSoP with GPMC clients, you can follow the detailed process mentioned here: `https://technet.microsoft.com/en-us/library/dn789183(v=ws.11).aspx`.

Finding Issues with GPResult

GPResult can be referred to as the command line version of RSoP. RSoP provides a rich GUI to verify policies, and GPResult provides additional information with the help of extensive possible parameters. In this way, GPResult can provide you with more information than RSoP can deliver. Here is a summary of the output that you can obtain with GPResult tool in addition to using RSoP:

- History that shows the previous time when the Group Policy was applied, plus details of the domain controller that applied it

- A complete list of those devices and users that have been affected by applying Group Policy

- Details about the registry setting(s) that are affected by applying the policy

- Information about folder redirection in an operation (if any)

- Software applications that have been assigned or published via Group Policy can be identified with the help of GPResult.

- Details of IPSec protocol if it is being used

- GPResult can provide you with information relating to the scripts that are being called by Group Policy.

- Disk quota information

To use GPResult, open the command prompt and type this general command after substituting suitable parameters:

```
GPRESULT [/S system [/U username [/P [password]]]] [/SCOPE scope]
        [/USER targetusername] [/R | /V | /Z] [(/X | /H) <filename> [/F]]
```

Please refer following online documentation about GPResults parameters: https://technet.microsoft.com/en-in/library/bb490915.aspx.

To obtain RSoP summary data, run the **GPRESULT /R** command. You can see the results in Figure 5-8.

Figure 5-8. *Locating results with the GPResult tool in the command prompt*

Enabling Verbose Logging

If you are looking for even more detailed logging than the default logs available through Event Viewer, RSoP, or GPResult, you can enable verbose logging. *Verbose logging* provides you with detailed information about Group Policy events so that you can track issues better. However, this logging may consume more disk space and reduce system performance. It is therefore recommended to use this settting only when required.

Verbose logging basically provides you with userenv.log files. It contains all the extended information you need in order to troubleshoot policies. The *userenv* term here indicates an event source. The main event sources for processing of Group Policy are mentioned in Table 5-1. Here it is worth mentioning the fact that Group Policy clients use *client-side extensions* (CSEs), while servers use *server-side extensions* (SSEs). CSEs are directly linked to the Group Policy Engine, whereas SSEs are produced and viewed through Group Policy Object Editor.

Table 5-1. *List of Event Sources for Group Policy Events*

Event Source	Role
userenv	Logs related to Core Group Policy processing (Inclusion: Administrative Templates)
DiskQuota	Logs about Disk Quota CSE processing
Userinit	Logs about Scripts CSE processing
Appmgmt	Logs about Software Installation CSE processing
Folder Redirection	Logs about Folder Redirection CSE processing
SceCli	Logs about Security CSE processing

Since the *userenv* source provides information about Core Group Policy processing, its logs are often used for fixing GPO issues. So to generate the userenv.log file on your server, you need to perform the following registry manipulation:

1. Log onto the client computer as an administrator and open the registry editor.

2. Navigate to the following key: HKEY_LOCAL_MACHINE\ Software\Microsoft\Windows NT\CurrentVersion\ Winlogon.

3. Now right-click the **Winlogon** key and select **New ➤ DWORD Value**.

4. Name the newly created registry *DWORD* (*REG_DWORD*) as **UserEnvDebugLevel**.

5. Double-click on this *DWORD* and set its *Value data* to **30002**. Make sure you selected *Hexadecimal Base*. Click **OK**.

6. Close the registry editor.

Run the **gpupdate /force** command to ensure a full listing of total Group Policy processing. This writes the *userenv* into userenv.log, located in the %windir%/debug/ usermode directory. This log file can be opened in Notepad, as shown in Figure 5-9.

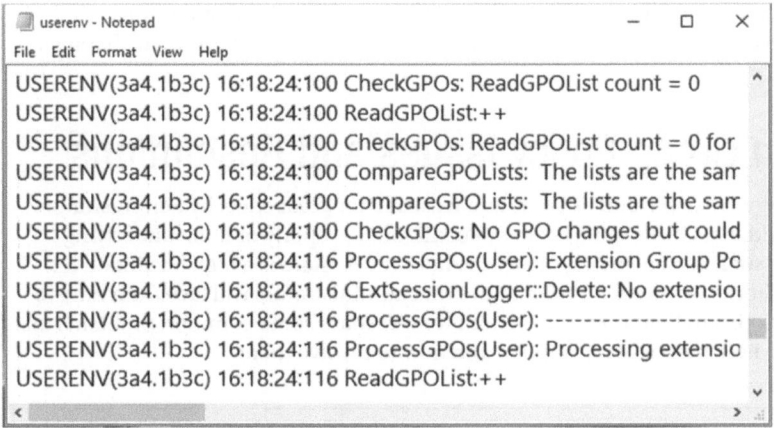

Figure 5-9. *Generated userenv.log file*

The *userenv* log files contain information about the following:

- Group Policy settings not processed/applied.

- Failed folder redirection.

- Failurers in loading and unloading registry hives and profiles.

- When a "slow link" is detected, default behaviors come into play. Details about slow links are provided in Chapter 6.

- Roaming or temporary profile issues.

- If logon is slow as compared to standard ones.

- Checks if a GPO is accessible or not. If it inaccessible, the cause is detected.

- If scripts are not applied as expected, especially logon scripts.

- Information about which DC is accessing SYSVOL.

■ **Note**   Verbose logging to the usernv.log was removed in Windows Vista SP1. In earlier editions of Windows, the same source name, userenv, was shared by many other components as well as Group Policy. This made it complicated to locate only Group Policy issues in these logs. Group Policy logs are now collected by a source named "Group Policy" directly into the Event Viewer. This removes any confusion of having multiple inputs into a log, and helps administrators focus on events related to Group Policy. You need to re-enable the userenv. log feature in the registry if this is required, using the steps shown in this section.

We have covered the basic approaches that you can use to find and resolve issues with Group Policy. We will cover more advanced approaches, in subsequent chapters.

Common Group Policy Issues and Resolutions

Group Policy is very stable and reliable, and it is used for great effect by administrators across the world. If a GPO's settings are not configured properly or if the underlying infrastructure, such as networking or DNS, is not robust, there is a high likelihood for GPO failure. There are many common issues that administrators will face from time to time relating to Group Policy. In this section, we will share some common problems that prevent Group Policy from being applied and how to resolve them.

■ **Info**   The common issues mentioned in this section can be avoided by properly planning and conducting pilot test for a design prior to deployment. This online guide gives you complete information about testing, staging, and production of GPO deployments: https://technet.microsoft.com/en-us/library/cc787823(v=ws.10).aspx.

Group Policy Not Being Applied

If the Group Policy is not applied, or you are not getting the expected results, then you should review the following steps:

1. In a mixed operating systems environment, make sure you have applied the setting to the correct OS for which it is supported. This is mentioned in each policy's configuration window under the *Supported on* section, as shown in Figure 5-10. Also make sure you read the complete policy explaination prior to making any changes in the configuration.

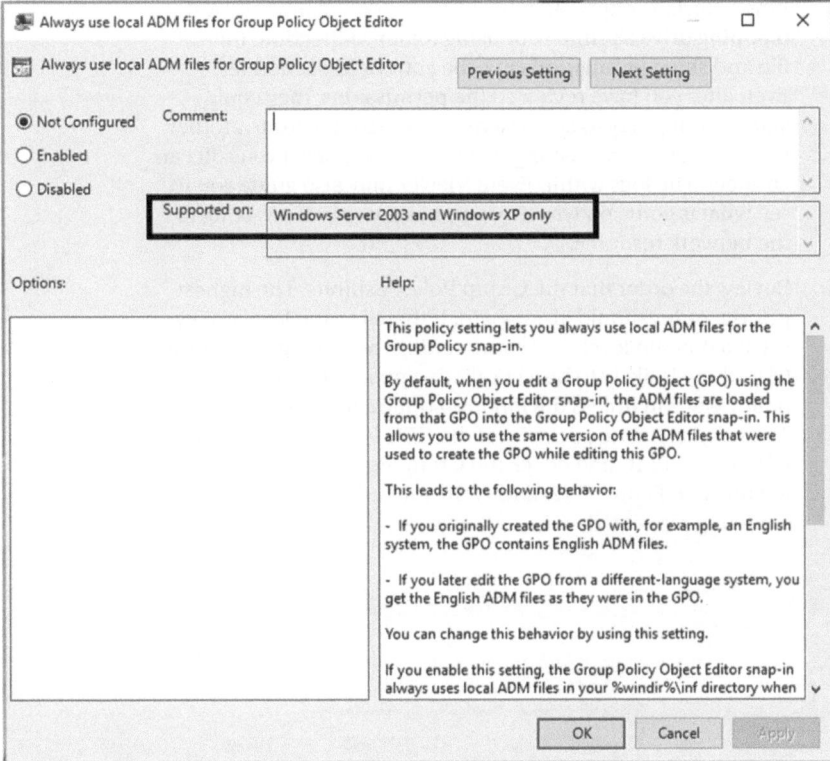

Figure 5-10. *The "Supported on" section of the Policy Configuration window*

2. Some policies do require a reboot of the system to make changes effective. Make sure you restart the machine and verify if the error is still present. If you don't want to reboot the system, you can run the **gpupdate /force** command, as shown in Figure 5-11, to make a background refresh of all Group Policy settings in effect.

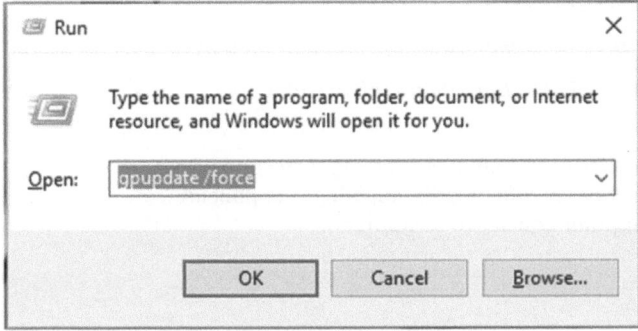

Figure 5-11. *Running the **gpupdate /force** command to refresh Group Policy forcefully*

3. When storing scripts outside of SYSVOL, deploying software, mapping drives/printers, or using folder redirection, then file and share permissions may be your biggest enemies. Even after you have reviewed the permissions, they could still be wrong. Try to access a network resource from another machine, or try connecting to it manually to see if you still can connect. The logs within Event Viewer may also guide you to see what is going on when a computer/user is connecting to the network resource.

4. Review the order that the Group Policy exhibits. The highest priority order should always win. If there is a top level policy set at a domain level, and some settings are configured within OUs, there is likely to be a conflicting policy. The lowest linked policy will win unless the *Enforced* option has been checked. To establish that the priority of the GPO is correct, view the OU in the GPMC and check the Group Policy *Inheritance* tab, as shown in Figure 5-12, and verify the order in which policies are being processed.

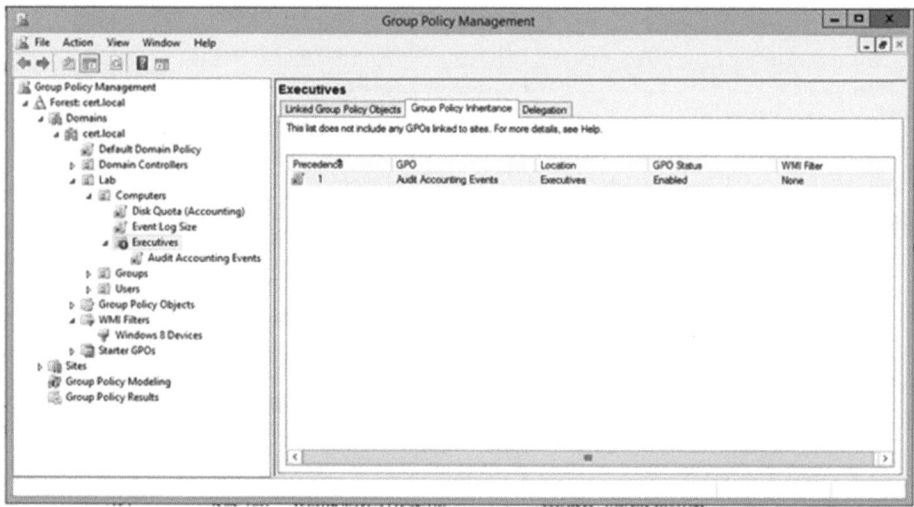

Figure 5-12. *Locating the Group Policy Inheritance tab in GPMC*

5. You need to verify that the system is applying correct policies to correct object type (in other words, applying user policies to users and computer policies to computers).

No User Policies in Group Policy Loopback Processing

In a public environment such as organizational units, laboratories, computer classes, Group Policy loopback processing can be useful. Loopback processing is special way to apply user policies to computer objects.

The main purpose of Group Policy loopback processing is to ensure that all users of a machine get a consistent experience, regardless of what user policies are applied. They are particularly useful for large organizations. You can spot this feature running on kiosks, library computers, terminal servers, and so on where applications should behave in the same way. It allows you to either completely replace (**Replace** mode) the user policies that have been assigned to the user or supplement them (**Merge** mode) with additional policies.

When you don't see user policies after applying Group Policy loopback processing, you need to reconfigure it and set it to **Replace** mode instead of **Merge** mode. To do so, launch the GPO editor and navigate to Computer Configuration ➤ Policies ➤ Administrative Templates ➤ System ➤ Group Policy ➤ Configure user Group Policy loopback processing mode.

In the window, shown in Figure 5-13, set the policy to **Enabled**, and in the option, make sure you select **Replace** mode.

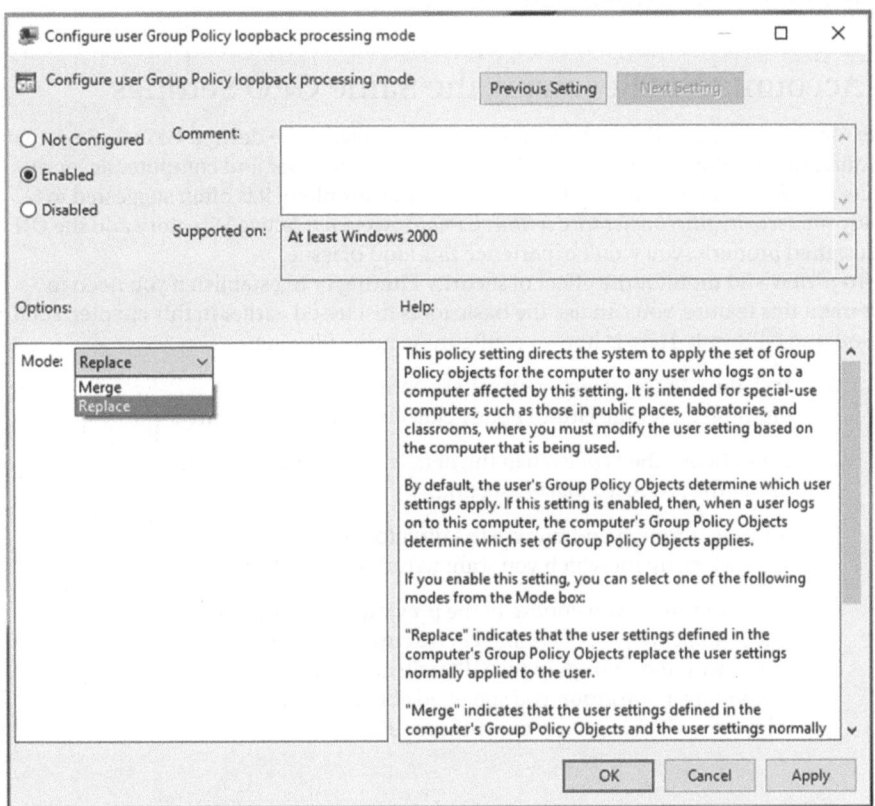

Figure 5-13. *Group Policy loopback processing mode configuration window*

Misallocation of User Accounts in Organization Units (OUs)

OUs are the containers in the directory that are used for scoping policy and permissions to multiple objects. They're present for managing user and computer accounts within Active Directory. If any user account is not placed in the correct OU, then settings configured for this user account may not apply correctly. The common factors responsible for the placing of user accounts in an incorrect OU are the following:

- Issues with provisioning and automation processes

- Accidental moves by administrators

- Accounts that were recently created or those accounts that are new but are not transacted to the correct OU

To avoid problems with OUs and object placement, it is very important that you have clear understanding about the desired objective of each GPO and how its application will affect the underlying object. As mentioned, user policy should be targeted to users only. If policies are being misapplied to incorrect users, you should carry out an audit on the objects in each OU that has GPOs linked to them.

All Accounts Not Receiving the Same GPO Settings

There may be scenarios when all accounts are not receiving the desired GPO settings that are configured for them. This typically happens when both user and computer account objects are located in the same OU. To overcome this problem, it is often suggested to employ the *security filtering feature within GPO*. However, if Active Directory and the OU are designed properly, you won't experience this kind of issue.

To review and monitor the effect of security filtering or to establish if you need to implement this feature, you can use the basic tools discussed earlier in this chapter, such as RSoP, and GPResult. Here is how to configure security filtering:

1. Pick the GPO for which you want to configure security filtering, under the Group Policy Objects node in the GPMC.

2. Now choose the *Scope* tab in the details pane, and click **Add** under the *Security Filtering* section.

3. Navigate through and browse the directory to select the security group for which you want to turn on the filter.

4. When the group you choose in the previous step is displayed, select *Authenticated Users* and click **Remove** (see Figure 5-14). In this way, the settings in the GPO will apply only to users and computers in the group you specified above. You may need to reboot the GPO engine to apply these settings.

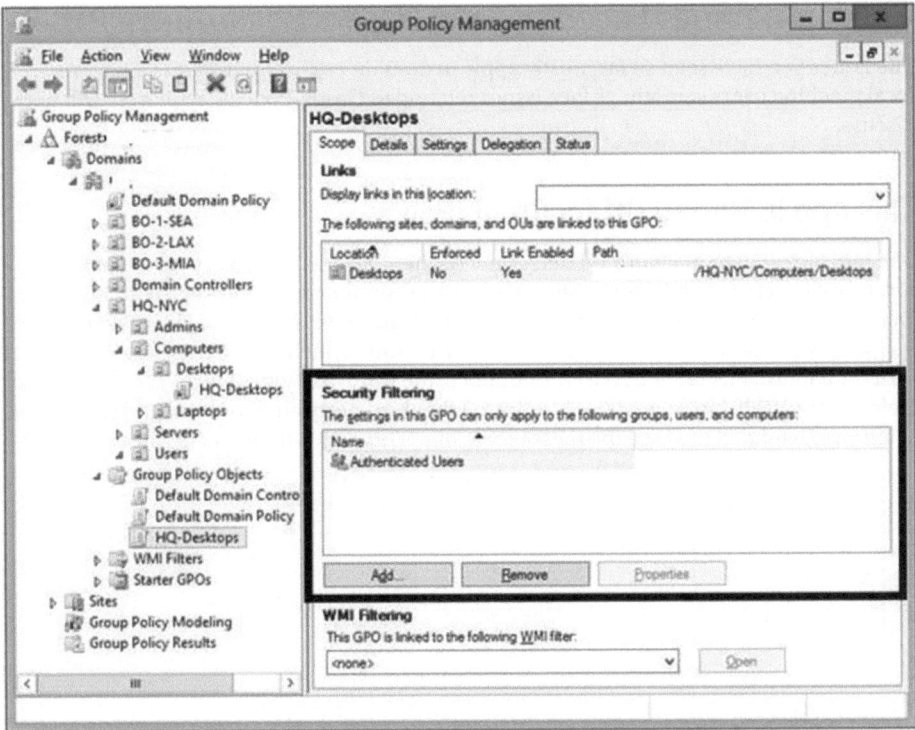

Figure 5-14. Configuring security filtering in GPMC

Issues Arising Due to Folder Redirection

When migrating to a new file server via folder redirection, you may find that your users experience issues as a result of moving to the new location. In this scenario, users may complain about missing or duplicated files. To reduce the likelihood of this happening, you should make sure that you have disabled the option to move user files to the new location while you are moving the files.

Sometimes administrators find that the move option is disabled and this can leave users in a dilemma because they can still see the old files when they sign in for the very first time after migration. Once the migration is complete, you should delete those old folders and move the content inside to the appropriate folder.

When redirecting the My Documents folder, which can be located in arbitrary locations, make sure you review the naming convention that the GPMC uses. If your file server is still using the old My Documents folder, the GPMC may try to change that to use the name of Documents.

Common Issues Faced by Local Users Regarding GPO

The issues you have seen so far mostly apply to domain environment users. However, local machine users sometimes face issues relating to Group Policies, which we will now discuss.

This App Is Turned Off By Group Policy

The message shown in Figure 5-15 is received when the app you are trying to open is turned off by its own dedicated policy. Users can experience this message with Windows Defender, but it can also be observed when other programs are blocked by a GPO. This happens when users install a third-party security suite/antivirus and they forget to turn off Windows Defender. As a consequence, the third-party suite turns off Windows Defender by itself. Now when users uninstall the third party antivirus tool and try to open Windows Defender, they see the message saying "This app is tuned off by Group Policy."

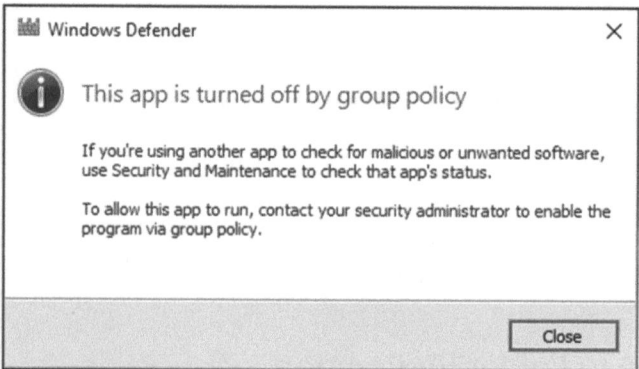

Figure 5-15. *This app is turned off by Group Policy*

Resolution is quite simple for this type of scenario. You should open the GPO and go to Computer Configuration ➤ Administrative Templates ➤ Windows Components ➤ Windows Defender. Set the *Turn off Windows Defender* policy to **Not Configured,** as shown in Figure 5-16.

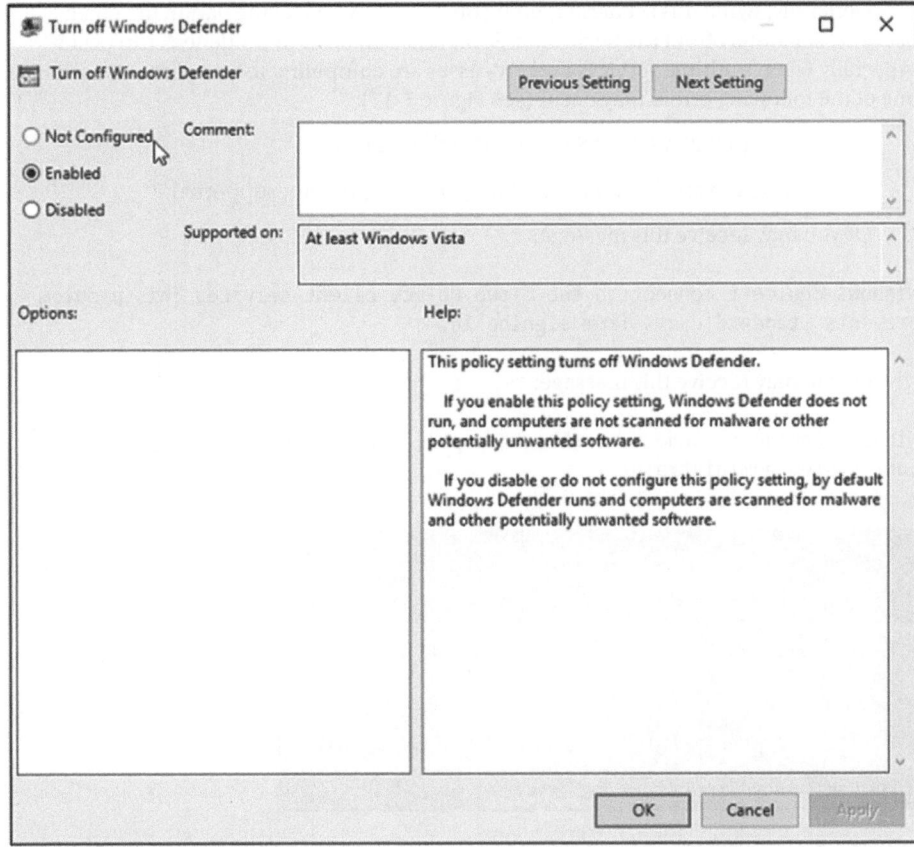

Figure 5-16. *Configuring the Turn off Windows Defender policy in a GPO*

Although the example provided is quite simple, you can face this type of message with any of the features that can be configured using Group Policy. We listed the available features in the "Managing Windows Features with GPOs" section, earlier in chapter 3.

Group Policy Client Service Failed During the Sign-on Process

While logging into Windows, there are some crucial background processes that propagate during logon. The *Group Policy Service* (GPSVC) is part of one of those processes in which this service communicates with the Winlogon service via a *Remote Procedure Call* (RPC). The aim of this communication is to make a cross check on the computer configuration and user configuration of Group Policy Objects and load the correct policies accordingly.

Generally, while this scenario is going on, the GPSVC is taking part in the chain of events separately from the beginning. Sometimes an error or bottleneck can occur, especially when multiple services and processes are competing to complete. Chances are one of the following errors may occur (see Figure 5-17):

- Group Policy Client Service failed the sign-in.

- The universal unique identifier (UUID) type is not supported.

Or you may receive this message:

Windows couldn't connect to the Group Policy client service. This problem prevents standard users from signing in.

Or you may receive this message:

Windows couldn't connect to the group policy client service. Please consult your system administrator.

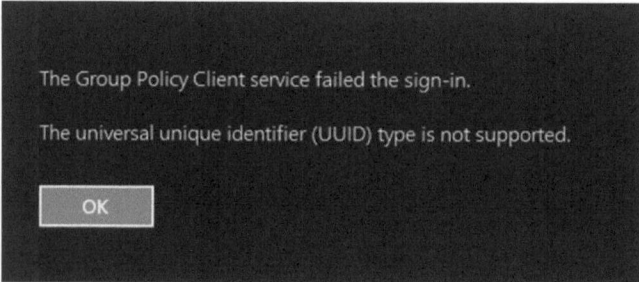

Figure 5-17. *"The Group Policy Client service failed the sign-in" error message*

To resolve this problem, open an administrative command prompt and type following command and then press **Enter**:

```
reg add "HKLM\SYSTEM\CurrentControlSet\Services\gpsvc" /v Type /t REG_DWORD
/d 0x10 /f
```

Executing this command will separate the Group Policy service into a separate SVCHOST instance, and therefore the issue will be resolved.

Key Points

- Common Group Policy issues include GPOs not being applied, folder redirection issues, and settings configured for the wrong version of Windows.

- Good planning and piloting can avoid most of these common issues.

- Configure and apply GPOs from the correct location (such as the computer or user configuration) to achieve the desired policy results.

- Network connections and permissions on SYSVOL are a common fault if you experience issues applying policy.

- GPResult is command line version of RSoP. It can provide you more information than using RSoP.

- Consider switching the Group Policy Loopback Processing policy to *Replace mode* to resolve loopback processing issues.

- To avoid folder redirection issues, make sure you have disabled the option to move user files during the migration to a new server.

- When you enable *userenv* logging, you can perform detailed debug logging of the user profile and the system policy processes.

Summary

This chapter introduced common Group Policy issues and how to resolve them. Group Policy can be complex, and as the enviroment grows larger, issues relating to GPOs will inevitably materialize. Group Policy issues commonly occur when they have been misconfigured or the network is not working properly. By using the tools discussed in this chapter you should have gained enough understanding to trace and troubleshoot common GPO issues that you will encounter. In the next chapter, we shall guide you through the AGPM, a very helpful tool in managing GPOs within a domain environment.

CHAPTER 6

■ ■ ■

Advanced Group Policy Management

In preceding chapters, you saw many concepts regarding GPOs and learned how to effectively use this awesome feature to set controls and consistency in an environment. In this chapter, you will learn advanced management of Group Policies.

After reading this chapter you will have a clear idea about how to manage GPOs in a complex environment and effectively deal with any issues that may arise. A major part of this chapter is dedicated to the Advanced Group Policy Management (AGPM) tool, which is used extensively for managing GPOs. We'll tell you in detail about AGPM features, applications, and how to effectively troubleshoot AGPM procedures. In the second half of this chapter, you'll learn how to employ advanced troubleshooting methods for fixing core and client-side extension-based Group Policy problems.

Introducing the Advanced Group Policy Management Tool

AGPM provides extensive capabilities over the standard GPO management tool GPMC introduced in Chapter 2. With AGPM, you can:

- Take full control of GPOs, either online or offline.

- Create a group of administrators, editors, reviewers, and approvers, and share the responsibility for corresponding operations with GPOs via role-based delegation throughout your organization.

- Create and test GPOs offline, so that there are no problems when you deploy settings to production.

- Archive changelog versions of GPO, such that if a problem occurs, you can go back to an earlier version and fix it.

- Document GPOs with comprehensive change control, which allows compliance with standards such as *Information Technology Infrastructure Library* (ITIL) Change Management.

© Kapil Arya 2016
K. Arya, *Windows Group Policy Troubleshooting*, DOI 10.1007/978-1-4842-1886-0_6

- Eradicate the possibility of multiple Group Policy administrators overwriting each other's work by using a check-in/check-out capability for GPOs.

- Create GPOs in a more straightforward way as part of a workflow using AGPM.

- Easy comparison of GPOs, version by version, in order to analyze the changes made in different iterations of the same GPO.

- Latest version of AGPM (part of *MDOP 2015*) provides Windows PowerShell support. You can control AGPM with cmdlets as well as with user interface (UI).

AGPM was previously known as **GPOVault** and was developed by a software company named **DesktopStandard**. Later, Microsoft acquired this company and renamed the tool to AGPM and included it in **Microsoft Desktop Optimization Pack** (MDOP). The MDOP package is a set of applications summarized in Table 6-1, and it is available free for Software Assurance customers.

Table 6-1. *List of Apps Available in MDOP*

Application	Importance	Genre
Microsoft Application Virtualization (App-V)	App-v allows businesses to centrally manage apps and let their devices run apps without actually installing them to the machine. It allows multiple versions of an app to run concurrently on a PC without conflict.	Virtualization
Microsoft User Experience Virtualization (MUE-V)	This is the part of MDOP for virtualizing the user desktop and applications. It is a complete solution, replacing roaming profiles. Here, manipulated user settings can be found in a centralized location, such as a DC. These settings can then be applied to the different computers that the user accesses, including desktop computers, laptop computers, and Virtual Desktop Infrastructure (*VDI*) sessions.	Virtualization
Microsoft Enterprise Desktop Virtualization (MED-V)	This technology uses Microsoft Virtual PC to provide an enterprise solution for desktop virtualization, which is especially useful when an organization is faced with the need to upgrade to a modern version of Windows, but they have incompatibility issues with legacy applications.	Virtualization

(continued)

Table 6-1. (*continued*)

Application	Importance	Genre
Microsoft Advanced Group Policy Management (AGPM)	Useful application for taking control of GPOs, performing their offline editing. The tool also provides role-based delegation facility for Group Policy Objects (GPOs).	Management
Microsoft BitLocker Administration and Monitoring (MBAM)	BitLocker is a drive encryption feature available with Windows Vista and later. MBAM provides enterprise management capabilities for *BitLocker* and *BitLocker To Go*. MBAM simplifies the deployment and key recovery, provides centralized compliance monitoring and reporting, and minimizes the costs associated with provisioning and supporting encrypted drives.	Management
Microsoft Diagnostics and Recovery Toolset (DaRT)	DaRT is basically a set of troubleshooting tools helpful in diagnosing misconfigured machines. It also provides desktop recovery services. This is quite similar to the tools like Startup repair/ system restore which we get when we boot into the Windows Recovery Environment (RE).	Restoration

If your organization is licensed to use MDOP, you will benefit greatly from the power tools listed in Table 6-1 because each of them has special offerings and importance. Of these applications, AGPM is of our prime interest and we will now discuss the AGPM tool in more detail.

Installing and Configuring AGPM

Installing the AGPM client and the server snap-in is quite easy. First, download the **MDOP ISO file** from Microsoft's Volume Licensing Center (www.microsoft.com/Licensing/servicecenter/default.aspx) or download the file from your organizational MSDN subscription.

Once extracted, you will find separate folders for each of the applications mentioned in Table 6-1. Choose the AGPM folder and locate the Installers folder. Here, you will find the Client and Server application setup files that you should install. *AGPM Server* must be installed on a DC or member server and *AGPM Client* can be installed on a machine running AGPM Server. AGPM Server helps you to deploy, offline edit, and roll back GPOs, while AGPM Client works similar to standard GPMC and helps you to manage GPOs.

As part of the installation and configuration of AGPM, you should know that AGPM directly integrates with GPO. After installing AGPM Client- and Server-based programs, you should open GPO and click **Change Control** in the console tree (left pane) of GPM window, as shown in Figure 6-1. In the right pane, you'll see the **AGPM Server** tab. In the AGPM Server tab you will manage the host and delete the old versions of GPOs from the archive.

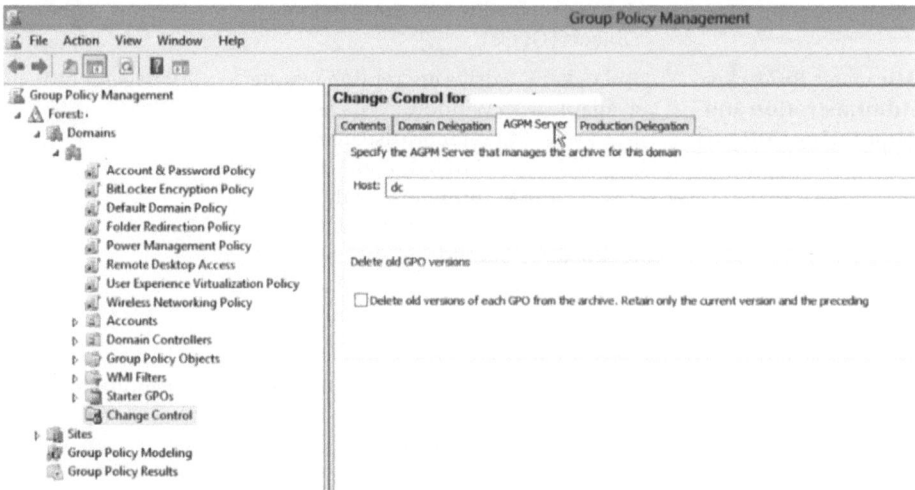

Figure 6-1. *Locating AGPM Server settings in the GPMC snap-in*

Taking Control of GPOs Using AGPM

AGPM is designed to take full control of GPOs and integrates itself into the GPMC tool. For taking control of GPOs, you need to click on **Contents** tab in the window shown in Figure 6-1 and then click **Uncontrolled**. Here you can select the GPOs that you want to take control of and right-click to select **Control**. You'll see a progress bar and each GPO listed with **Succeeded** term against it (see Figure 6-2), which confirms that you've successfully taken control of those GPOs.

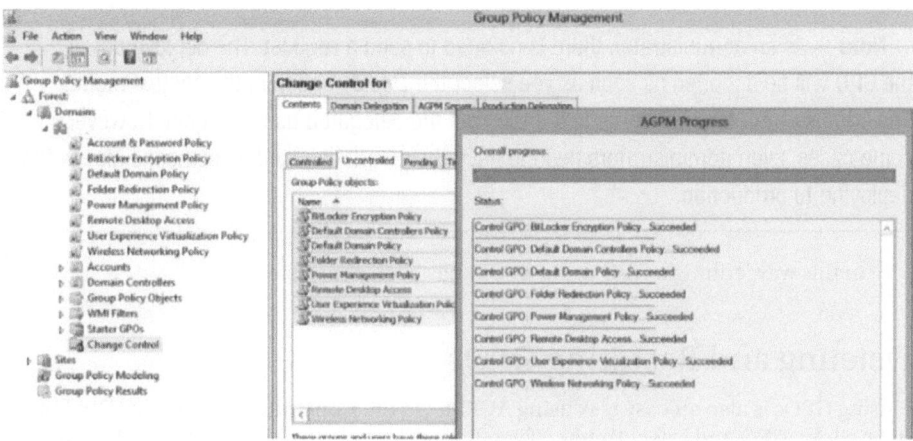

Figure 6-2. *Taking control of GPOs in AGPM*

Editing GPO Using AGPM

Once you have taken control of the GPOs, you can edit them directly and any changes will be reflected immediately within the tool. If you've assigned a delegate, they can edit the GPO. When GPOs are edited, notifications about those edits are sent to the assigned administrator, whose e-mail address is linked under the snap-in. Follow these steps to edit a GPO as a delegated user:

1. Open AGPM snap-in and click **Change Control**.

2. Then on the **Controlled** tab, right-click the policy you want to edit and select **Check out**. You'll receive a *Succeeded* notification.

3. Right-click the same policy and then select **Edit**. Now the GPO snap-in will open and you can change the policy status.

4. After configuring the policy, right-click the updated policy and select **Check in**.

5. Finally, right-click the policy and select **Deploy**. In the next window, hit **Submit** and AGPM will send a notification to the administrator as you are using delegated access. Note that deployment will make the GPO live in production, whereas a Check in doesn't.

■ **Note** As an administrator, there is no need to send a request. The deployment of the GPO will be actioned as soon as you select the *Deploy* option in the context menu. The administrator has full rights to the GPO but the delegated user does not. However, in some cases, even administrators need to have their work checked by someone else before deploying to production.

In this way, editing a GPO using AGPM has been completed.

Deleting and Restoring GPOs

Erasing GPOs is also an easy task using AGPM. On the **Controlled** tab under AGPM, just right-click a GPO and select **Delete**. If you have privileges to delete a GPO (link), it will be moved to the Recycle Bin immediately; however, the actual associated GPO is not deleted and it still remains in AD. This was explained in Chapter 2 under the "Deleting GPOs Using the GPMC" section. If you don't have full control, the notification will be sent to the admin or user who has full control of the corresponding GPOs. Once the GPO has been deleted, you can select the domain name in the left pane and press the **F5** key, which will refresh the list of GPOs applied. You'll find that the GPO you just erased no longer appears in the list.

To restore a deleted GPO (link) back to the production, go to the Recycle Bin, right-click the GPO, and select **Restore** (see Figure 6-3). Refresh the screen and the GPO should be restored back to the Control tab. If the changes are not reflected immediately, you can refresh policies by pressing **F5** or exiting and reloading the MMC.

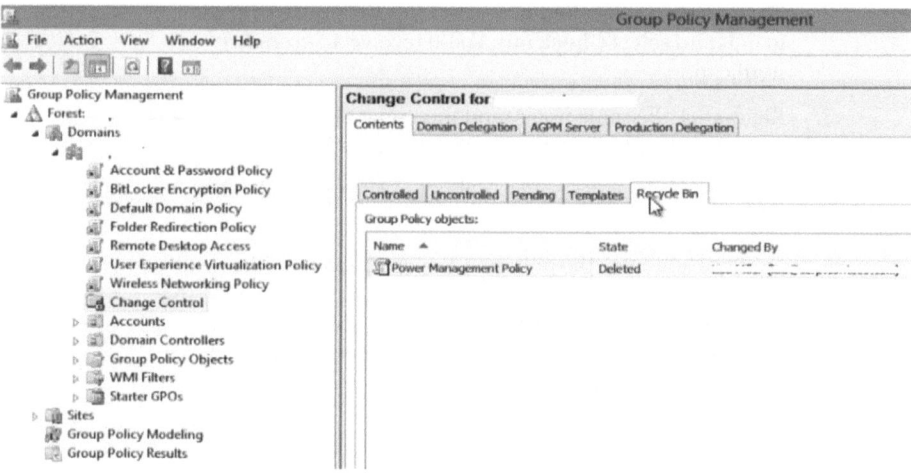

Figure 6-3. *The deleted GPO appears in the Recycle Bin tab*

Restoring GPOs to Previous Versions

With the help of AGPM, it is quite easy and straightforward to restore GPOs to their earlier editions. Follow these steps:

1. To restore a GPO to an earlier edition, under the **Controlled** tab, right-click the GPO and then select **History**.

2. In the History window, switch to the **Unique Versions** tab.

3. Right-click the earlier date version to which you want to roll back and select **Deploy** (refer Figure 6-4). The AGPM Progress window will return a *Succeeded* message.

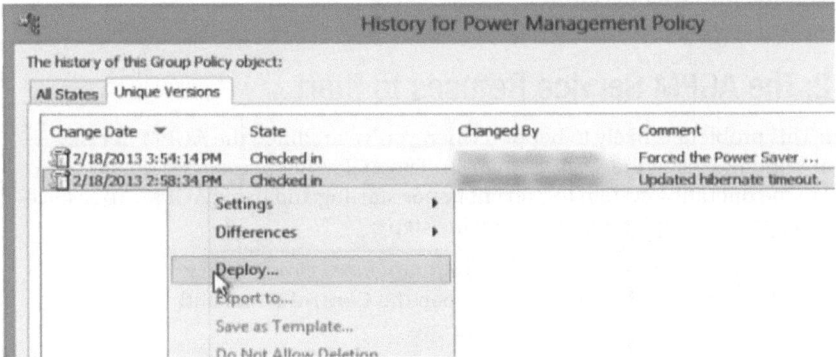

Figure 6-4. *Restoring a GPO to earlier version from the History window*

In this way, you have restored a GPO to its earlier edition.

Troubleshooting AGPM Problems

There are some common problems that administrators often encounter when using AGPM. In this section, we will review these common issues and the corresponding resolutions.

Issue 1: When You're Not Able to Edit, Create, Delete, or Modify GPOs and Templates

Solution: This can be possible when you don't have the required privileges. You need to ensure that you have control over the GPOs to carry out these types of actions. As an administrator, follow these steps to ensure you have full control:

1. Choose the forest or domain for which you want to manipulate GPOs and click **Change Control** for it, under the GPMC window.

2. Next, click **Domain Delegation ➤ Advanced**.

3. Under **Permissions**, check the roles you have assigned to individuals and press the **Advanced** button.

4. In the **Advanced Security Settings** dialog box, choose a GP administrator and click **Edit.**

5. For **Apply onto**, select **This object and nested objects**, configure any special permissions beyond the standard AGPM roles, and then click **OK** in the **PermissionEntry** dialog box.

6. Click **OK,** and **Apply**, and **OK.**

If you're not the administrator, you need to contact the administrator and explain the issue you are experiencing so that they can assign the required delegated permissions for your user account.

Issue 2: The AGPM Service Refuses to Start

Solution: This problem is likely to happen when you've modified the **AGPM Service** settings in Windows using the *Services* snap-in. The AGPM Service should not be modified in the operating system to prevent issues starting and using AGPM. To resolve this problem, you can implement the following steps:

1. On the computer that has *Microsoft Advanced Group Policy Management - Server* installed, open the **Control Panel** and then open **Add or Remove Programs.**

2. Right-click *Microsoft Advanced Group Policy Management - Server*, and then click **Change** (see Figure 6-5).

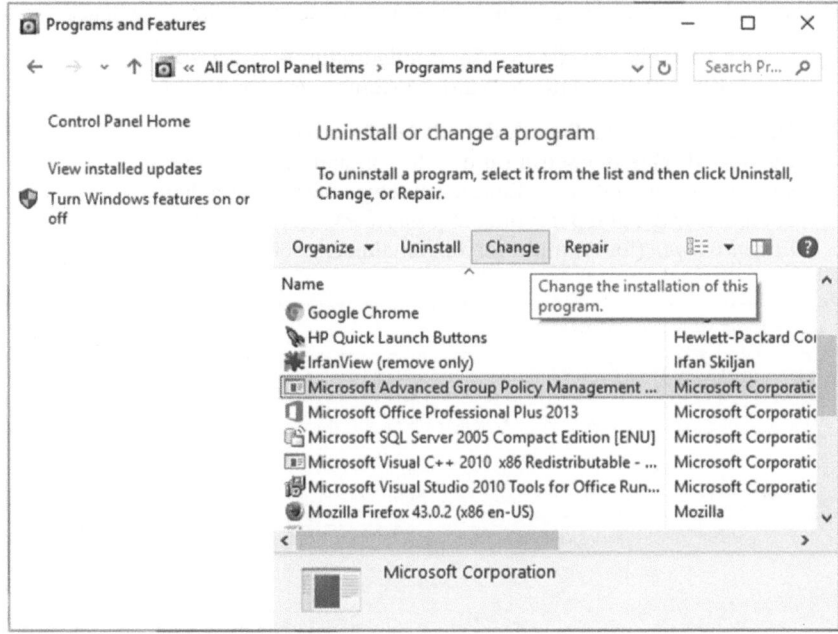

Figure 6-5. *AGPM Server entry in Add or Remove Programs*

3. Click **Next**, and then click **Modify.**

4. Follow the instructions on the screen to configure settings for the **AGPM Service**. This operation will restore the correct settings for the application, which should ensure that AGPM will start normally.

5. Click **Change**, and when the installation is complete, click **Finish.**

Issue 3: You Can't Access the Archive

Solution: There may be two possible causes for this. Either the AGPM Service is not running or you have specified invalid settings for the server and port when configuring the AGPM.

Run the **services.msc** command and verify the AGPM Service status under the Services snap-in. You may find the service has stopped. Right-click the service and select **Start**.

You should review the next steps while logged in with administrative privileges:

1.   Open *GPMC* and navigate to User Configuration ➤ Policies ➤ Administrative Templates ➤ Windows Components ➤ AGPM.

2.   Double-click **AGPM: Specify default AGPM Server (all domains) policy setting** and in the configuration window shown in Figure 6-6, select **Enabled** and type the fully-qualified computer name and port under *Default AGPM Server for all domains input* (for example, server.domain.com:4600).

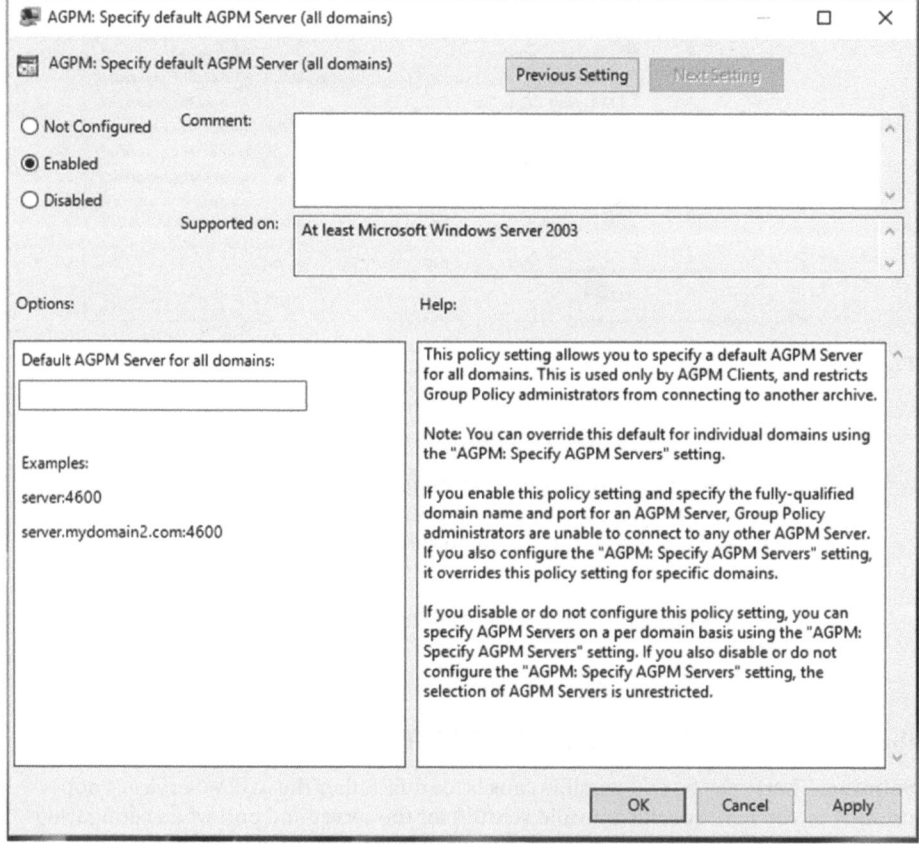

Figure 6-6. *The AGPM: Specify default AGPM Server (all domains) policy window*

3.   Click **OK**. Unless you want to configure additional AGPM Server connections, close the GPMC and deploy the GPO.

If you don't have administrative control, you will need to discuss this with an administrator.

Issue 4: You're an Administrator and You Aren't Receiving Notification Mail from AGPM

Solution: This can happen when you've haven't provided the correct SMTP email server and e-mail address details. You should verify the mail settings. You also need to make sure that any delegated users that you've assigned also have the correct SMTP email server and e-mail address settings.

Issue 5: You Can't Use Port 4600 for AGPM Service

Solution: By default, AGPM corresponds to port 4600, so you need to modify each archive index file to use another port and then update the AGPM Server for all Group Policy administrators. Figure 6-7 shows the AGPM port exception prompt.

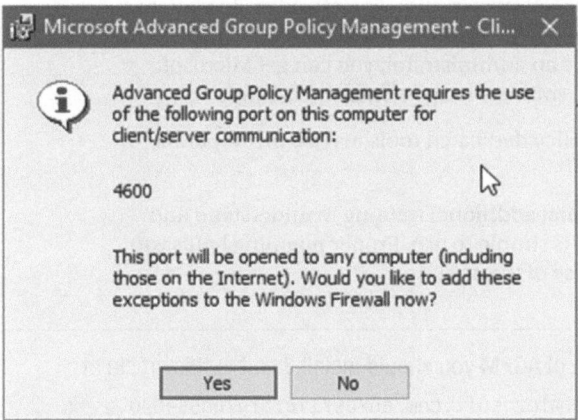

Figure 6-7. *AGPM port exception prompt*

To specify another port, follow these steps:

1. Go to the machine hosting the archive and open the archive index file named **gpostate.xml** in a text editor such as Notepad. This file is located in the folder entered as the archive path during the installation of AGPM snap-in. It must be located by default at %CommonAppData%\Microsoft\AGPM\ gpostate.xml path. You should back up this setting before making any edits.

2. In the file, search for **agpm:port="4600"**.

3. Replace **4600** with your desired one, then save and close file.

4. On the AGPM Server, reboot the *AGPM Service*.

5. Modify the port in the AGPM Server connection for each Group Policy administrator.

6. Repeat for each archive and AGPM Server.

In this way, you can enable the AGMP Server to listen to the port you have set.

Additional Information About AGPM

AGPM is robust offline tool with in-depth integration with GPMC. It provides you with comparisons between *live* and *offline* GPOs. The following are some additional facts about AGPM:

- AGPM isn't a free tool. You get it when you subscribe to Software Assurance licensing. You can download this under the MDOP package from your MSDN subscription to test and evaluate it, but you need to ensure you are licensed to use AGPM in a production environment. If you're an administrator, you can get Microsoft support to ensure the software usage terms and conditions.

- Third-party Group Policy dedicated tools may be incompatible with AGPM.

- AGPM requires minimal additional training to understand and use it because AGPM is simple to use. Proper planning helps you to make productive use of this tool.

■ **Note** To decide which version of AGPM you should install, head to this article at TechNet library: `https://technet.microsoft.com/en-us/library/dd553090.aspx`.

Advanced Group Policy Troubleshooting

In earlier chapters, you saw some common and basic approaches to deal with Group Policy-related issues. This section takes you into more depth; you'll learn more technical-level procedures to troubleshoot Group Policies. This section is divided into three parts:

- Understanding Group Policy processing

- Tools to help identify Group Policy issues

- Troubleshooting Group Policy issues

Understanding Group Policy Processing

Before you tackle Group Policy issues and start troubleshooting them, you must obtain sufficient information to understand the problem. Sometimes the lack of knowledge may make the issues more complicated and the results could damage your environment. You need to understand how Group Policy processing works in-depth.

Let us understand Group Policy processing with the help of explaination provided below. The example environment is a domain-connected client machine and a domain controller server.

There are *Client* and *Server* sides, and each has an important contribution to processing. Basically, Group Policy processing covers two different phases:

- **Core Group Policy Processing**: According to Microsoft (https:// technet.microsoft.com/en-us/library/cc779077(v=ws.10). aspx), "Core Group Policy or the Group Policy (GP) engine is the framework that handles common functionalities across Administrative Template settings and other client-side extensions." When the client is logged in, the GP engine attempts to determine whether it can reach the domain controller or not. This is done to check and confirm if any GPOs are manipulated and which GPOs needs to be processed. When the GP engine is initializing, the core Group Policy engine performs these checks.

- **Client-Side Extension (CSE) Processing**: Group Policy is a repository for holding settings in GPOs that will be applied to a machine or a user. This repository also holds server- and client-side components. When you are about to deploy a GPO, the client-side components may make suitable changes to the local environment, and these components are known as client-side extensions (CSEs) in the science of Group Policy. A CSE can be identified with its 128-bit **Globally Unique Identifier** (GUID). Group Policy settings are grouped into several categories, such as **Administrative Templates** (aka registry-based policy), **Security Settings**, **Folder Redirection**, **Disk Quota**, and **Software Installation**. This categorization aids our understanding and provides easier navigation. The settings in each category require a specific CSE to process them, and each CSE has its own rules for processing settings. The core Group Policy engine calls the CSEs that are required to process the settings that apply to the client.

■ **Note** A detailed explanation about how the core Group Policy engine works can be found at https://technet.microsoft.com/en-us/library/cc784268.aspx.

While Group Policies are being processed, each CSE is passed with a GPO list via the *Winlogon* process. The work of CSE is to process the correct policy when required. You can use the commonly used CSE GUIDs mentioned in Table 6-2 to spot their activity under the logs generated by GP processing.

Table 6-2. *List of GUIDs for CSE Components*

GUID	Component
25537BA6-77A8-11D2-9B6C-0000F8080861	Folder redirection
3610EDA5-77EF-11D2-8DC5-00C04FA31A66	Microsoft disk quota
42B5FAAE-6536-11D2-AE5A-0000F87571E3	Scripts
827D319E-6EAC-11D2-A4EA-00C04F79F83A	Security
B1BE8D72-6EAC-11D2-A4EA-00C04F79F83A	Recovery
C6DC5466-785A-11D2-84D0-00C04FB169F7	Application management
A2E30F80-D7DE-11d2-BBDE-00C04F86AE3B	Internet Explorer settings
35378EAC-683F-11D2-A89A-00C04FBBCFA2	Registry settings
e437bc1c-aa7d-11d2-a382-00c04f991e27	IP security

When viewing event log entries and log files recorded by Group Policy and CSE, an administrator can identify an extension by its GUID.

When an extension is installed by any third-party tool or by a service, its registry entry is created under the following location (refer Figure 6-8):

HKEY_LOCAL_MACHINE\SOFTWARE\Microsoft\Windows NT\CurrentVersion\Winlogon\GPExtensions

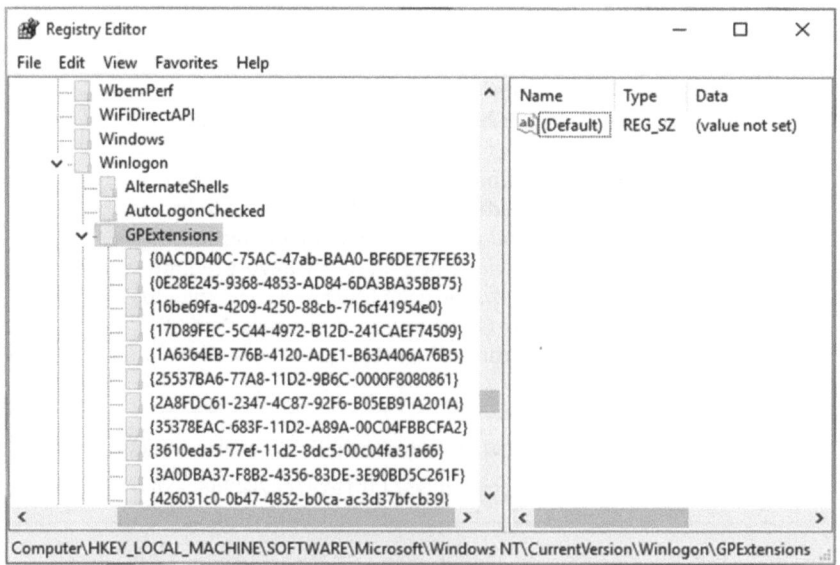

Figure 6-8. *Registry entries for GP extensions*

Registry Values for CSEs

You can maintain CSEs with direct registry manipulation. This may help you deal with a particular extension if you are comfortable using the registry. Table 6-3 lists the registry values presented in CSEs. It is not mandatory that all of these values are present. In this case, the default specified is used by the client extensions.

Table 6-3. *List of Registry Values Present for Each CSEs*

Value	Importance	Type*	Data
Dllname	--	*REG_EXPAND_SZ*	<Client-side extension DLL>
ProcessGroupPolicy	--	*REG_SZ*	CSE function needs to be called while GP passes to this extension.
NoMachinePolicy	This helps to check the client extension, whether or not to process GP as it is applied to the machine.	*REG_DWORD*	0 or value not present = Process *(Default)* 1 = Do not process
NoUserPolicy	This helps to check the client extension, whether or not to process GP as it is applied to the user.	*REG_DWORD*	0 or value not present = Process *(Default)* 1 = Do not process
NoSlowLink	If this value is present and set to 1, when a slow link is detected, the category it belongs will not be processed. The reverse happens when the value is 0.	*REG_DWORD*	0 or value not present = Process *(Default)* 1 = Do not process
NoBackgroundPolicy	It checks whether or not the client-based extension will process GP when a background refresh of the GP engine occurs.	*REG_DWORD*	0 or value not present = Process *(Default)* 1 = Do not process

(continued)

Table 6-3. (*continued*)

Value	Importance	Type*	Data
NoGPOListChanges	When there is no change in processing or if this value is set to 1, it tells Windows that it does not need to call the call back function in order to reload policy.	*REG_DWORD*	0 or value not present = Process *(Default)* 1 = Do not process
PerUserLocalSettings	This value decides whether to process user policies on a per-user or per-computer basis.	*REG_DWORD*	0 or value not present = Enabled *(Default)* 1 = Disabled
RequiresSuccessful Registry	When the registry extension has successfully processed the client, the callback function can be called, if this value is set to 1 or disabled.	*REG_DWORD*	0 or value not present = Enabled *(Default)* 1 = Disabled
EnableAsynchronous Processing	Checks whether or not a GP will continue processing while the client extension is performing operations.	*REG_DWORD*	0 or value not present = Synchronous *(Default)* 1 = Asynchronous

* *Value type should be interpreted as:*
REG_DWORD= registry DWORD, REG_SZ= registry string, REG_EXPAND_SZ=
Expandable registry string.

Tools to Help Identify Group Policy Issues

In an earlier chapter we suggested that you can examine Group Policy problems using *Event Viewer* logs and the *RSoP* and *GPResult* tools. All of these are useful from the troubleshooting point of view and they make a firm base for further analyzing issues. In this section, we're going to highlight other advanced-level diagnostic tools that may help you to troubleshoot issues with GPOs.

Group Policy Management Console (GPMC)

Since AGPM is fully integrated with GPMC, this is the first place you should look when you're troubleshooting Group Policy issues. The console helps you to take control of GPOs and allows you to perform editing tasks even if you are offline. GPMC is also useful because of the following two featured tools which we introduced in Chapter 2:

- *Group Policy Modeling*
- *Group Policy Results*

GPOTool.exe

GPOTool.exe is a useful command-line tool which can be found in the *Windows Server 2003 Resource Kit Tools* (see Note below for downloading link). It has been around for many years and is used in domains that contain more than one domain controller such as in *replicated domains* environments.

■ **Note**   To download Windows Server 2003 Resource Kit Tools, point your browser to
www.microsoft.com/en-us/download/details.aspx?id=17657.

GPOTool reviews all of your domain controllers and will check each DC for consistency between the Group Policy containers (that is, information contained in the directory service) and the Group Policy templates (that is, information contained in the SYSVOL share on the domain controller). This powerful tool helps you to check the consistency and validity of GPOs across all of your domain controllers. It also displays detailed information about the GPOs that have been replicated between the domain controllers.

If you suspect that you are having problems with replication of Group Policy information, this tool helps you diagnose and isolate where Group Policy is not being replicated properly. This is illustrated in Figure 6-9, where GPOTool validates the consistency of GPOs across your environment. When the consistency is found to be operational and everything is alright, the tool will result a "*Policies OK*" message.

Figure 6-9. GPOTool.exe command line tool

Enable Advanced Auditing and Logging

Group Policy should be considered a technical feature within Windows and especially when deployed in a domain environment. You have seen how errors can occur, and there are various tools that you can use to investigate and isolate issues. At the first sign of problematic networking, login issues, or GPO failures, you should enable auditing and logging because this will create a tracking mechanism that may provide useful hints to you and may help you to fix problems. We have already covered how to enable logging and auditing under the following sections:

- "Auditing User Activities with Security Policies" in Chapter 3

- "Using Event Viewer for Tracing Group Policy Logs" in Chapter 5

- "Enabling Verbose Logging" in Chapter 5

Flow Chart Approach for Verifying GPO Issues

Group Policy problems are often solved by using a flow chart approach. By flowcharting you can sometimes simplify the way to troubleshoot and find the issues and then fix them accordingly.

The flowchart approach can be explained as follows:

While troubleshooting Group Policy issues, your main concern should be to first check whether GPO is applied or denied. If GPO is denied or filtered out, there may be causes behind it such as WMI filtering, security filtering, an empty GPO, inaccessible data, etc. You can use the tools discussed earlier, such as Group Policy Results (discussed in the "Using GPMC Reports for Troubleshooting" section in Chapter 2) to find out which GPOs are applied.

If you realize that not all settings are applied, factors such as Group Policy refresh, replication, User Mode GP loopback processing, or slow link over connection may be used. You should compare the results for each of the policy settings with the help of a flow chart. It is often recommended that you solve core Group Policy problems first. For this, you may need to recheck the core configuration deeply. Steps like reconnecting the computer to the domain, ensuring the correct time and date on system, and verifying network connectivity are part of this session. If the issue still persists, CSE(s) might be the culprit. Make the best use of GPOTool.exe, GPResults, and of course the GPMC to locate the issue. If you're still in a dilemma and have no clue, head over to CSE logs, userenv logs, and event logs to determine the exact cause and troubleshoot accordingly.

■ **Note** To learn about each component of the flow chart in detail, visit
`https://technet.microsoft.com/en-us/library/cc779631.aspx`.

Troubleshooting Group Policy Issues

You now have several tools and processes to allow you to effectively troubleshoot GPO issues. The flowchart approach should help you to locate Group Policy problems with the help of the dedicated GPO tools, auditing, and logging shown in this chapter.

We will now guide you through how to fix the component-based problems. We will also assume that you have gained a good understanding of your infrastructure and how your environment has been configured. The key areas that we will explore are as follows:

1. Fixing core Group Policy or Group Policy Engine problems; divided into four parts:

   • Processing issues: Problems related to the processing of the GP engine

   • Networking issues: Fixes for issues relating to network connectivity

   • Scoping issues: Issues arising due to incorrectly applied filtering

   • Structural issues: Solutions to GP infrastructure-related problems

2. Various problems: Discussion about problems due to extensions and scripts

Fixing Core Group Policy Issues

Processing Issues with GPOs

When you have issues with the processing of Group Policies, you should verify the processing order and look for applied exceptions. The correct order of processing GPOs is as follows:

Local GPO ➤ Site ➤ Domain ➤ OU ➤ Order specified by administrator for Linked GPOs tab of OU.

■ **Note** The lower link order is processed at the end, so it will have highest precedence. In other words, a lower link of order 1 will be processed last, so if settings from this GPO have been specified in GPOs that have been applied previously in processing, the values for those settings in this GPO win.

Table 6-4 lists the common problems when GPOs are not processed and some of their resolutions.

Table 6-4. Processing Issues with GPOs

Issue	Resolution
GPO Policy not being supported	When you configure GPOs, make sure you check the *Supported on* section. You also need to confirm that the OS requirements mentioned in this section and the target OS to which you're deploying the GPO match.
Not getting expected values from GPOs	Check the GPO processing order. You may want to change precedence order and see if this resolves the issue. Try disabling only the computer or the user settings and verify the status of issue.
GPOs not refreshing	The refresh interval by default is 90 minutes (1.5 hours). You should try to manually refresh the policies by running the **gpupdate /force** command either from the affected machine or by triggering remotely.
Loopback processing did not work	Read the detailed fix in the section "No User Policies in Group Policy Loopback Processing" in Chapter 5.

Networking Issues with GPOs

When the network is the cause of a problem, clients may not receive GPO settings correctly. This is due to an obstruction in the path or flow of settings via the network, and you must diagnose and resolve it. Although outside of the scope of this book, you can use various network troubleshooting tools such as the command line tools **ping** and **netdiag**. Simply type **ping** in the command prompt window and press **Enter**. You'll get list of all available parameters for ping, which can then be used to direct your ping request to a nearby DC. The **Netdiag** command-line diagnostic tool helps to isolate networking and connectivity problems by performing a series of tests to determine the state of your network client.

■ **Note**　To learn about Netdiag in detail and to learn about the series of tests that can performed with Netdiag, refer to `https://technet.microsoft.com/en-us/library/cc731434.aspx`.

In addition to the built-in network troubleshooting tool within Windows, you may also want to use third-party tools for checking network connectivity. There are many software tools available for troubleshooting networking issues. Analyzing event logs on a client machine can also help you locate and resolve problems. General troubleshooting steps taken to solve network connections include:

- Running the Windows Network Diagnostics/Network Adapter/ Internet Connections troubleshooters.

- Checking, resetting, or reinstalling the TCP/IP configuration.

- Reinstalling or rolling back network drivers.

- Updating the network drivers to the latest version.

- Checking whether the network card is installed and corresponding hardware working properly.

You will find some common GPO-related networking problems and their remedies in Table 6-5.

Table 6-5. *Networking Issues with GPOs*

Issue	Resolution
Unable to access domain controller	If the network is working but the client can't access specified server, then issue most likely resides with the DNS. Use the **ping** command against the computer using NetBIOS name. Use the **ping** command against the domain name in the target machine. If the first ping succeeds but the later one doesn't, it confirms there is problem with DNS. You can then use the **Netdiag. exe** tool to perform various tests to examine the root cause of problem and then resolve it.
GPOs changes are not applied	See the suggestions mentioned in the "Group Policy Not Being Applied" section under "Common Group Policy Issues and Resolutions" in Chapter 5.

(continued)

Table 6-5. (*continued*)

Issue	Resolution
GPOs don't react when you connect remotely on a slow link	Some GPO may not be applied when they're below a threshold preset value, such as 500 kbps. Such GPOs are referred to as a **slow link**. This means when your client is applying policy settings, and if available bandwidth between him and the DC is lesser than 500 kbps, only important GPO settings will be downloaded, although administrative templates and security settings may still get an update over a slow link. But settings such as software installation, folder redirection, disk quota, etc. are not processed over a slow link. To solve this problem, follow these steps and see if they help: **Open GPMC.** **Navigate to** Computer Configuration ➤ Policies ➤ Administrative Templates ➤ System ➤ Group Policy. In the right pane, double-click *Configure Group Policy slow link detection* and select **Enabled**. In the Connection Speed option, try setting a lesser value below which the connection can be flagged as slow. Click **Apply**, followed by **OK**, and reboot to apply the setting.
One or more protocols are missing on this computer	When registry entries are corrupted, you may get this error. If you fix this issue by attempting to reinstall the TCP/IP configuration, you may receive a "This program is blocked by Group Policy" error. To resolve this issue, you must reset Windows Sockets. You can use the **netsh winsock reset** command. If the problem still persists, you can try rebooting, and then reinstalling the network driver and see if that helps. For detailed fix, check following link: *http://www.kapilarya.com/windows-sockets-registry-entries-required-for-network-connectivity-is-missing.*

Scoping Issues with GPOs

The process of identifying which user and computer received the settings under GPO is called **scoping**. Factors that can affect how scoping works on a GPO are listed here:

- Site, domain, or OU (where GPO is linked)

- Security filtering on GPO

- WMI filtering on GPO

If security filtering and WMI filtering have been configured incorrectly, the results are likely to be poor. When either of these filtering types return false values, GPOs are often not processed at all. To tackle issues for both of these types of filtering, you can try the suggestions mentioned in Table 6-6.

Table 6-6. *Scoping Issues with GPOs*

Issues	Resolution
GPOs applied/denied on the verge of WMI filtering	Check the WMI filter and edit it, if required. Open GPMC, click the GPO that you want to troubleshoot, and then click the **Scope** tab. The **WMI Filtering** section shows whether a WMI filter is linked to the GPO. If you need to edit the filter, click **Open**, and then click **Edit**. If you're using Windows 2000, then WMI Filtering is ignored and GPO is applied regardless. On later editions, WMI filtering works as usual.
GPOs applied/denied on the verge of security filtering	You can restrict an application using a security filter in applied GPOs. When GPOs are not working as expected with security filtering, you need to check the following set of permissions. But before that, you may also try rejoining the issued specific machine to the domain, in case it helps. If not, follow these steps: Open GPMC, click **Group Policy Objects**, and select the GPO with which you are having issues. In the corresponding right pane, select **Scope**. You can then check the *Security Filtering* and *WMI Filtering* sections to see what settings are applied. Then go to the **Delegation** tab to review the set of permissions applied so far. Choose the computer/user/security group for which you want to review the set of permissions. Please keep in mind that minimum permissions should be set to *Read*, if the GPO is applied to computer/user/security group. So basically here you need to add authenticated users to GPO with the *Read* permissions. In some cases, you may also need to add *Domain Controller* (DC) group with *Read* permissions.

Structural Issues with GPOs

Earlier you saw the order in which GPOs are processed. The *Sites*, *Domains*, and *OUs* are the elements under which *User* GPOs are applied to all *users*. The *Computer* GPOs are applied to all *computers* in the element. However, if your GPOs are not being delivered, you may have to deal with some well-known problems. Those structural issues and fixes are discussed in Table 6-7.

Table 6-7. Structual Issues with GPOs

Issue	Resolution
GPO policy does not react to specific user/machine	Confirm that the user/computer is located in the correct *Site, Domain, and OU*. If there is more than one conflicting GPO, review any GPO inheritance rules in place. You can also test this scenario by adding a new user/computer to the OU and reviewing the results once the GPOs are initiated.
Critical files are corrupted	You should check the integrity of the GP engine files and other system files. These suggestions may help: If the issue is related to DC, use **GPOTool.exe** to check the integrity of registry.pol file in SYSVOL share. **Userenv.log** (available at %windir%\debug\usermode\Userenv.log) can help you to reference this file. Administrative templates are processed with the help of registry.pol via registry-based CSEs. To resolve corrupted system files on a client computer and check for missing system files in the %windir%\system32 folder, you may try the **SFC /SCANNOW** command and it will fix or replace any corrupted/broken system files found.
Trust relationships not working	Avoid linking a GPO from a forest, site, and domain to GPO to another corresponding element. If the GPO cannot be applied due to lack of trust, it will appear in the list of *Denied GPOs* in the Group Policy Results report and the reason given will be *Inaccessible*. Use Active Directory Domains and Trusts or **nltest.exe** to verify the trust relationship, and to repair it if necessary.
GPOs not working after user/computer migration	Check for a broken domain trust relationship. If there is no trust, you should try to copy the GPO directly. Once trust is restored, you can import the GPO.

■ **Info** **Nltest.exe** is a command-line tool useful in querying GPO structural issues. It is available in Windows Server editions and if you've got AD DS or the AD LDS server role installed. Read more about it at https://technet.microsoft.com/en-us/library/cc731935.aspx.

Miscellaneous Issues

We have reviewed the Core Group Policy problems. Other issues that administrators may come across include the Group Policy CSE processing categories including Administrative Templates, security settings, folder redirection, disk quota, and software installation. Most issues attributed to these categories can be referred as problems due to extensions. Review the problems and possible solutions shown in Table 6-8.

Table 6-8. *Various Issues/Extension-Based Problems*

Problem	Possible Solution
When Disk Quota CSEs fails to operate	Review the Event Viewer for events logged by the Disk Quota CSE and use the information in the event description to troubleshoot the problem. Also confirm the existence of the dskquota.dll file under %SystemRoot%\ system32. You may also want to reregister the dskquota.dll file using the **regsvr32. exe** command-line tool.
Folder redirection issues	These suggestions may help: Ensure that the folder redirection configuration is correct and that you are not redirecting parent folders to subfolders. Confirm that no files to be moved are locked by an application or service. This article may be helpful if you need to understand more about *folder redirection* permissions: https:// technet.microsoft.com/en-us/library/ cc781907%28v=ws.10%29.aspx.
Software Installation CSE background problems	If software installation changes are not reflected after logon, you may turn Off the *Always wait for the network at computer startup and logon Group* policy. This setting determines whether Group Policy processing is synchronous. Software installation may also fail whenever an incorrect path is provided for the destination directory. Administrators are suggested to provide the correct path and should ensure that the necessary privileges on the target folder are in place.

(*continued*)

Table 6-8. (*continued*)

Problem	Possible Solution
Scripting issue: Windows cannot obtain the domain controller name for the computer network. (The specified domain either does not exist or exist or could not be contacted.) Group Policy processing aborted.	This error is often found while examining logs within the Event Viewer. A quick resolution to this issue is to add the GpNetworkStartTimeoutPolicyValue registry entry at HKEY_LOCAL_MACHINE\SOFTWARE\Microsoft\WindowsNT\CurrentVersion\Winlogon. The entry should be a registry DWORD (REG_DWORD) with Value data set to 60 (Base: Decimal).
Security settings are propagated with warnings	When you observe this problem and review the event logs, you may see event ID1202. You will also obtain an error code, for example *0x6fc*. Refer the following support article and perform the troubleshooting steps suggested regarding the error code: https://support.microsoft.com/en-us/kb/324383.
Password policy is not applied	You may try a manual refreshing of GP engine using the **gpupdate /refreshpolicy** command.
The following entry in the [strings] section is too long and has been truncated	Obtain the hotfixes from Microsoft Support article from https://support.microsoft.com/en-us/kb/842933.
Custom ADM Settings are not displayed in the GPO snap-in	Open the GPO snap-in and right-click Administrative Templates, select View ➤ Filtering options. Now set the *Managed* policies option to **Yes**.

Key Points

- MDOP is available to Software Assurance customers and includes six powerful applications for virtualizing, managing, and repairing Windows.

- AGPM is part of MDOP and integrates fully into GPMC and can be used to manage GPOs offline.

- The AGPM Service is required to run after you install AGPM.

- When a GPO is applied, the CSEs interpret the policy and make the appropriate changes to the environment.

- You can identify CSEs under the registry with the help of their GUIDs.

- GPMC Modeling is used to predict policies, while GPMC Results is used to obtain information about policies in effect.

- GPOTool.exe is a troubleshooting tool useful within domain environments that have multiple domain controllers.

- Lower link orders have the highest precedence when deducing GPO processing.

- If the network speed drops to lower than a rate of 500 kbps, only GPOs referred to as "slow links" will be processed. Administrative Templates and security settings are processed as slow links.

- Auditing and logging should be configured in advance, as a precaution to troubleshooting GPO issues.

Summary

Administrators may find this chapter useful because we reviewed the AGPM and also because we reviewed several GPO issues and resolutions. It is not possible to cover each and every issue but we have included some of the most common issues and their fixes. We also focused on various troubleshooting tools and processes that should help you when you are troubleshooting advanced GPO issues. In the next and last chapter, we'll share with you some interesting tips and tricks that you can use with GPOs.

CHAPTER 7

Group Policy Tips and Tricks

In the preceding chapters, you saw that Group Policy offers great flexibility and reliability when customizing and enhancing Windows for your users and devices. The ease in which you can configure and deploy any of the 3,500-plus policy settings to a single or multiple devices within your environment is something no other operating system can compete with. Once you have configured your business-critical end user or computer settings, you should explore how to use Group Policy to modify and tweak Windows settings. This chapter introduces many popular and well-known GPO tricks and tips.

This final chapter will cover the following category areas:

Popular GPO tweaks in Windows:

1. Customize the way you get Windows Updates in Windows 10.

2. Force Windows to display the delete confirmation prompt.

3. Rename the administrator account in Windows.

4. Hide specific tabs in the Internet Properties window.

5. Remove Help Tips in Windows 8.1.

6. Disable user access to the Control Panel and Settings app.

7. Force the requirement to enter a password when you resume from sleep/hibernate mode.

8. Set a custom logon screen background wallpaper.

9. Show a custom message to users attempting log on.

10. Set Minimized as the default mode for the File Explorer ribbon.

11. Enable the sideloading of apps in Windows 8 or later.

12. Prevent deleting of download history for Microsoft Edge and Internet Explorer.

Must-know GPO tweaks for Office applications:

1. Allow or block access to the Office Store.

2. Specify Microsoft telemetry settings for Office.

3. Force Outlook to be your default app for e-mail, calendar, and contacts.

4. Disable all application add-ins in Office.

5. Assign your choice of shortcut key to open the Menu or Help in Excel.

Popular GPO Tweaks for Windows

In this section, we are going to unpack some very popular and often configured GPOs for your Windows devices. They can be used to customize your user experience, enhance device security, and increase productivity while working.

Customizing the Way You Receive Windows Updates in Windows 10

If you are using Windows 10, you might have noticed that you can no longer prevent Windows Updates, even if you do not want them (although corporate editions, such as the Enterprise SKU, allow administrators to use WSUS to receive, approve, and publish Windows updates manually). In earlier editions of Windows, you were able to entirely prevent Windows from checking with the Windows Update site. This was achieved by configuring settings in the Control Panel. Additional options available included the ability to prevent Windows from downloading and installing Windows Updates.

With Windows 10 this is no longer the case. Windows Updates settings are no longer available within the Control Panel; they have been moved to the **Settings app**. The settings available for Windows Updates in this app prevent you from disabling updates. This behavior is designed to ensure that the Windows 10 installation remains in the most secure state and that users are kept safe from malware.

If you use a version of Windows prior to Windows 10, you can use either the Control Panel or Group Policy to prevent Windows Updates from being detected and installed automatically on your machine.

A GPO can be used to enforce the update behavior that you want to achieve. To see how this can be done, open Group Policy and navigate to Computer Configuration ➤ Policies ➤ Administrative Templates ➤ Windows Components ➤ Windows Update (in GPMC) or Computer Configuration ➤ Administrative Templates ➤ Windows Components ➤ Windows Update (in LGPO).

Locate the *Configure Automatic Updates* policy, as shown in Figure 7-1, and double click it.

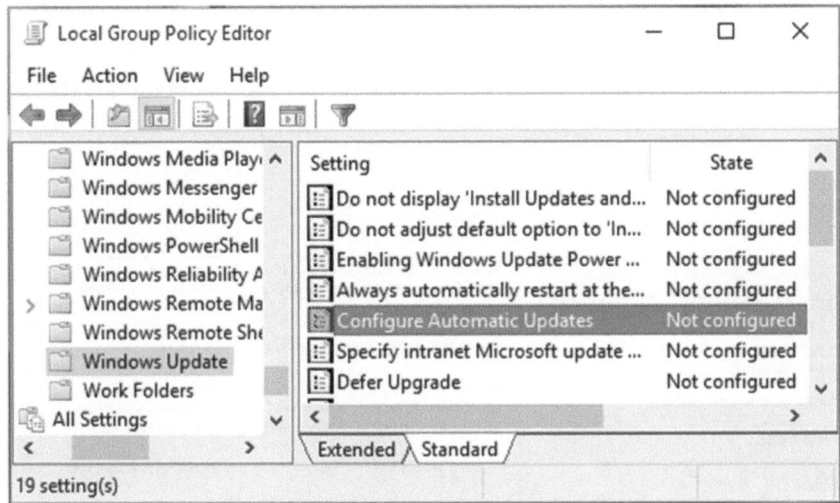

Figure 7-1. *Locating the Configuring Automatic Updates setting in a GPO*

Once you have opened the policy, as shown in Figure 7-2, set the policy to **Enabled** and choose the **2 = Notify for download and notify for install** option within the *Configure automatic updating* section. You can also modify the schedule of updates from within this window. Click **OK**.

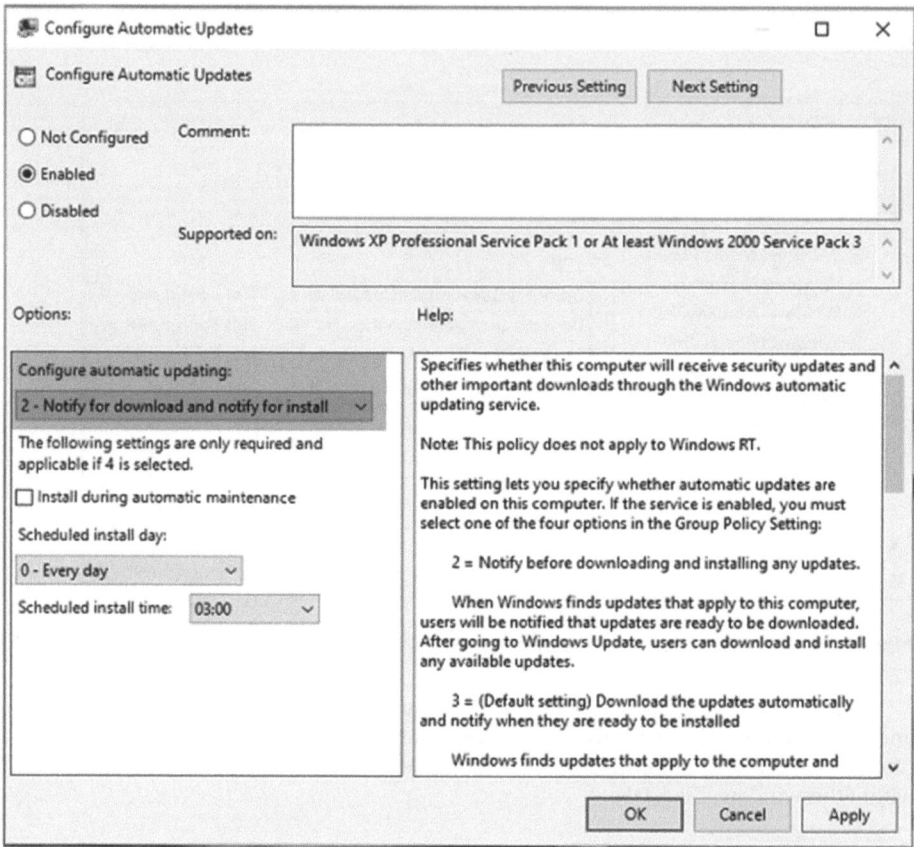

Figure 7-2. *The Configuring Automatic Updates policy configuration window*

In order to make the setting effective, you must reboot the machine. This action is applicable whether you are applying it for a local computer or in a domain environment. In practice, we have seen that some systems may take few reboots to make this policy effective. When the policy is in operation, you will find that Windows Updates now detects automatically, as normal, but Windows 10 will notify you to download and install (as shown in Figure 7-3). The updates will now install only when you wish them to be installed. However, we strongly recommended that you install the latest updates that are available to you in order to be safe and secure.

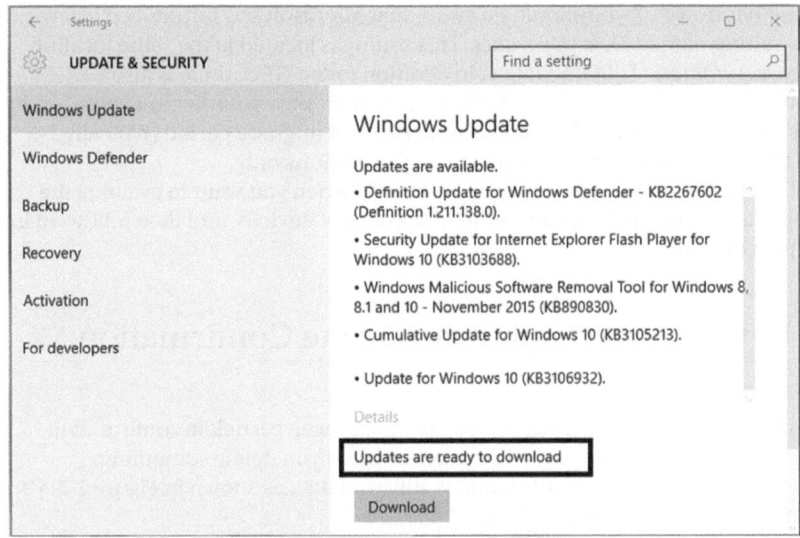

Figure 7-3. *Windows Updates notifies you before download in the Settings app*

It is best practice to leave Windows Updates turned on, unless absolutely necessary.

You can also treat the Configure Automatic Updates policy as a way to force users to use the Windows Update settings that you want for them. You should configure the GPO in the computer section; this way users won't be able to modify the Windows Updates settings manually. They will see the statement that "Some settings are managed by your organization," as shown in Figure 7-4.

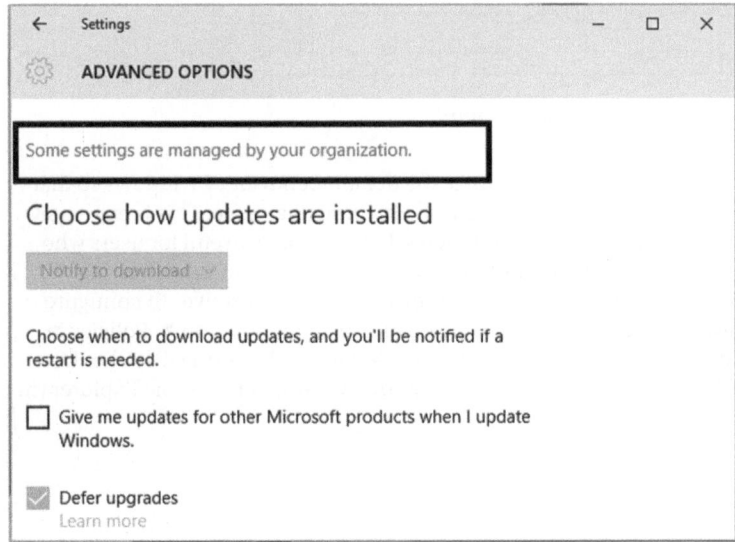

Figure 7-4. *Windows Updates setting to preventing user configuration*

Regarding Windows 10, you should be aware that Microsoft has introduced a new Group Policy setting named *Defer Upgrades*. This setting is located at the same location as the *Configure Automatic Updates* policy. In addition to the GPO, there is also a GUI configuration option, which is found in the *Settings app*, as shown earlier in Figure 7-4. By enabling this policy, you can defer upgrades until the next upgrade period (typically 2-3 months); this is valid for Windows Enterprise and Pro editions only.

The ability to defer upgrades is particularly helpful when you want to evaluate the Windows upgrades by testing them on a limited number of devices, and then follow up in a phased roll out or pilot.

Forcing Windows to Display the Delete Confirmation Prompt

On Windows 8 or later operating systems, you no longer receive a delete confirmation prompt, asking you to move a file to the Recycle Bin, when you delete something. However, the ability to receive a confirmation is still available, as shown in Figure 7-5; you just need to enable it with the correct GPO.

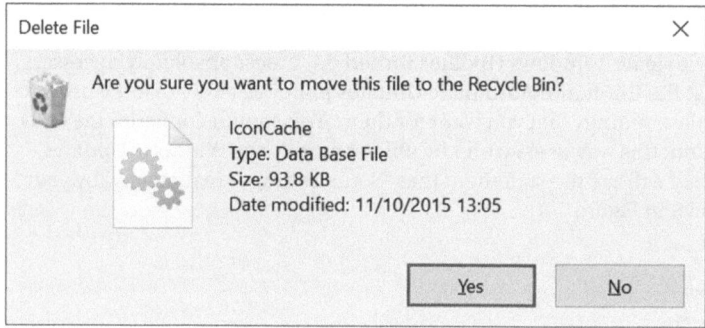

Figure 7-5. *Delete confirmation dialog/prompt*

With the help of GPOs, you can customize the default behavior of Windows so that it looks for your confirmation when you delete an object such as a file. This is extremely useful for users who are not proficient in Windows. It is especially useful for users who have upgraded from Windows XP or Windows 7, as it may help them from deleting files accidentally. We often ask our helpdesk if they want this GPO active. To configure this policy, open Group Policy editor and navigate to User Configuration ➤ Policies ➤ Administrative Templates ➤ Windows Components ➤ File Explorer (in GPMC) or User Configuration ➤ Administrative Templates ➤ Windows Components ➤ File Explorer (in LGPO).

In the left pane, locate the *Display confirmation dialog when deleting files* policy
setting, as shown in Figure 7-6.

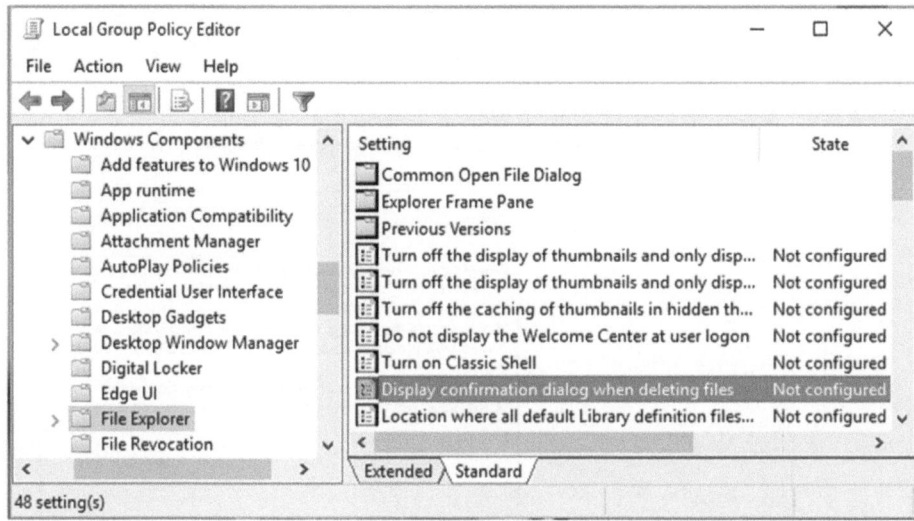

Figure 7-6. *Locating the Display confirmation dialog when deleting files setting in a GPO*

As with all GPOs, there is useful help text displayed in the GPO. As a best practice,
you should refer to the help text that is available to ensure that the correct setting is
applied. To apply this GPO, set the policy to **Enabled** (as shown in Figure 7-7); once
configured, users will receive the delete confirmation prompt.

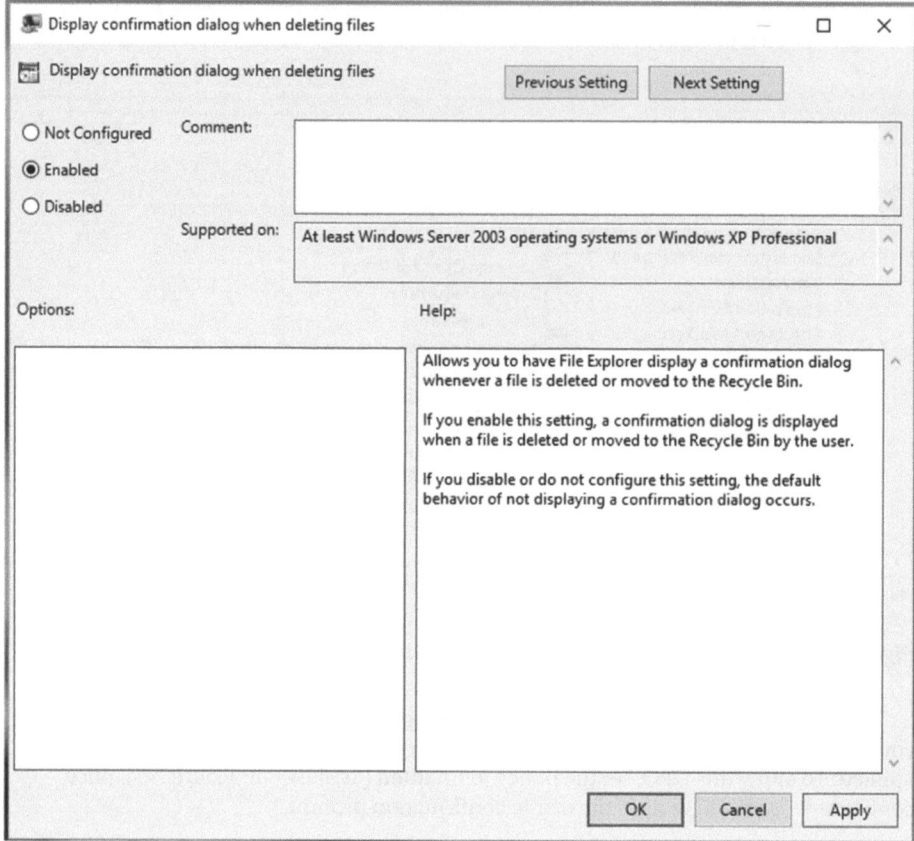

Figure 7-7. Configuring the Display confirmation dialog when deleting files setting in a GPO

Renaming the Administrator Account

We think that this is one of the best security policy settings you can configure. By default, the built-in administrator account name is called *Administrator*. The Administrator account is associated with a specific security identifier (SID) key. Windows will verify that the SID that is associated with the built-in Admin account. This policy setting can be configured in the *Security Policy snap-in* (**secpol.msc**). It is located at Security Settings ➤ Local Policies ➤ Security Options.

In the policy setting window shown in Figure 7-8, you can type your desired name by replacing *Administrator*. By doing so, you can enhance your Windows system security and prevent hackers from searching out your default Administrative account on your PC. You will need to reboot the machine to make this change effective.

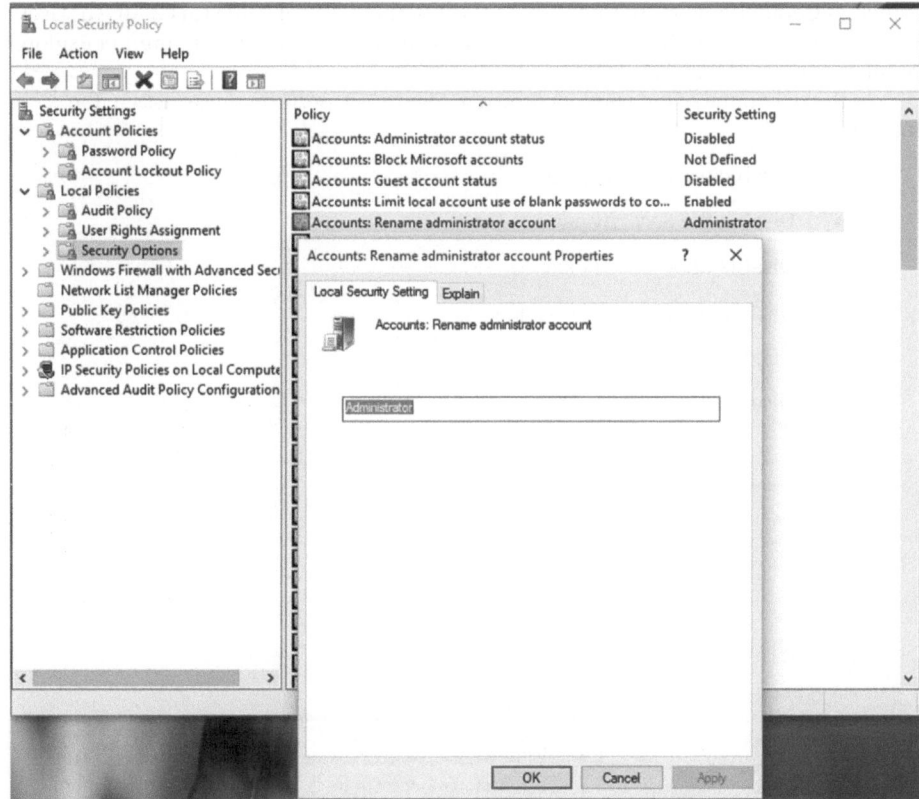

Figure 7-8. *Renaming the Administrator account*

■ **Note**   Renaming the Administrator account should be done only when it is badly required. Sometimes it may cause breaking of services, or result in losing the ability to install or use programs. Hence, be careful when renaming the Admin account.

Restricting a Particular Tab in the Internet Properties Window

The *Internet Properties (inetcpl.cpl)* window in the Control Panel helps you to manage a broad number of settings. Using this dialog box, you can create or edit many settings, as well as manage connections, browsing with Internet Explorer, and security certificates for web sites. You can also allow or prevent features like GPU rendering, etc.

When you need to disable a specific tab within *Internet Properties* for a user or computer, you can use Group Policy to restrict access to one or more of the tabs. In the GPO snap-in, navigate to User Configuration ➤ Policies ➤ Administrative Templates ➤

Windows Components ➤ Internet Explorer ➤ Internet Control Panel (in GPMC) or User Configuration ➤ Administrative Templates ➤ Windows Components ➤ Internet Explorer ➤ Internet Control Panel (in LGPO).

In the right pane of the window shown in Figure 7-9, perform these tasks to the following policies:

- Disable the *General* page

- Disable the *Security* page

- Disable the *Content* page

- Disable the *Connections* page

- Disable the *Programs* page

- Disable the *Advanced* page

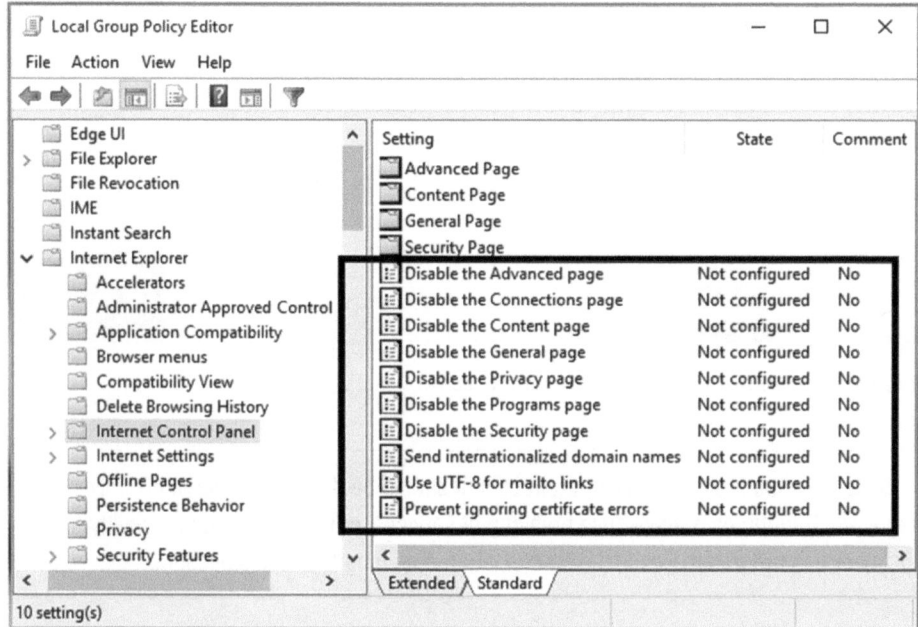

Figure 7-9. *Internet Control Panel policies*

There are policy settings for each tab of the Internet Properties dialog box. When any of these policies are set to **Enabled**, your users will not be able to see the corresponding tab when they open the Internet Properties dialog box, as illustrated in Figure 7-10.

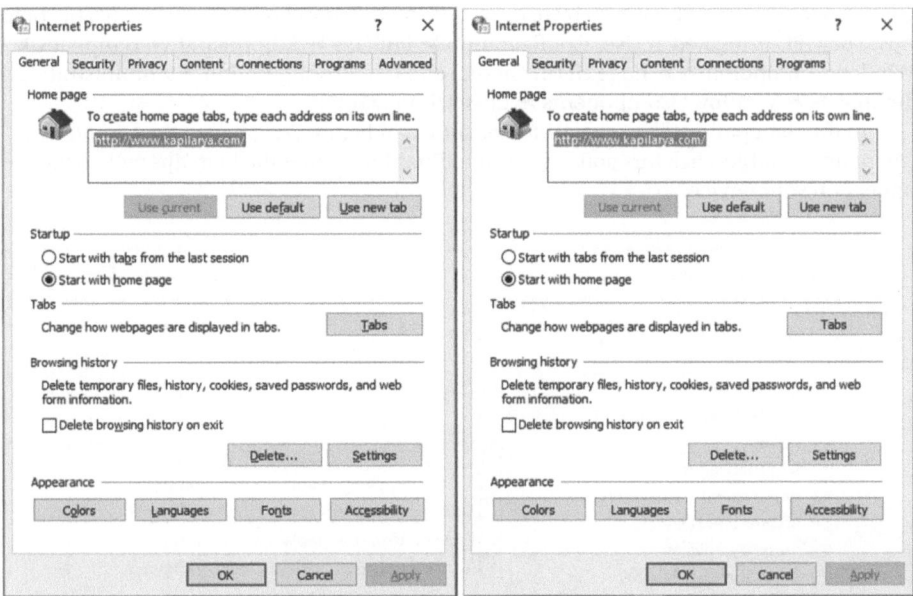

Default (All policies disabled)   Modified (Advanced page policy *Enabled*)

Figure 7-10. *Advanced tab page missing from Internet Property sheet*

Disabling Help Tips in Windows 8.1

During the initial weeks of new ownership, many Windows 8.1 users reported irritation with the Windows feature called *help tips,* shown in Figure 7-11. Microsoft implemented this feature so that new users could discover the new features of Windows 8.1 and get tips on how to use them, such as how to use charms. Many power users didn't find the tips useful; also the tip notification popped up often and became very distracting.

Figure 7-11. *Help tip in Windows 8.1*

This problem can be solved by using a dedicated Group Policy setting to disable help tips. The GPO is located at User Configuration ➤ Policies ➤ Administrative Templates ➤ Windows Components ➤ Edge UI (in GPMC) and User Configuration ➤ Administrative Templates ➤ Windows Components ➤ Edge UI (in LGPO).

In the right pane of the Edge UI folder shown in Figure 7-12, locate the *Disable help tips* policy. Double-click this policy to set it to **Enabled** so that the help tips will no longer appear on your device.

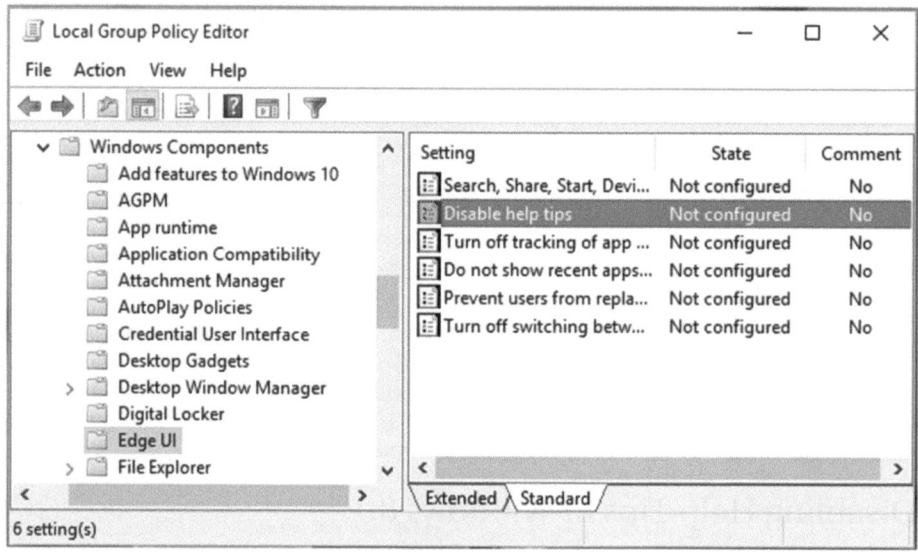

Figure 7-12. *Locating the Disable help tips policy*

Disabling Access to the Control Panel and Settings App

The Control Panel, as we all know, is the popular location for managing settings in Windows. With the release of Windows 10, Microsoft has shifted and even duplicated many of the options found in the Control Panel to a new Settings app. For the time being, the Control Panel will still offer the same functionality as it did in previous versions of Windows, and for many people this will be the default location for Windows settings.

You can modify access to the Control Panel and the Settings app feature by using Group Policy as required. The relevant policy setting can be found at following path and can be seen in Figure 7-13: User Configuration ➤ Policies ➤ Administrative Templates ➤ Control Panel (in GPMC) and User Configuration ➤ Administrative Templates ➤ Control Panel(in LGPO).

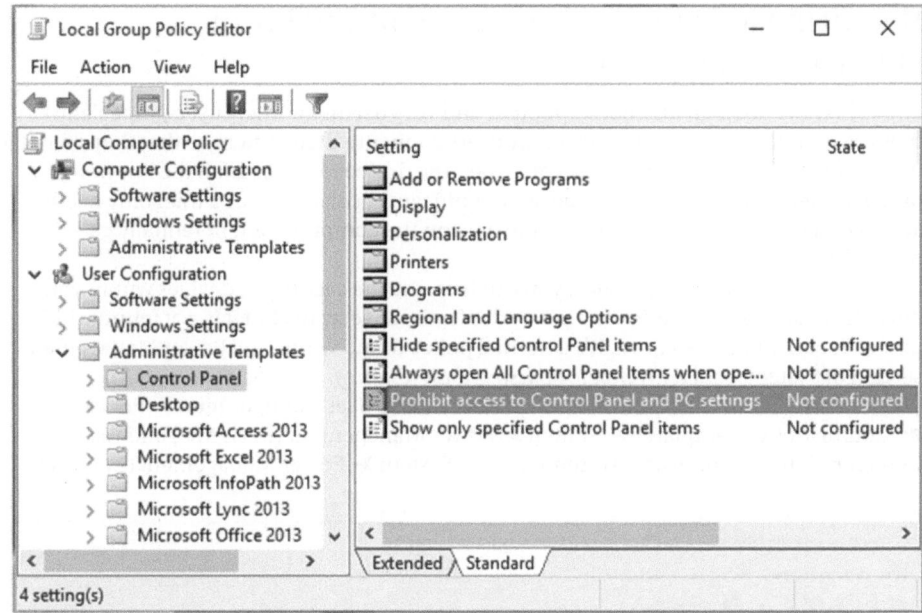

Figure 7-13. *Locating the Prohibit access to Control Panel and PC Settings policy*

In the right pane of the Control Panel folder, locate the *Prohibit access to Control Panel and PC Settings* policy and set it to **Enabled**. Before configuring this GPO, you should ensure that the Control Panel and the PC Settings app are not open. The policy takes effect immediately after you configure it; it doesn't require a reboot to become effective. When the GPO is set to Enabled, and if any user tries to open the Control Panel or the Settings app, they will receive the error message shown in Figure 7-14.

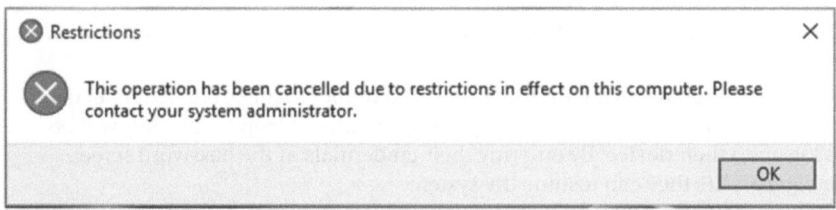

Figure 7-14. *Error when accessing Control Panel*

Rather than turning the feature access on or off, you will see from Figure 7-13 that you can also configure a GPO to restrict individual items within the Control Panel .

Requiring a Password When Resuming From Hibernate/Sleep Mode

The Hibernate or Sleep function is popular and very useful for many users, especially if they are mobile workers. However, many users configure their system so that they do not need to enter their username/password when the device resumes from the low power or hibernated state. This scenario poses a significant security risk, as a thief only needs access to the device to gain control of the data on the computer and potentially gain network access.

With the help of Group Policy, you can increase the security of devices within your environment. You can configure a policy dedicated to security, but it is not found within a part of Security Policy snap-in. It's a normal policy found within the Power Management section of System, called *Prompt for password on resume from hibernate/suspend* (as shown in Figure 7-15). The full path to this GPO is User Configuration ➤ Policies ➤ Administrative Templates ➤ System ➤ Power Management (in GPMC) and User Configuration ➤ Administrative Templates ➤ System ➤ Power Management (in LGPO).

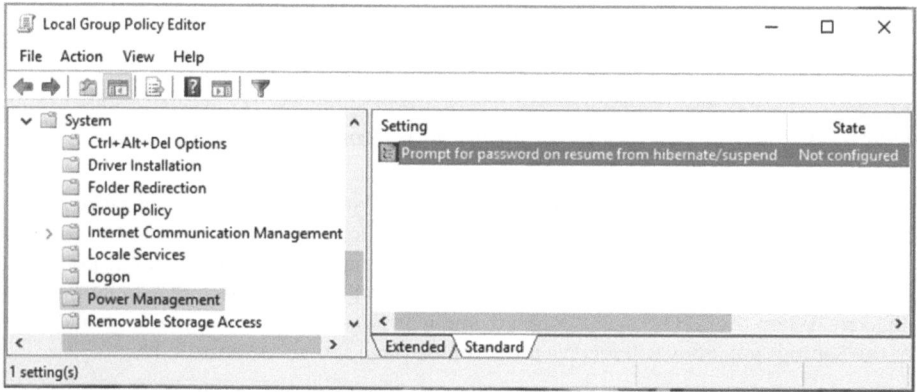

***Figure 7-15.** Locating the Prompt for password on resume from hibernate/suspend setting*

You can set this policy to the **Enabled** state and reboot to make changes effective. Now when users resume their machine from Hibernation or Sleep mode, they will be forced to log on to their device. By entering their credentials in the password screen shown in Figure 7-16, they can resume the system.

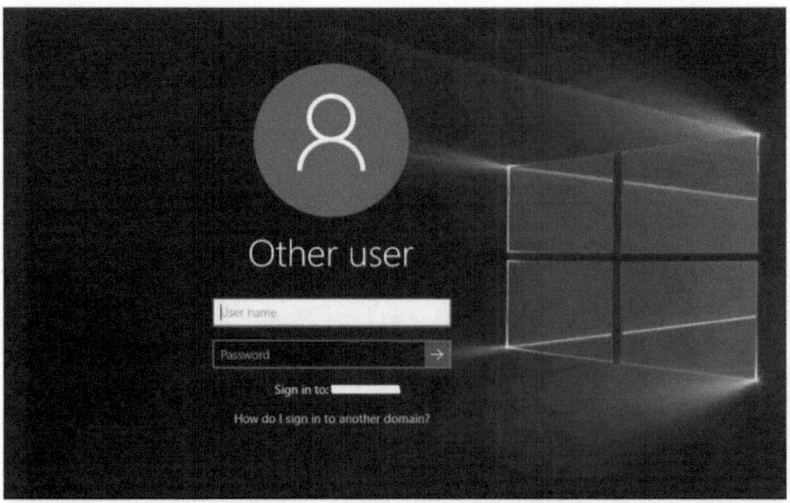

Figure 7-16. *Prompt for password on resuming from hibernate/suspend*

Setting Custom Logon Screen Background Wallpaper

With the help of this Group Policy tweak, you will be able to replace your wallpaper from the current default logon screen background wallpaper to a choice of wallpaper of your own. All you need to do is to configure the *Always use Custom logon background wallpaper* (as shown in Figure 7-17) setting and set it to **Enabled**. The policy can be found at Computer Configuration ➤ Policies ➤ Administrative Templates ➤ System ➤ Logon (in GPMC) and Computer Configuration ➤ Administrative Templates ➤ System ➤ Logon (in LGPO).

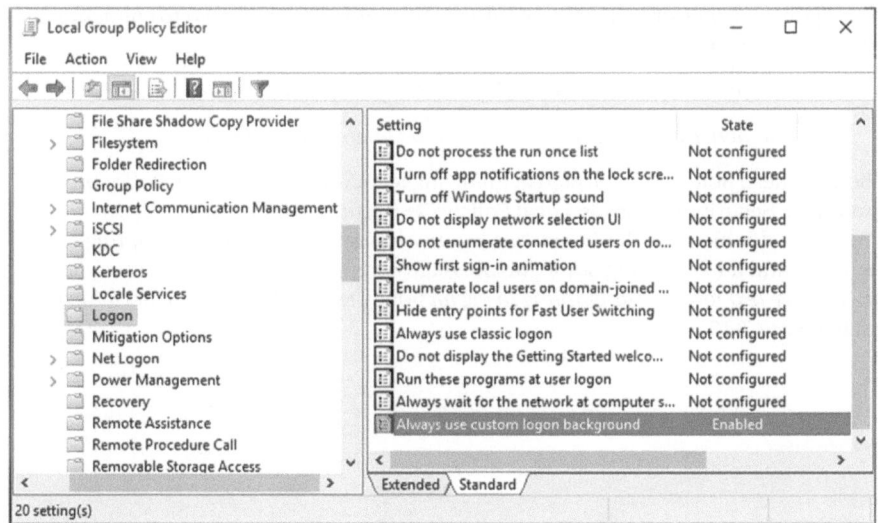

Figure 7-17. *Always use the custom logon background policy*

The next step is to let Windows see if there is a custom wallpaper present in the default custom folder (C:\Windows\System32\oobe\info\backgrounds).

You will find that under the oobe folder, there is no info folder. Simply create a new folder and name it info and add a backgrounds subfolder. Into the backgrounds folder you should put your custom background image. The change should take effect immediately. The next time you log on/off your machine, your logon background should change to your custom background image, as shown in Figure 7-18.

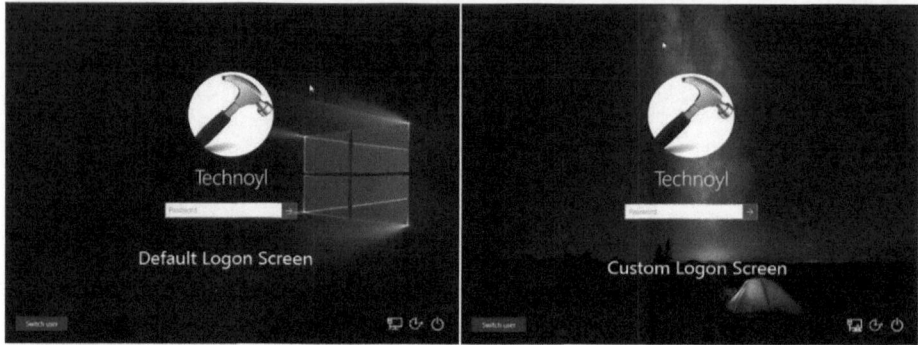

Figure 7-18. *Default and custom logon screen in Windows 10*

Displaying a Custom Message to Users During Attempted Logon

When a user is presented with the device logon screen and attempts to sign in, you can allow Windows to display a custom text message to him/her. This message could be a company policy or rule, or a tip or warning, etc. To enable this, you need to configure one or both of the following security policies:

- *Interactive logon: Message title for users attempting to log on*

- *Interactive logon: Message text for users attempting to log on*

Both of these policies are located at following location in the *Security Policy snap-in* (**secpol.msc**): Security Settings ➤ Local Policies ➤ Security Options.

You must double-click the *Interactive logon: Message title for users attempting to log on* policy and add a title to your logon message and then double-click the *Interactive logon: Message text for users attempting to log on* policy to add the message body/text, as shown in Figure 7-19.

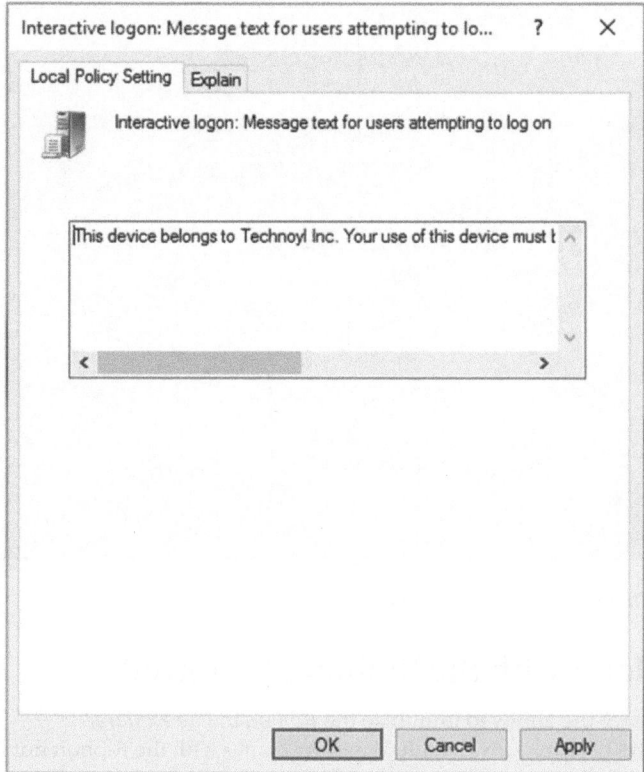

Figure 7-19. *The Interactive logon: Message text for users attempting to log on policy configuration window*

Once you have configured both of these the policies, you can log out. On the logon screen, you will see the custom sign-in message shown in Figure 7-20.

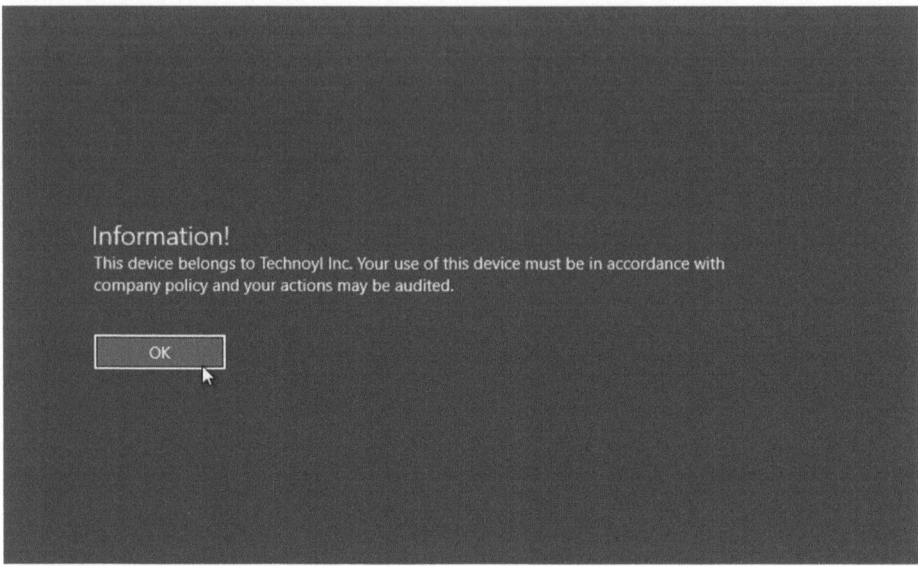

Figure 7-20. *Custom sign-in message at logon screen*

Opening File Explorer with the Ribbon Minimized

In Windows 8 or later, you have the ability to minimize the *Ribbon* in *File Explorer* (formerly known as Windows Explorer). By default, Windows comes with the Ribbon not minimized. Using the Group Policy, you can set your preferences for this option so that client machines will see the Ribbon minimized when they open File Explorer. This policy should only be configured for proficient users because some users may not be able to find the Ribbon manually. In Figure 7-21, File Explorer is shown with and without the Ribbon for comparison.

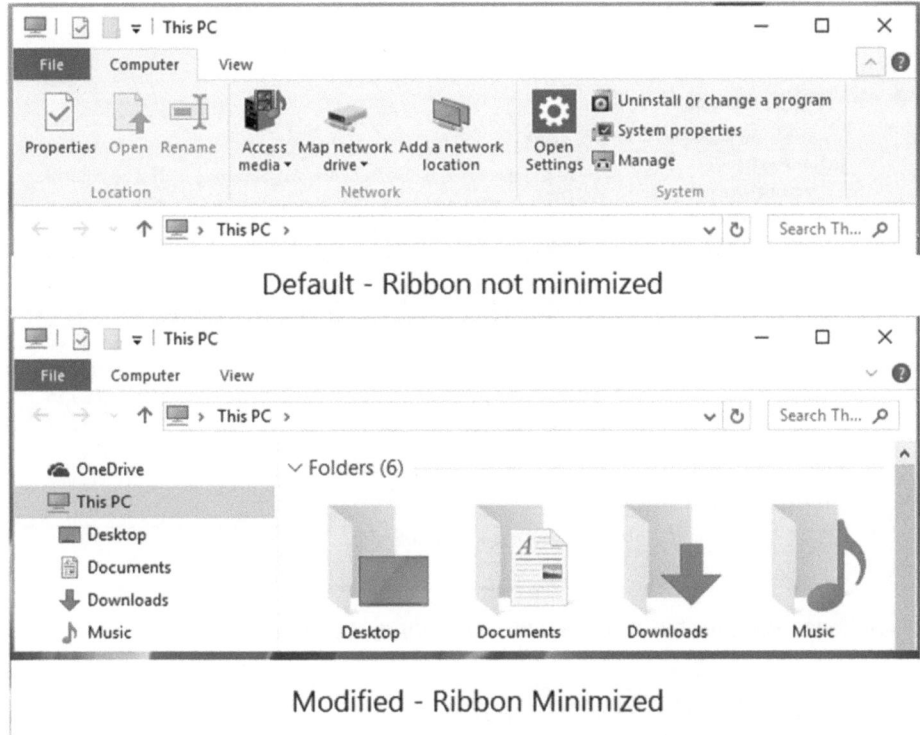

Figure 7-21. *File Explorer with Ribbon not minimized and minimized*

To accomplish this configuration, navigate to the following location in the GP Editor: User Configuration ➤ Policies ➤ Administrative Templates ➤ Windows Components ➤ File Explorer (in GPMC) and User Configuration ➤ Administrative Templates ➤ Windows Components ➤ File Explorer (in LGPO).

In the right pane of File Explorer (shown in Figure 7-22), find the GPO setting named *Start File Explorer with ribbon minimized,* which should be set to **Not Configured** status by default. Double-click the policy and set it to **Enabled** status. Click **Apply**, followed by **OK**. You may need to reboot to make the changes effective.

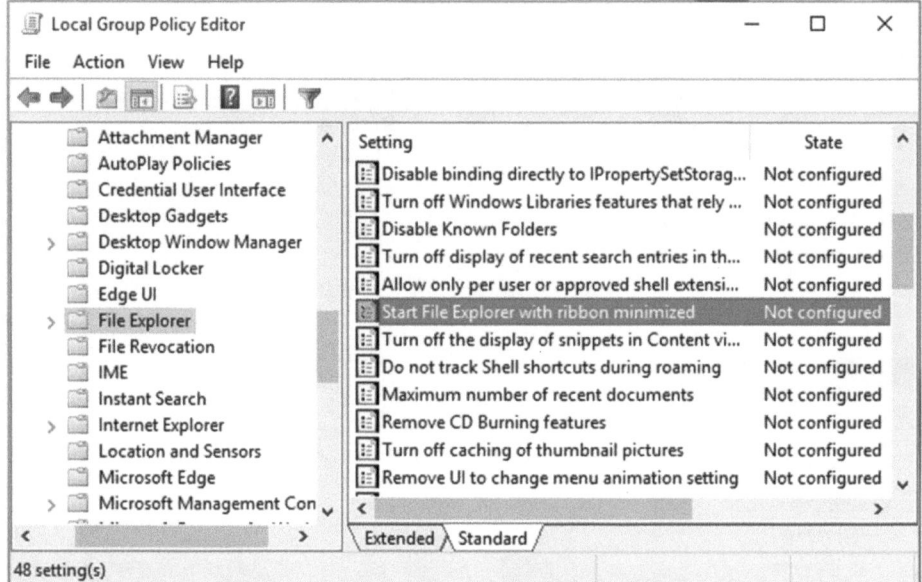

Figure 7-22. *The Start File Explorer with ribbon minimized policy*

Enabling Sideloading of Apps

Sideloading allows administrators to install their own corporate line of business (LOB) apps, similar to those found in the Microsoft Store apps, without first needing to publish them to the Company or Microsoft Store and then downloading them individually. With Windows 8 or later, which support Modern or Universal Apps, you must first configure the GPO setting named *Allow all trusted apps to install* so that you can sideload applications, as shown in Figure 7-23.

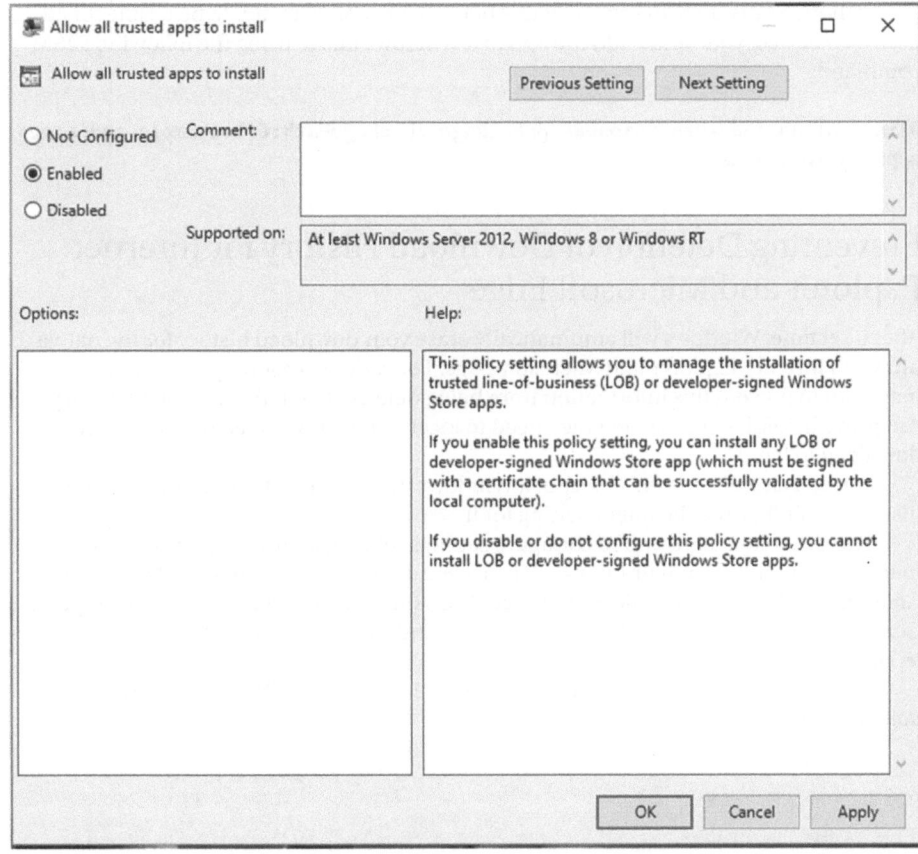

Figure 7-23. *The Allow all trusted apps to install policy configuration*

The setting is available at Computer Configuration ➤ Policies ➤ Administrative Templates ➤ System ➤ Logon (in GPMC) and Computer Configuration ➤ Administrative Templates ➤ System ➤ Logon (in LGPO).

A valid certificate, derived from a trusted root certificate, is also required to be installed on the device, prior to being able to sideload the apps on your machine. If you are considering testing sideloading, your app developer can obtain a temporary (30 day) developer license from Microsoft. Once you have configured the GPO setting and installed the certificate, you should be ready to sideload apps.

Sideloading is achieved by using PowerShell. Enter the following command in an administrative *Windows PowerShell* console to sideload an app onto your device:

```
Add-AppxPackage C:\<example app name>.appx
```

The app will then be installed and ready for testing. To remove any sideloaded app, right-click the app and click **Uninstall** and confirm your actions.

Although outside of the scope of this book, to provision an app to be usable for all users of a device, you would add the app to a Windows image using the following DISM command:

```
DISM /Online /Add-ProvisionedAppxPackage /PackagePath:C:\<example app name>.
appx /skiplicense
```

Preventing Deletion of Download History for Internet Explorer and Microsoft Edge

After a set time, Windows will automatically erase your download history for the native browsers Internet Explorer and Microsoft Edge. For various reasons, you or your users may want to prevent this information from being deleted. Often the download history can prove helpful to users when they need to locate a recently visited web site or track a downloaded file.

You can also disable the ability of a Windows device to delete your downloading history by configuring the policy setting for it.

The GPOs that allow you to configure settings relating to browsing history are found at Computer Configuration ➤ Policies ➤ Administrative Templates ➤ Windows Components ➤ Internet Explorer ➤ Delete Browsing History (in GPMC) and Computer Configuration ➤ Administrative Templates ➤ Windows Components ➤ Internet Explorer ➤ Delete Browsing History (in LGPO).

You configure the setting shown in Figure 7-24, which is called *Prevent deleting download history*.

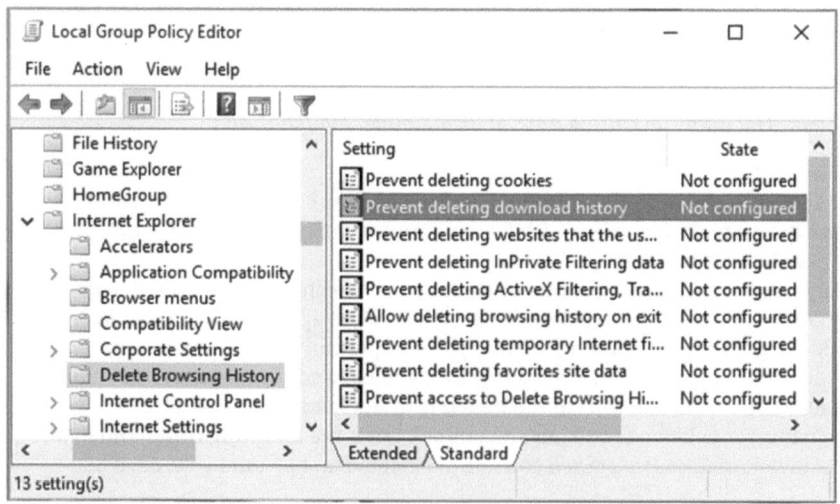

Figure 7-24. *The Prevent deleting download history policy*

Once the policy is set to **Enabled**, your downloading history will not be deleted automatically.

■ **Tip** You can also prevent deleting of cookies and your site favorites and other settings for IE and Edge under the *Delete Browsing History* node of the GPO snap-in.

Useful Tweaks for Office Apps

Microsoft Office can increase the productivity of Windows users. In this section, we will share with you the most commonly configured Office application Group Policy settings. In order to configure these settings, you must first install the Office-based Administrative Templates relating to the version of Office that you are administering, into the GPO editor as described in Chapter 4.

Allowing or Blocking Access to the Office Store

Microsoft Office can be extremely extensible by allowing users to access and utilize the diversity of add-ins that are available via the Office Store, as shown in Figure 7-25.

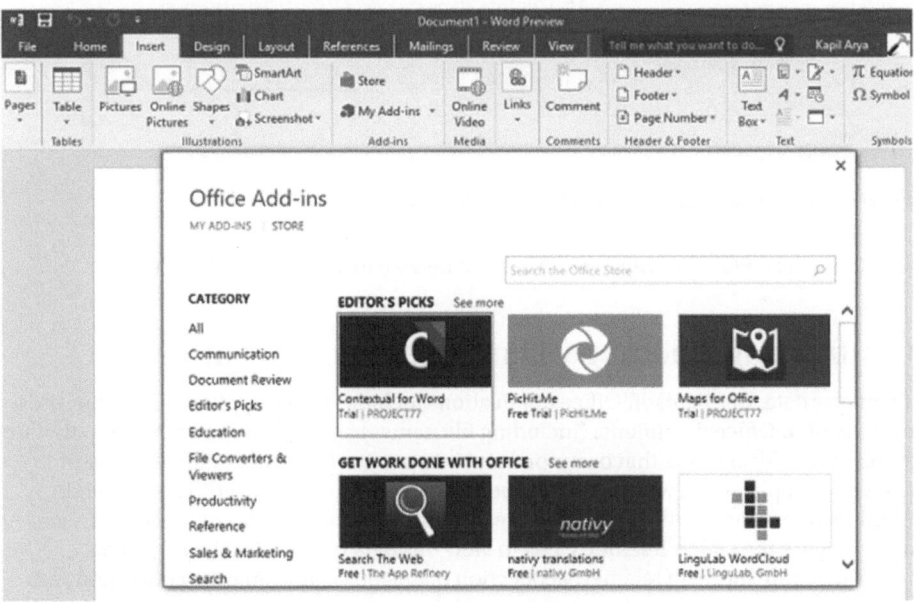

Figure 7-25. *Office Store feature snapshot on Word 2016*

Your users may find that their capabilities and productivity while using Office 2013 or above increases greatly when they are exposed to these extra tools and add-ins. The add-ins can be directly installed from Office Store across all Office apps.

You can use Group Policy to block or allow usage of the Office Store in your organization, which can enable or disable the ability for users to install add-ins. The dedicated policy setting, shown in Figure 7-26, is *Block the Office Store* and it is available under User Configuration ➤ Policies ➤ Administrative Templates ➤ Microsoft Office (Edition) ➤ Security Settings ➤ Trust Center ➤ Trusted Catalogs (in GPMC) or User Configuration ➤ Administrative Templates ➤ Microsoft Office (Edition) ➤ Security Settings ➤ Trust Center ➤ Trusted Catalogs (in LGPO).

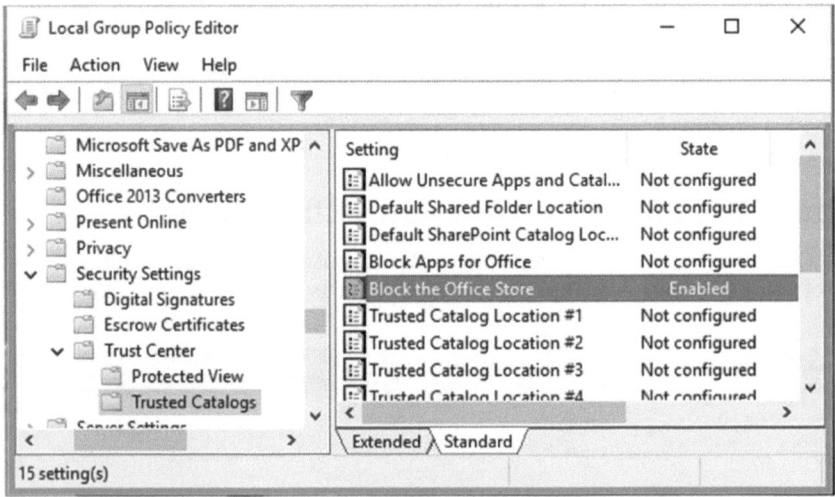

Figure 7-26. *Locating the Block the Office Store policy in LGPO*

Once the GPO is **Enabled**, users will not be able to access the Office Store.

Configuring Telemetry Data Collection in Office

Telemetry data for Microsoft Office applications includes Office applications usage, most recently used Office documents (including file names) and solutions usage, compatibility issues, and critical errors that occur on local computers. The Office Telemetry Agent and Office applications will collect telemetry data if the telemetry setting is enabled. Administrators can use the Office Telemetry Dashboard to view this data remotely, and users can use the Office Telemetry Log to view this data on their local computers.

If users are aware of telemetry collection taking place, they may be concerned with the privacy of sharing this telemetry data. This concern is justified because telemetry data may share filenames from your documents, which can be regarded as sensitive or private. If you want to disable telemetry data collection, you must configure the relevant GPO, shown in Figure 7-27 and located at User Configuration ➤ Policies ➤ Administrative Templates ➤ Microsoft Office (Edition) ➤ Security Settings ➤ Trust Center ➤ Trusted

Catalogs (in GPMC) or User Configuration ➤ Administrative Templates ➤ Microsoft Office (Edition) ➤ Security Settings ➤ Trust Center ➤ Trusted Catalogs (in LGPO).

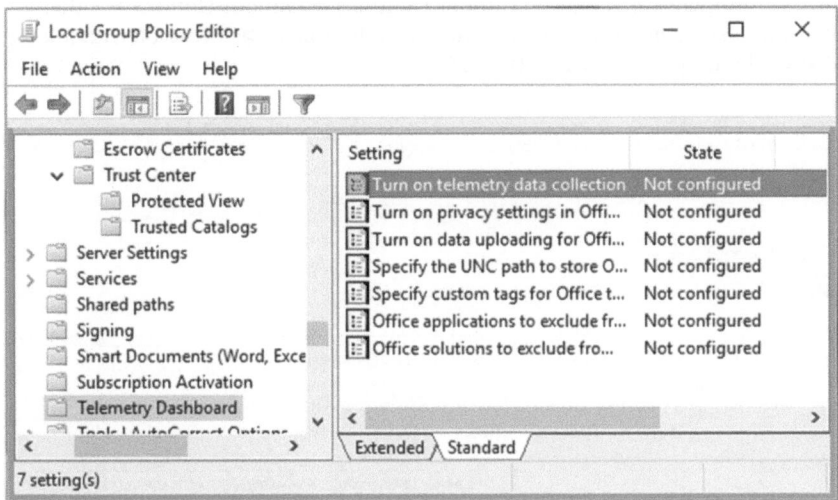

Figure 7-27. *Locating the Turn on telemetry data collection policy*

In the right pane if the Telemetry Dashboard folder, locate the *Turn on telemetry data collection* policy and set it to **Disabled**. Close the GPO editor and reboot the machine to make the changes effective.

You may also want to configure the *Turn on privacy settings in Office Telemetry Agent* policy located at same node. By configuring this setting, you can configure the Office Telemetry Agent to disguise, or obfuscate, certain file properties that are reported in the telemetry data.

■ **Info**   To explore more about telemetry, interested readers can go to the following page at the TechNet Library: https://technet.microsoft.com/en-us/library/jj863580. aspx.

Forcing Outlook to be the Default Program for E-Mail, Contacts, and Calendar

Sometimes administrators may want to force users to use Outlook as the default program for all e-mail and for managing contacts and calendar events. This can be useful to standardize training; it may also reduce support calls if users aren't allowed to use third-party software.

To force users to use Outlook as their primary communication application, you can configure the *Make Outlook the default program for E-mail, Contacts, and Calendar* Group Policy, shown in Figure 7-28 and located at User Configuration ➤ Policies ➤ Administrative Templates ➤ Microsoft Outlook (Edition) ➤ Outlook Options ➤ Other (in GPMC) and User Configuration ➤ Administrative Templates ➤ Microsoft Outlook (Edition) ➤ Outlook Options ➤ Other (in LGPO).

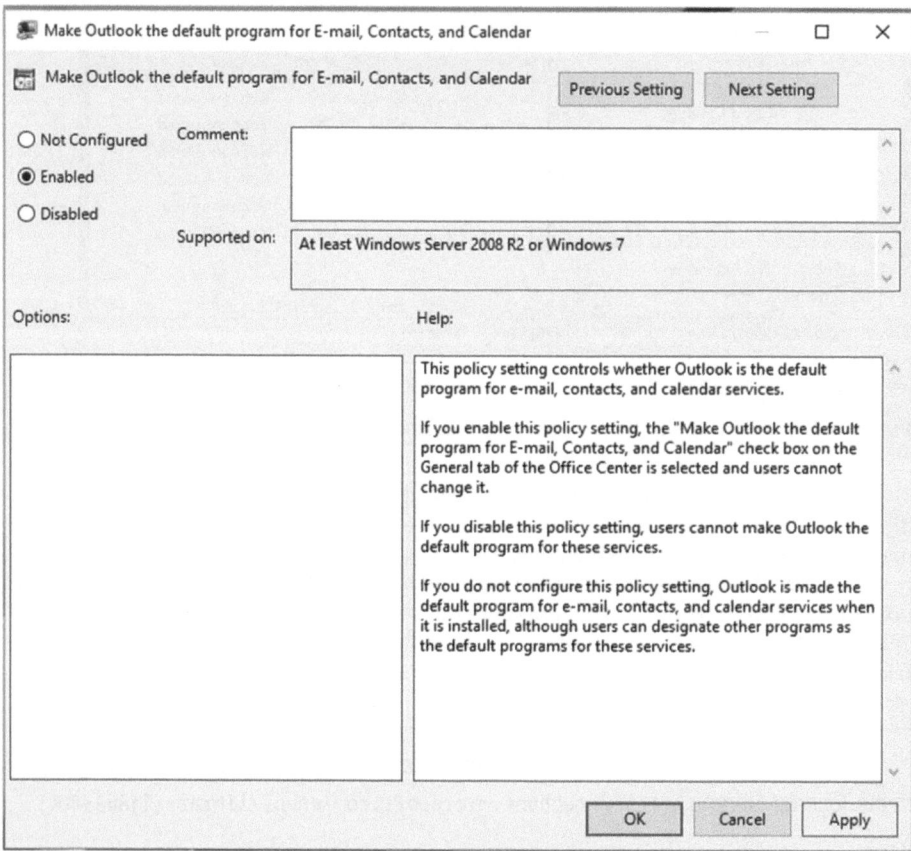

Figure 7-28. The Make Outlook the default program for E-mail, Contacts, and Calendar policy in GPO

When this policy is set to **Enabled**, users won't be able to select a different mail client program and Outlook will be set as the default program.

Disabling All Application Add-ins For Office

Add-ins are written by developers to extend Office application productivity and are then made available via the Office Store. Some add-ins are free to use, while others may incur a fee. Users may need to install a new add-in if they encounter a shortfall in the application or they need added functionality and that requirement can be fulfilled by available add-in. Example add-ins include the Wikipedia add-in, a Random Generator for Excel, or a Translator add-in.

Corporations will often prevent users from installing add-ins because a poorly written add-in may create problems for the user, and it can be easier when troubleshooting Office issues for a particular user if add-ins are blocked.

If you are looking to disable add-ins from being installed in your Office application, you can set the *Disable all application add-ins* policy setting to **Enabled**, as shown in Figure 7-29. The policy is available is available in the following locations: User Configuration ➤ Administrative Templates ➤ Microsoft <Application> (Edition) ➤ <Application> Options ➤ Security ➤ Trust Center (Options) (in GPMC) and User Configuration ➤ Administrative Templates ➤ Microsoft <Application> (Edition) ➤ <Application> Options ➤ Security ➤ Trust Center (Options) (in LGPO).

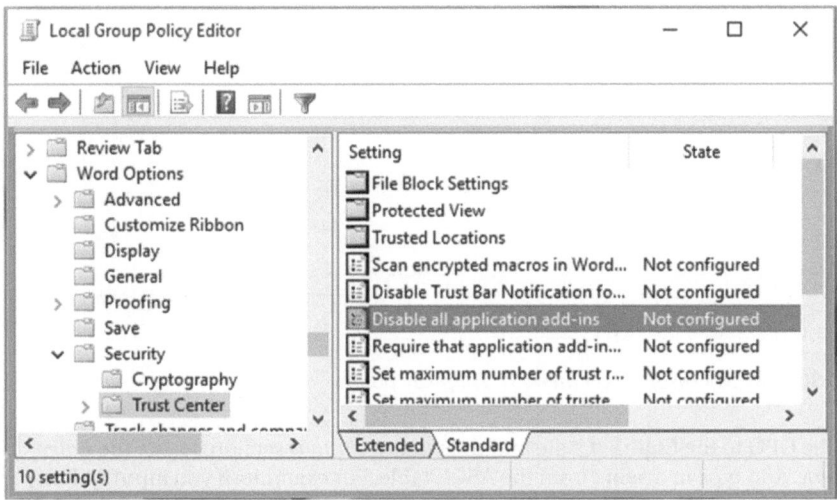

Figure 7-29. *The Disable all application add-ins policy in GPO*

After configuring the policy setting, you may need to reboot the machine in order to make the changes effective.

Assigning Your Choice of Key to Open Menus in Excel

Using this setting, you can assign your choice of a key to open the Excel menu or Help in Excel. This is useful in scenarios where the default F1 key is assigned to another task. The GPO for this is named *Microsoft Excel menu or Help key*, as shown in Figure 7-30, and it can be located at User Configuration ➤ Policies ➤ Administrative Templates ➤ Microsoft Excel (Edition) ➤ Excel Options ➤ Advanced (in GPMC) and User Configuration ➤ Administrative Templates ➤ Microsoft Excel (Edition) ➤ Excel Options ➤ Advanced (in LGPO).

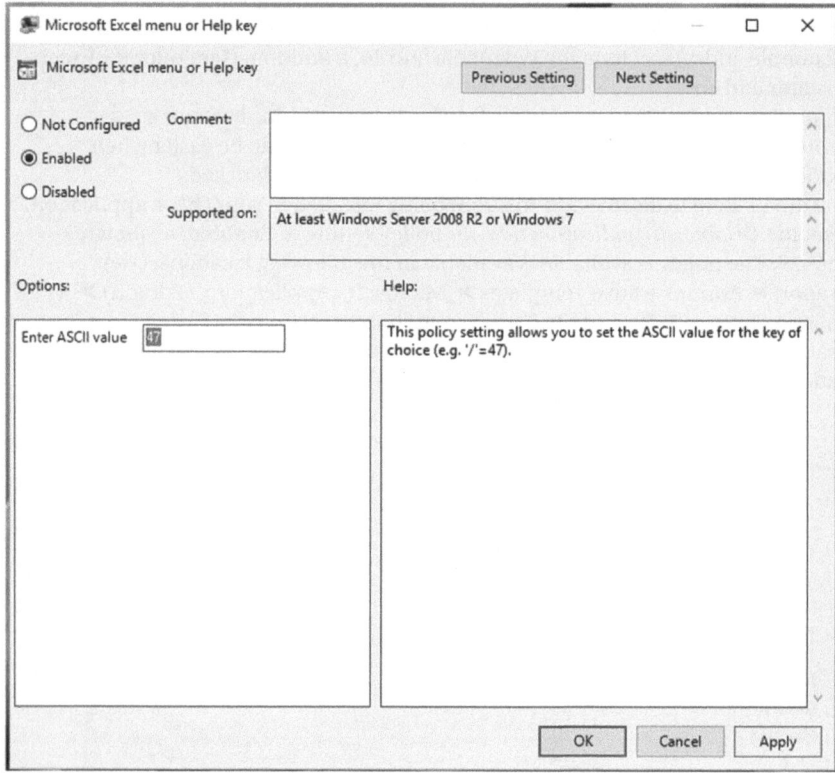

Figure 7-30. *The Microsoft Excel menu or Help key policy*

Set the GPO to the **Enabled** state and then in the *Options* section, locate the *Enter ASCII Value*, and type in a value from the ASCII table. For example, if you input 43 here, entering '+' as first character in a cell of a Microsoft Excel worksheet will bring up the menu or Help.

Key Points

- You can prevent automatic download of Windows Updates in Windows 10 using Group Policy.

- Renaming the Administrator account should be done carefully and only when it is required badly.

- You can use Group Policy to sideload apps or allow trusted apps to install in Windows.

- In your organization, you can provide custom messages to users attempting to log on, by configuring security policies.

- Telemetry data is collected to track applications usage and analysis performance. You can prevent the collecting of telemetry data at your end via Group Policy.

Summary

In this chapter, you learned various concepts about Group Policy settings that may be useful in your day-to-day work. Many times users want to configure Windows to work in the way they need, but the lack of manual settings makes this difficult, as you saw in the case of getting automatic updates, which can be prevented easily using GPO settings. A GPO has been always a beneficial way to enable/disable features, whether you are on a local machine or you are managing a corporate environment. We believe that, if properly used, Group Policy is something that can make your work easy, fast, and reliable. Hopefully, you enjoyed this book and found it useful!

Index

A

Active Directory, 1, 13
Active Directory Directory
        Services (AD DS), 8
Active Directory Domain Services, 36
Active Directory Objects (ADOs), 103
Add-ins, 205
Administrative command, 148
Administrative template
    admin and admx folders, 108
    customization, 112
    error, 110
    GPO-based, 108
    language-specific folders, 108
    license agreement, 108
    location, 109
    Microsoft Office, 107
    OfficeXX.admx, 106
    UAC permissions, 107
Administrative templates, 5, 163, 174
Administrator
    configuration window, 122
    error message, 120
    feature, 122–124
    LGPO, 121
    managed add-ins, 121
Administrator account, 186–187
Advanced Group Policy
        Management (AGPM)
    administrative privileges, 160
    changelog versions, 151
    client-side extensions, 163
    configuration, 153
    CSE components, 164
    Edit, Create,
        Delete/Modify GPOs, 157–158
    editing GPO, 155

GPOs deletion, 156
GPOs management, 151
installation, 153
notification mail, 161
offline tool, 162
port 4600, 161
power tools, 153
processing, 163–164
service settings, 158–159
Software Assurance licensing, 162
troubleshooting, 151, 162
AGPM Server tab, 154
Allowing/blocking access, 201–202
Animation, 80
Attempted Logon, 194–195
Auditing, 168
Auditing policies, 95, 97
Audit policies, 94
Autoplay, 86

B

Backup, 49–52

C

Calendar, 203–204
Client-side extensions (CSEs)
        processing, 8, 137, 163
Command line version, 136
Computer configuration, 4
Configure automatic updates, 182, 183
Confirmation dialog/prompt, 184–185
Contacts, 203–204
Control Panel, 190–191
Cookies, 6
Custom logon screen, 194

■ D

Delegation tab, 173
Deploying policies, 20–21
Desired state configuration (DSC), 29
DesktopStandard, 152
Display, 184–185
Domain Controller (DC), 12, 173
Domain Name System (DNS), 12
Domain user, 11
Dynamic Host Configuration
      Protocol (DHCP), 12

■ E

E-Mail, 203–204
Event Viewer, 132–133, 166
Excel menu, 205–206

■ F

F5 key, 156
File explorer, 196–197
Flow Chart Approach, 168–169
Folder redirection, 145, 174–175

■ G

Globally unique identifier (GUID), 14, 163
gpedit.msc, 5, 111
GPMC modeling
    DC selection screen, 55
    GPMC window, 53
    Loopback processing, 56
    production environment, 53
    report, 61
    scripts, 66
    security groups, 57
    Slow network connection, 56
    Wizard, 54
    WMI Filter, 58
gpmc.msc command, 39, 74
GPOs
    deletion, 48–49
    inheritance, 23–24
    link, 46, 48
    networking issues, 170–172
    processing issues, 170
    scoping issues, 172–173
    settings, 144–145
    structural issues, 173–174

    subset, 87–88, 90
    Tool.exe, 167, 169
    vault, 152
gpupdate /force, 111
gpupdate /force command, 75, 170
Group Policy
    administrators, 1
    command prompt, 8
    computer-specific settings, 1
    configurations, 2
    connection
        account type, 10
        communication, 12
        computer account, 13
        computer boot-up process, 12
        computer object, 12
        DNS database, 12
        domain, 13
        domain credentials, 9
        domain-joined workstation, 12
        domain, tree, and forest, 13
        vs. DSC, 29
        hierarchical structure, 14
        IP address, 12
        (OU), 13
        registry configuration, 14
        restart, 11
        site, 13
        third-party security, 146
        user account, 14
        Windows 10 machine, 9
        workstation to AD, 12
    copying, 25–26
    deploying policies, 20
    enforcing, 24–25
    gpedit.msc, 8
    importing, 26
    Microsoft Office, 21–22
    mirror images, 2
    permissions, 30
    security and networking, 1
    security templates, 19
    software, 1
    Windows administration, 71
Group PolicyWindows
Group Policy deploying policies, 21
Group Policy Management
      Console (GPMC), 2, 4, 167
    backup, 49–52
    configuration, 31
    creation and edition, GPO, 43–46

deployment, 31
GPO link, 46, 48
GPO settings, 31
logging, 66
report, 62
user/computer, 65
user selection screen, 64
Windows Server, 31
wizard, 62
Group Policy Management Tools, 41
Group Policy Object (GPO)
command prompt, 3
configuration, 4–7
gpedit.msc command, 2, 3
system root drive, 3
Group Policy Service (GPSVC), 147
Group Policy tips
in Windows, 179

H

Hibernate/Sleep Mode, 192
HomeGroup, 85

I, J, K

Information Technology Infrastructure
Library (ITIL), 151
Installation, GPMC
client device, 32
command prompt, 42
configuration, 42–43
confirmation screen, 39
destination server, 34
domain environment, 36
feature-based installation, 33
role-based, 33
RSAT, 40
Server Manager Dashboard, 32
Wizard, 35
Internet Explorer, 200–201
Internet Properties, 187–189
Internet Protocol (IP), 12
IPSec protocol, 136
Issues/extension-based
problems, 175–176

L

Line of business (LOB), 198–200
Local audit policies, 94–95

Local Group Policy
Editor (LGPO), 3, 31, 74
Local users, 146
Logging, 168
Loopback processing, 143
lusrmgr.msc, 23

M

Microsoft Advanced Group Policy
Management - Server, 158
Microsoft Desktop Optimization Pack
(MDOP), 152–153
Microsoft Download Center, 7, 107
Microsoft Edge, 5, 6, 200–201
Microsoft Management
Console (MMC), 2
Microsoft Office, 21–22
administrative template, 105, 106
Group Policy settings, 105
Microsoft Windows
operating systems, 1

N

NETLOGON service, 12
Network lists, 100–102

O

Office clients, 125–127
Office- dedicated policy settings
administrative templates, 112–116
configuration, 112
Microsoft Office, 113–116
Office-specific GPOs, 106
Organizational Unit (OU), 13, 144

P

Password policies, 93, 192
Password Reveal Button, 75–77
Performance and display, 125–127
Port 161, 4600
PreviewHandlers feature, 117–119, 120
Process Monitor Filter dialog box, 16
Process Monitor window, 17

Q

Query tab, 53

R

RegEdit /s filename.reg, 78
Registry
    Editor window, 19
    filter prompt, 16, 17
    GPO setting, 15, 17
    hierarchical database, 15
    Process Monitor, 18
    Procmon.exe, 15
    RegSetValue criteria, 17
    select Jump To, 18
    troubleshooting system, 19
Registry Editor, 2
Registry manipulation, 77–79
Registry values, 165–166
Remote Server Administrative
        Tools (RSAT), 32, 40
Renaming, 186–187
Restore GPOs, 49–52, 157
Resultant Set of Policy (RSoP), 133–135
Ribbon, 196–197

S

Scoping issues, GPO, 172
Screen/Menu configuration XML file, 73
secpol.msc command, 87
Security filtering, 28, 145
Security policies, 87–88, 90, 94, 100–102, 103
ServerManagercmd.exe, 40
Server-side snap-in
        extensions (SSEs), 8, 137
Service Resource Locator (SRV), 12
services.msc command, 159
Settings App, 180, 190–191
Sideloading, 198–200
Software installation, 163
Specific security identifier (SID), 186
Start Menu Layout File, 74
Start screen layout, 72–74
Start Screen/Menu, 72
subnet mask, 12
Sysinternals, 15
System security enhancement, 87–88, 90

T

taskmgr.exe, 86
Telemetry data collection, 202–203
Total cost of ownership (TCO), 105

Troubleshooting, 53
    approaches, 130–131
    client service, 131
    domain, 131
    Excel file, 117–119, 120
    mechanisms, 129
    misconfigured policy settings, 130
    network connection, 131
    target, 129
Troubleshooting AGPM, 157
Troubleshooting Group Policy, 169

U

Universal unique identifier (UUID), 148
User Account Control (UAC), 90–92
User configuration, 4, 183
userenv log files, 139–140
Userenv.log, 174
User policies, 143

V

Verbose logging, 137–138

W

Wallpaper, 193–194
Windows
    customization
        benefits, 71
        GPO policy settings, 80–83
        group policy, 72
        password,
            enabling/disabling, 75–77
        registry editor, 77–78
        Start Menu, 72–73
    features management, 84–86
Windows 8.1, 189–190
Windows 4, 10, 180–182
Windows defender policy, 147
Windows features, 84–86
Windows Firewall, 98–100
Windows PowerShell, 73
Windows Server 2012 R2, 67–68
Windows updates, 180–181
WMI Filter, 26–27

X, Y, Z

XML handler, 73

Get the eBook for only $5!

Why limit yourself?

Now you can take the weightless companion with you wherever you go and access your content on your PC, phone, tablet, or reader.

Since you've purchased this print book, we're happy to offer you the eBook in all 3 formats for just $5.

Convenient and fully searchable, the PDF version enables you to easily find and copy code—or perform examples by quickly toggling between instructions and applications. The MOBI format is ideal for your Kindle, while the ePUB can be utilized on a variety of mobile devices.

To learn more, go to www.apress.com/companion or contact support@apress.com.